THE PURPOSE AND MEANING OF
JEWISH EXISTENCE

To Rivkah

THE PURPOSE
AND MEANING
OF JEWISH EXISTENCE

A People in the Image of God

by

MORDECAI M. KAPLAN

The Jewish Publication Society of America

PHILADELPHIA

5724–1964

PREFACE

The major portion of this book deals with Hermann Cohen's exposition of Judaism as a rational religion. Hermann Cohen (1842–1918) was a Professor of Philosophy at the University of Marburg, Germany. There he succeeded in reviving and deepening the philosophy of Kant and creating the Neo-Kantian School of Thought. His interest in Judaism, which had remained dormant during his incumbency at the Marburg University, was re-awakened when, on retirement from active teaching, he joined the faculty of the Akademie für die Wissenschaft des Judentums in Berlin. The product of his lectures there was his book *Religion der Vernunft, aus den Quellen des Judentums* ("Rational Religion, in the Light of the Source-Material of Judaism"), published post-humously in 1918.

It may shock the reader to learn that, in my opinion, Hermann Cohen's treatise is based on a misunderstanding of Judaism. Why then go to the trouble of publicizing it? The answer is that Cohen's misunderstanding has been, and still is, generally prevalent. It is deeply ingrained in the consciousness of both Jews and non-Jews, as well as of both Jewish believers and non-believers. That misunderstanding is fatal to the spiritual readjustment which Judaism must undergo, if it is to survive. For the sake of Judaism's survival, therefore, it is vitally important to eradicate that misunderstanding, by indicating the false premises and assumptions on which it is based.

All the more amazing, then, is the fact that Cohen's treatise expresses his utmost love for Judaism and his passionate eagerness to prove that it is compatible with absolute reason. He

v

stresses there the primacy in Judaism of its ethical values, the significance of its God idea as a correlate of what is most spiritual in man and, above all, its universalism as emphasized in its Messianism. Does it not then seem absurd to accuse Hermann Cohen of misunderstanding Judaism?

On second thought, however, certain questions come to mind: If Judaism is, or can be, as rational and as ethical as Cohen proves it to be, can we not learn to think rationally and act ethically just as Cohen himself did, for the most part, without the aid of Judaism? Secondly, in Chapter XVI of his book, Cohen states that as long as, on the basis of its sources, Judaism can be shown to be a rational religion, the need for preserving it is self-evident. In order, however, to have those sources prove that Judaism is a rational religion, Cohen submits them to a process of reinterpretation. These sources by themselves, without his reinterpretation, would never yield the high moral and spiritual values which he reads into them. Why go to all the trouble of reinterpreting the source material of Judaism, when reason by itself can generate the moral and religious ideas that are essential to human life?

Actually, Cohen's position with regard to Jewish intermarriage with the majority population would hardly help to perpetuate Judaism, although in his last years he did recommend that Jews should retain their communal separateness. On the face of it, his treatise seems to voice an ideology of Judaism, which the Reform Movement should have adopted as its *vade mecum.* Yet his treatise has not had any impact on the Reform Movement. Even the few Jewish intellectuals who became his ardent disciples are said to have been influenced more by his ardour and spirituality as a Jew than by the plausibility and relevance of his exposition of Judaism.

The prevailing misunderstanding of Judaism, Cohen's included, stems from the following three misconceptions: 1) Judaism is a religion, and a religion only; 2) A religion is a personal philosophy of life; and 3) Ideationism (= philosophical idealism) is the most rational approach to reality.

It is beyond the limitations of this book to enter into a detailed discussion of each of these misconceptions. All that it attempts is to set forth as much of the development of Judaism as will, in part indirectly, and in part directly, prove the following counter propositions: 1) Judaism is a religious civilization; 2) A religion is the third, or spiritual, dimension of a civilization, the other two dimensions being the politico-economic (= somatic) and the cultural (= psychic); and 3) Functionalism, rather than ideationism, is a rationally reliable approach to reality.

Instead of attempting a summary of Hermann Cohen's philosophy of Judaism, I have thought it best to reproduce the contents of his *Religion der Vernunft* in epitomized form. I am grateful to Dr. Trude Weiss-Rosmarin for having taken the trouble to read the Epitome and for having eliminated from it all traces of Cohen's heavy German style.

The subtitle, "A People in the Image of God" is a phrase borrowed from the writings of the Zionist pioneer, A. D. Gordon.

The letter "P" in "Jewish People" is capitalized in this book wherever its context requires that the reader have in mind the restructured and reconstituted body of World Jewry as the form of Jewish existence in the future.

M.M.K.

Contents

PART THREE
MODERN RATIONALES OF JUDAISM

PART ONE

Judaism in Search
of a Rationale

CHAPTER I

INTRODUCTION

The most significant term in the title of this book is *"Jewish Existence."* Whether justly or arbitrarily, the only way the term "existence" can express a communicable fact is to use it in the sense of "functioning." For anything to exist, it has to function in some specific manner. Whatever performs a function of any kind exists. In that sense even a dream has existence, as a dream, though its substance does not have existence, because as the object of a dream it does not function the way it does as an object of the mind when awake.

"Jewish Existence," accordingly, means "functioning as Jews." Jews can function as Jews only by virtue of their belonging to the Jewish People, just as a soldier can function as a soldier only by virtue of his belonging to an army. When the army is disbanded, the units are no longer soldiers; they become veterans. For an army to *exist,* it has to *function* as an army, either by actively engaging in war, or by preparing itself for war through various drills and maneuvers. Likewise, for the Jewish People to exist, it has to *function* as a people. The unpleasant, and therefore readily forgettable, truth is that we Jews have ceased to function as a people. The most that can be said of us is that we function as a *veteran* people.

Jews ceased to be a people as soon as they failed as a body publicly to denounce the action of the so-called Sanhedrin, which in 1806 at the behest of Napoleon I, renounced in the name of all Jews, their Jewish nationhood. The Jews, as a body, have even permitted that renunciation to go unchallenged, when it was voluntarily confirmed and adopted by a rabbinical conference which took place in 1844 at Braun-

3

schweig. The only action since then through which Jews have functioned actually in the capacity not of an existing, but of a veteran, people has been the Zionist Movement. Since the establishment of the State of Israel, however, the Zionist Movement has been on the decline, so that even that veteran capacity may be said to have been abandoned. All that exists at present is a miscellany of human beings, who call themselves Jews by virtue of their being third or fourth generation descendants from Jews who were authentically such because there was then a Jewish People to which they belonged.

There can be no doubt as to the existence of the Jewish People, despite its lack of a State, before Jews began to be emancipated from their medieval disabilities. Jews then functioned as a people, because they professed and practised wholehearted allegiance to the Written and Oral Torah and submitted to the coercive authority of those who were duly authorized to administer the way of life decreed by that twofold Torah. Only those Jews, who to this day continue to live the same way of life and to maintain the same religious outlook as did their forebears during the pre-Emancipation centuries, are entitled to claim that they belong to an existing or functioning Jewish People. That, however, is cold comfort to the overwhelming number of Jews who cannot subscribe to the Orthodox version of Judaism. They find themselves in the limbo of uncertainty, where they have to endure the liabilities of a status which is more of a fiction than a reality. The worst of that situation is that among that overwhelming number of Jews there are very few, indeed, who have the least idea of what there is to them that is essentially Jewish.

The unique fact concerning the past existence, or functioning, of the Jewish People is that it was always attended by a keen awareness of purpose and meaning. Before the nineteenth century all Jews had a rationale which justified their Jewish existence. The Jewish People thus resembled a mature person. It was always aware of itself. It recalled its past career, as soon as it had a career to look back to. Seldom, if ever, content with its present conditions, it always looked forward to an illustrious future. Like an individual, the Jewish People had an overruling purpose, which gave direction to its existence, or functioning, and it had no doubt as to the most effective means whereby to achieve this purpose. Thus did its life achieve meaning as well as a sense of purpose.

The purpose of its existence as a people, as conceived by our ancestors in Bible times, is clearly stated in Isaiah 43.12. Thus, one text reads: "You are My witnesses, that I am God"; and another text reads: "This people I have formed, in order that they make known My greatness" (43.22). The *meaning* of ancient Israel's national existence during Bible times was expressed through conformity to the prescribed order of worship and ritual practice and to the regulations pertaining to the inter-personal relations. By those means, together with the expected consequence in the form of well-being and national prestige, the foregoing purpose of testifying to the righteousness and unlimited power of their God was to be achieved. The ancients were not given to abstract reflection. They did, however, assume that there was a necessary connection between the degree to which they obeyed the laws of God and the events in their own life as a people. God had long ago apprised them of that inevitable connection (Lev. 26. 3 ff.)

In time, there evolved, out of the collective self-awareness of our ancestors as a people, a personal self-awareness which is of supreme significance for the spiritual growth of the human being. With the emergence of personal self-awareness, the assumed correlation between conformity to the prescribed way of life and its consequence in terms of well-being and national prestige no longer seemed to obtain. That in no way affected the idea either of the purpose or of the meaning of Jewish existence. Those remained in force as they had been formulated in the very beginning of the existence of our ancestors as a people. But the failure of the individual to experience in his own person, or in that of other individuals, the expected consquence of living up to the traditional purpose and meaning of Israel's national existence at first led either to some wrong conclusion or to outright scepticism. The Psalmist, for example, was certain that the prosperity of the wicked was only a prelude to their utter destruction (Ps. 92.7-8). The author of Job, in veiled fashion, and the author of Kohelet, in bold strokes, declared their disbelief in any actual correlation between, on the one hand, living up to the purpose and meaning of the collective life of their people and, on the other hand, what befell the individual person, either of good or evil fortune.

This condition of spiritual life for the Jewish People could not go on too long without completely undermining its faith in what it assumed to be the purpose and meaning of its existence. Fortunately for the survival of the Jewish People, due to its contact with the Persian civilization (after it had been transformed by Zoroastrian religion), a way was at last found out of the predicament caused by the failure of the individual to expereince any connection between deed and meed. The belief in the post-mortem survival of the soul and in the resurrection of the dead supplied the imagination of the learned among the Jews with a conception of a very much greater vista for the enactment of human life than that provided by the tradition inherited from biblical times. With immortality and bliss in the hereafter in the offing, and with this transitory world as nothing more than a portico to the world to come, the God of righteousness could be trusted to straighten out in the world to come the account of the individual person. No one would have any reason to feel himself aggrieved.

By the time this new outlook on the destiny of the human being sank into the consciousness of the Jewish People through the spread of the Pharisaic movement during the middle of the era of the Second Commonwealth, the original purpose, which underlies the biblical writings, was gradually and unconsciously replaced by a radically different purpose. Originally the purpose of ancient Israel's existence was to make God known to the rest of the world. With the rise of Pharisaism, the purpose of Jewish existence came to be the salvation of the individual Jew. Salvation was understood specifically as immortality and bliss in the hereafter. The clearest formulation of this new purpose of Jewish existence is the statement in the Mishnah of Sanhedrin, which reads: "All of Israel [all Jews] are entitled to share in the world to come" (X. 1). That privilege is forfeited by Jews who are guilty of the particular heresies which this same Mishnah enumerates. As a result, also the original meaning of Jewish existence gave way to the one which was related to the new purpose of Jewish existence. The study of Torah, worship, the observance of ritual practices and adherence to the laws pertaining to inter-personal relations thenceforth functioned as a means to other-wordly salvation.

A fact seldom noted is that this radical transformation of the purpose and meaning of Jewish existence, from a God-centered to a man-centered rationale, transformed the status of the Jewish People itself. From that time on, the Jewish People figured in the consciousness of the Jew not only as a nation, but also as an *ecclesia* (= Church). Whereas the solidarity that united Jews as a nation was essentially political, the solidarity of the Jews as an *ecclesia* was essentially salvational or religious. In the rabbinic tradition, the Jews figure more often as an *ecclesia* (*Knesset Yisrael*) than as a political nation, for the simple reason that the Jews had lost their State before the rabbinic era. The rabbis therefore resorted to the common interest of all Jews in their own personal salvation as a means of keeping the Jews united as a nation and as an *ecclesia*. It is doubtful, however, whether the Jews could have survived as a People after the destruction of the State if they had not achieved also the status of an *ecclesia.*

When we pass on to the early centuries of the Christian Era, we find that once again the condition of mankind contributed to Jewish survival. At the very time the Second Commonwealth was destroyed, the Mediterranean peoples, among whom the Jews found domicile, had among them vast numbers who were in passionate search for a way of life, or for some theurgic procedure whereby they could be assured of salvation in the form of eternal life. That situation gave rise to the spread of Christianity. Pharisaic Judaism had long prepared the Jews for that conception of salvation. As a consequence, the Jews found themselves in a world which, in spite of its hostility, confirmed them in their purpose to continue living as a people.

In theory and officially, Jewish existence continued to be both national and ecclesiastic. The fulfillment of the national aspect was to take place with the coming of the Messiah; that of the ecclesiastic aspect was the attainment of bliss in the hereafter for each Jew individually. In practice, however, the ecclesiastic aspect functioned in their daily activities, while the national aspect functioned only as passive waiting for the Messiah to come. The most telling statement in the medieval writings, which reveals the extent to which the national aspect of Jewish existence became dormant, is the one in the *Kuzari*. There its author, Judah Hallevi, describes the attitude of his fellow-Jews as parrot-like in their repetition of prayers for the return to Zion, without doing anything about it.

It was during the centuries of sojourn in the Diaspora that the Jews led this bifocal existence, national-ecclesiastic, with the national rather dormant and the ecclesiastic fully active. During these centuries, the Jewish intellectuals encountered the challenge of the Gentile intellectuals, mainly with regard to the following theological problems: 1) The anthropomorphic representations of God in the Bible; 2) the suspension of the laws of nature ascribed there to God; and 3) the belief in individual experience of Divine Providence. To be an intellectual in those days meant to subscribe to one or another of the classic philosophies which had their origin in ancient Greece. Armed with these philosophies, they challenged the traditional solutions of those theological problems.

There were two long periods of several centuries each in the career of Diaspora Judaism when intellectual challenge and response played an important role. The outstanding name of the first long period was Philo of Alexandria, whose response to classical philosophy set the keynote for Christain theology, but whose influence on Judaism was short-lived and confined to the Jews of Alexandria. The outstanding name of the second long period was Maimonides, the influence of whose response to the philosophic challenge is still felt in our day. In each case the response consisted in the reinterpretation of the traditional beliefs which had been under attack. Those beliefs were so reinterpreted as to express ideas in keeping with the authoritative teachings of the philosophers. Here and there, a traditional belief is upheld and defended, despite its deviation from philosophic doctrine.

The knowledge of the foregoing facts concerning the radical changes which the conception of the purpose and meaning of Jewish existence underwent is indispensable if Jewish existence is to have a future. That knowledge can imbue us with the feeling that, if we are determined to survive as a people and to do all in our power to put that determination into effect, we need not fear changing the purpose and meaning of Jewish existence in conformity with the most tenable outlook of our day. This means that we Jews are confronted again with the need of revaluating and reinterpreting the purpose and meaning of our survival as a people.

There are, however, serious differences between our situation now and what it was in the past, when Judaism encoun-

tered challenge. The radical change which took place under
Pharisaic influence in the traditional conception of reward
and punishment, and which completely revolutionized the
purpose and the meaning of Jewish existence, then came
about so slowly as to be imperceptible. Nowadays, a change
in Jewish ideology has to take place forthwith and with full
awareness that it is, from the standpoint of world outlook,
a break with the kind of religious rationale that was accepted
by our ancestors or forebears. Moreover, in the past, all that
was needed to meet challenge was to reinterpret the traditional ideas about God, the world and man. Nowadays the
Jewish situation is such that reinterpretation is far from
enough. What is urgently needed is a social structure, or
polity, that would enable the Jews throughout the world to
function as an organic people. They cannot function as a
nation in the modern sense of the term, nor as a church in
the modern sense of the term. They have to find a way of
functioning as a civilizational people, united by a bond of
voluntary allegiance to a civilization or *Torah,* the purpose
of which is to achieve fulfillment, both individual and collective, along lines which permit continuity in change and
unity in diversity. In other words, the Jews have to achieve
existence as a Torah people, with *Torah* understood as coming forth from a modern Zion. The establishment of the
State of Israel is only a spearhead of a movement to create
that new kind of social structure or polity. So far, no thought
has been given to the forging of the spear itself.

Once we know what we have to do to assure the existence
of the Jewish People, we can proceed to reinterpret the traditional values which spell out the purpose and meaning of
that existence. It is then that recourse to Hermann Cohen's
Religion der Vernunft will prove to be extremely illuminating. Its main value consists, on the one hand, in emancipating Jewish religion from its traditional commitment to
supernaturalism and, on the other hand, in redeeming

naturalism from the synonimity with crass materialism. In accentuating the dimension of purpose as the human differentia, Cohen makes naturalism compatible with spirituality and with all those values in human life that impel man to transcend that in himself which he shares with the beast.

Of all the works Jews have written that come in any way near to defining the purpose and meaning of Jewish existence in keeping with a tenable naturalist outlook of a spiritual character, few can surpass Hermann Cohen's *Rational Religion*. That is the reason an epitome of its contents, together with an introduction and commentary, constitutes a large part of the substance of this book. The remainder consists of summaries of responses to pre-modern challenges to ancient conceptions of the purpose and meaning of Jewish existence, and of two recent alternative responses to the one by Hermann Cohen, to meet the challenge of modern naturalism. Buber's response is summarized in the chapter on *Esoteric Rationalism,* and my own in the chapter on *Functional Rationalism.*

CHAPTER II

THE MOSAIC TORAH AS RATIONALE

The key to the understanding and appreciation of the Mosaic Torah is the fact that it represents the initial rationale for the high goal which the people of Israel set for itself: that of ultimately becoming "a people in the image of God." That goal, according to a proper understanding of the Torah, is not reserved exclusively for the people of Israel. On the contrary, all peoples are expected to emulate the people of Israel and also strive to reflect "the image of God."

The following is the barest outline of the Mosaic Torah as rationale: When God created the world, the crown of His creation was Man. In the ancient way of speaking, that statement means that God had expected the human species to lead the kind of a life that would be a true reflection of His own nature. Therein would man be different from, and superior to, the rest of creation.

According to what the Mosaic Torah tells us, first in the form of legend and then as literal fact, the human species became corrupt. Its way of life was dominated by violence. Thereupon God would have put an end to the human species, had not Noah, by his conduct, proved that mankind might yet turn out to be what God had expected. However, the only one of Noah's descendants who gave promise that his descendants might ultimately live up to God's expectation was Abraham. God therefore singled him out for the task of instructing those who were to come after him "in the way of righteousness and justice," and promised to make of his descendants a nation that would, in effect, constitute "a people in the image of God." For that purpose, Abraham's descendants needed a land of their own where they would be exempt from the corrupting influences of the rest of mankind.

The Mosaic Torah then goes on to point out that, despite all that God has done to nurture that people and to instruct it in the holy way of life, it turned out to be wayward and unreliable. However, God was determined not to reject His people, despite its recalcitrance, but to discipline it by means of exile from its land, persecution and torment at the hand of its enemies. In the end, however, God would restore His people to its land, where it would resume life anew. Two reasons are given for that act of God: One is His promise to the Patriarchs to make of their descendants a great nation, and a second reason is that God's name might not be profaned among the other nations. This second reason which is the theme of the Song of Moses (Deut. 31.19-22; 32.1-44) is elaborated by the Prophet Ezekiel, who reiterates the conclusion that had been arrived at by Jeremiah (31.26-32), to the effect that God would force those of the House of Israel to change their way of life by creating in them "a new heart and a new spirit" (36.16-28).

That doctrine, which summarizes the narrative part of the Mosaic Torah, is supplemented by the precepts of a cultic, legalistic and ethical character which were calculated to foster a way of life that would qualify the people of Israel to become "a kingdom of priests and a holy nation." It would in the end win the admiration of the nations and be emulated by them. The Mosaic Torah, by thus being both a kind of Declaration of Dependence upon God and a Divine Constitution regulating the people's way of life, functioned as the rationale whereby the Jewish People has articulated the conception of its own destiny.

A remarkable fact which has never been noted is that the significance of the God idea in the Hebrew Bible is virtually

identical with that of the God idea in the Western philosophic tradition. That philosophic tradition arose in ancient
Greece about the middle of the sixth century B.C.E. It had its
inception with the cosmological thinkers like Thales, Anaxi-
mander, Anaximines, Xenophanes and Heraclitus. They discovered, first, that nothing in human experience stands still
and that everything undergoes change, and, secondly, that as
a result apparently of the continuous process of change and
the ultimate evanescence of everything visible, nothing is
what it appears to be.

That awareness comes hard to man, who needs to feel secure in the world. If he is of a highly reflective turn of mind,
he begins to speculate and to search for something in his experience that he can regard as fixed, static and immutable.
Even Heraclitus, who was the only thinker that denied the
existence of anything that does not undergo change, had to
admit that the law of change itself does not change. In the
development of the philosophic tradition, however, Heraclitus was ignored for a long time by the thinkers. The
teaching of Parmenides, that only what is unchanging, fixed
or immutable is real or authentic, became the basic principle
of the philosophic tradition of the West. A further noteworthy fact is that those ancient philosophers termed what
they regarded as the reality behind all appearance and change
"Nature." Occasionally they also called it "God."

Now, let us turn to the Mosaic Torah and ask ourselves:
How did those who formulated the first verse conceive of
God, to whom they ascribed the creation of heaven and earth?
For an answer let us turn to some of the passages in the Bible
where the idea of God is contrasted with the idea of the
world. Thus we read in the ninetieth psalm: "Before the
mountains were brought forth, or ever Thou hadst formed
the earth and the world, even from everlasting to everlasting,
Thou art God" (v. 2). In the one-hundred and second psalm

(vv. 26-28) we read: "Of old Thou didst lay the foundation
of the earth; and the heavens are the work of Thy hands.
They shall perish, but Thou shalt endure; yea all of them
shall wax old like a garment; as a vesture shalt Thou change
them, and they shall pass away; but Thou art the self-same,
and Thy years shall have no end." Many similar passages
could be quoted to prove that the concept of God was clearly
identified in the minds of the biblical writers with the principle of authenticity. We can therefore get the full sense of
what they sought to convey in the opening sentence of the
Bible, if we understand that sentence as implying that
the God of Israel, who is the only *authentic* God, created the
heaven and the earth.

Those spiritual leaders to whom ancient Israel owed its
idea of God were evidently as much interested as were the
Greek thinkers in stressing the difference between reality
and appearance. Unlike those thinkers, however, who studied
general experience for the purpose of distinguishing in it
that which was real or authentic from that which was mere
appearance or illusory, the spiritual leaders of the House of
Israel confined their search, so to speak, to the *gods* men worshipped. They knew from experience that no visible object
of nature, much less any idol made by human hands, could
escape deterioration. The only god that could be authentic
was the one who, in the words of a later prophet, could be
represented as saying: "To whom then will ye liken Me, that
I should be equal? Lift up your eyes on high and see: who
hath created these?" (Isa. 40.25-26).

That unchanging, immutable, and therefore authentic,
character of the God of Israel constitutes His uniqueness. One
of Philo's works is entitled: *Quod Deus Sit Immutabilis.* By
the same token, the People of Israel, which as His Chosen
People is committed to Him, is bound to be both enduring
and immutable. It alone possesses that authenticity as a people which renders it unique among the nations of the world.

Thus the prophet Malachi says in the name of God: "I the Eternal change not, and ye, O sons of Jacob, are never to perish" (3.6). In the Book of Samuel we read that David prayed: "Who is like Thy people, like Israel a unique nation on the earth . . . Thou didst establish to Thyself Thy people Israel to be a people to Thee forever" (II Sam. 7.23,24). According to Hosea, God promised to renew His covenant with Israel which was never to be broken: "I will betroth thee to Me forever" (Hos. 2.21). According to Jeremiah, God said: "I will make an everlasting covenant with them" (Jer. 32.40).

In the Bible, the covenant between God and man is always associated with ordinances analogous to those associated with the covenant between God and Nature. Thus the fixed order of day and night is referred to as a covenant between them and God (Jer. 33.30). The covenant between God and Israel took the form of laws. Such was the covenant formally entered into between God and Israel at Sinai, where, we are told, Moses "took the Book of the Covenant and read in the hearing of the people, and they said 'all that the Lord hath spoken we will do and obey' " (Ex. 24.7). Thus we come upon the third referent, or matter of ultimate concern, in the initial and basic rationale of Judaism, namely, the Torah itself as sharing the eternity and authenticity which are the essence of Divinity. There is no adjective that is so often associated with those three main objects of Judaism's concern as the term *olam*, which means "everlasting."

It is not surprising, therefore, that one of the obligatory prayer-readings in our liturgy refers to the Torah, in terms found in the Torah itself (Deut. 30.20), as "our life and the length of our days." Here, then, we have the secret of the survival of the Jewish People under conditions of exile, dispersion, discrimination and persecution, which no other people has shown itself capable of withstanding. So long as Jews believed literally and wholeheartedly in the divine origin of the Torah as the covenant between them and the only true

God of the universe, none of the vicissitudes they experienced could destroy their loyalty to it. That loyalty enabled them to survive as a people, despite the worst that other nations inflicted on them.

CHAPTER III

PHILO'S RATIONALE

The first ideological challenge to Judaism took place in Alexandria during the first century before the common era. There the Jews who had migrated from Palestine encountered the culture and philosophy of the ancient Greeks, which had spread throughout the Near East in the wake of the conquests of Alexander the Great. A brief survey of the philosophical development up to the point where the Jews of Alexandria began to feel its impact will help us understand the role of Philo as author of the first rationale for Judaism outside the Mosaic Torah itself.

During the fifth century B.C.E. the Greek thinkers turned to speculating on human, particularly political, institutions and the laws governing them. No longer believing in the authenticity of the gods to whom those laws had been attributed, and assuming those laws to be man-made, they questioned their validity. Those were the Sophists, the most outstanding among whom was Protagoras. He is remembered by his motto: "Man is the measure of all things." Because of their subversive views, the Sophists acquired a bad name. Socrates, who had himself been known as one of them, tried to counteract their subversive influence. He thus arrived at the concept of justice as a criterion by which to judge the validity and authenticity of man-made laws and institutions. At the same time, he laid the foundation of a method of thinking, whereby the authenticity not only of political and economic laws, but of all human experience, might be discovered.

His disciple, Plato, built upon that foundation his philosophic system known as "idealism." A more correct term for that system, and one by which it is designated in this book, is "ideationism." The underlying principle of ideationism is that the *idea* of a thing, being free from the vicissitudes of time and place, is constant and unchanging, and therefore the most authentic part of it. On the other hand, the visible and tangible thing itself is only one of the many embodiments of that which is its idea; it cannot be authentic, because it is evanescent.

Being a poet, Plato became obsessed with his discovery that the idea of a thing was not only the most important aspect, but the only element of authenticity any thing could have. He, therefore, gave free rein to his poetic imagination, which transferred ideas as such to a "supercelestial place" (*Phaedrus* 247 C), where they were assumed to exist eternally as a kind of beings that had perfect form. That, in brief, is the approach to Reality, which Whitehead referred to when he said: "The safest general characterization of the European philosophical tradition is that it consists of a series of footnotes to Plato" (*Process and Reality,* New York, 1929, p. 53). Note Whitehead's use of the term "philosophical tradition." The authoritarian attitude has played as much of a role in the philosophical as in the revelational tradition.

Plato's profoundly ethical interest impelled him to project a perfect type of city-state, with an ideal social order and an ideal system of education, all in the interests of the task his master Socrates had undertaken to accomplish—the establishment of a political state based on justice. Only three or four centuries before Plato, a few hundred miles to the southeast, one great prophet after another had been clamoring that the Kingdoms of Israel and Judah should become states based on justice as the will of the only authentic God.

Both the prophets and Plato failed to accomplish what they had in mind and at heart. There is a difference, however, in the ultimate outcome of their respective visions. The prophets failed because mankind had not caught up to them.

It will ultimately have to catch up to them; otherwise it cannot survive. They had a more reliable sense of justice than did Plato, and could afford to speak in the name of God, whereas Plato could speak only in his own name. What assurance did the Greeks have that Plato's idea of social justice, based as it was on sharp class distinctions, was more authentic than that of any other philosopher? As a matter of fact, his own disciple, Aristotle, had a different notion of what constituted justice. Ideas, according to him, did not reside in some supercelestial space, apart from the changeable, mutable phenomena, but in and through them. His politics and ethics were built on entirely different lines from those of Plato.

Consequently, the inquisitive, speculative approach of the Greek thinkers to the problems of ethical conduct, of justice and injustice led to no unifying or solidifying principle that might have saved the Greeks from being absorbed by other states and nations. Those thinkers did, however, enable the human mind to advance beyond its childhood, into its adolescent stage. Without their contribution it could never have attained its present maturity.

At the time that the impact of Roman power on the eastern coastlands of the Mediterranean was breaking up the political unity of the Greeks, their heritage of philosophical speculation, in its most pervasive form, was encountered by the Jews in the Egyptian Delta, particularly in Alexandria. More threatening to the inner life and solidarity of the Jews than the Roman power was, in fact, the thought-universe of the Greek culture. Who could have foretold the outcome of the challenge of that thought-universe to the Judaism of the Egyptian Jews? There were Jews in Alexandria whose faith in the divine origin of the Torah was shaken; they were soon lost to Judaism. Most Alexandrian Jews, however, remained loyal to the Jewish People. They constituted a distinct and autonomous community. They assembled every Sabbath for worship and listened to the public reading of the Torah in Greek, which was followed by homiletical interpretation. They maintained contact with the Jews of Eretz Yisrael. Some pilgrimaged from time to time to Jerusalem. They must, on the whole, have led quite an intensive Jewish life for a Jew like Philo to have arisen among them.

Philo elaborated a rationale for Judaism that was not indigenous, as was that of the Mosaic Torah. His rationale is based on the world outlook of the Greek philosophers. He derived from the Stoics the method of allegorization, which is implicit in his interpretation of the Bible. Beginning with Euhemerus of the third century B.C.E., the Stoics had developed an allegorical interpretation of the Homeric myths and other religious legends, whereby they had tried to save their traditional pagan religion.

Philo had a much easier task in reconciling Judaism with Hellenic thought than the Stoics had in reconciling paganism with it. In the first place, there was the monotheism of Jewish religion, which had been motivated by a quest after authenticity like that of the Greek philosophers. Secondly, the high ethical traits, which the God of Israel demanded of the Jewish People as a prerequisite to the privilege of worshipping Him, exceeded both in scope and motivation those which Hellenic philosophy demanded of its adherents. Philo was thus able to reinterpret the contents of the Torah in such Hellenic terms as almost to transform it into a philosophic system that could compete with Stoicism in its appeal to reason or to the universal mind, and in its contribution to the moral life. That is evident from the hostility which the leading Stoics manifested at that time toward the Jews against whom they incited pogroms and whose religion they tried to defame. Apion, whom Josephus immortalized by his reply, *Contra Apionem,* was one of those leading Stoics.

It is noteworthy that Josephus, in interpreting Judaism to the Greco-Roman world, wrote in the same vein as did Philo.

Thus we read in his *Contra Apionem* the following: "The Laws we have given us are disposed after the best manner for mutual communion with one another, for a general love of mankind, and also for justice and for sustaining labors with fortitude and for contempt of death. And I beg of those that shall peruse this writing of mine to read it without partiality; for it is not my purpose to write an encomium upon ourselves, but shall esteem this as a most just apology for us and taken from those our laws, according to which we lead our lives, against the many and the lying objections that have been made against us" ("Against Apion," Book II, in *Complete Works of Josephus*, World Library, vol. 10, p. 497). If the term for "rationale" had existed in Josephus' time, he might have used it instead of his phrase "a most just apology for us."

*   *   *

The rationale which Philo formulated for Judaism, in order to prove that it was compatible with Hellenic philosophy, possessed two outstanding traits: one, it utilized the Hellenic criterion of immutability to stress the immutable character of the Torah as evidence of its authenticity; and, two, it read into the statements of the Torah the kind of Hellenic philosophy which was entirely alien to the Torah. An example of the first is the following statement by Philo: "The laws of the Greek legislators are continually subject to change; the laws of Moses alone remain steady, unmoved, unshaken, stamped as it were with the seal of nature herself, from the day they were written to the present day, and will so remain for all time as long as the world endures. Not only the Jews but all other peoples who care for righteousness adopt them. . . . Let all men follow this code and the age of universal peace will come about, the Kingdom of God on earth will be established" (*De Vita Mosis* II, 5).

An illustration of the way Philo read into the Torah the

Platonic theory of ideas as the eternal types that abide in the supercelestial sphere—those ideas of which the things on earth were imperfect copies—is the following: "Why does it say: 'And God made every green herb of the field, before it was upon the earth' (Gen. 2.5)? [This translation is based on the Septuagint which renders verse 5 as co-ordinate with verse 4, instead of as a parenthetical statement.] That suggests symbolically the incorporeal idea. The phrase 'before it was upon the earth' marks the original perfection of every plant and herb. The eternal types were first created in the noetic world, and the physical objects on earth, perceptible to the senses, were made in their likeness" (*De Mundi Opificio,* II, 30-31). So thoroughly Hellenized in his entire outlook on life did Philo become, as a result of having to find a rationale for Judaism, that he adopted the Hellenic goal of human existence as being "the contemplative life," instead of the Jewish goal, which is the "return to God and the performance of good deeds."

Jews whose destiny it is to live out their lives in the various lands outside Israel are confronted with a situation analogus in many respects to that of the Alexandrian Jews in the days of Philo. What can we learn from their history, and what warning, if any, can we infer from their disappearance from Jewish life? There can be no doubt that the cause of the disappearance of Alexandrian Jewry was not, as some maintain, their loss of the Hebrew. Nor was it their Hellenization, which necessitated their developing a rationale for Judaism based on a philosophy that was alien to the spirit of the Torah. The main cause was at first the pogroms which the Alexandrian Greeks waged against them and which grew in savagery whenever Roman rule relaxed. What led to the final ruin of the Jewish-Alexandrian community was the desperate revolt of the Jews during the reign of Trajan (114-117). They were then deprived of their political privileges and were treated as aliens. When Christianity made headway among the population of Alexandria, the Jews were subjected to frequent attacks and finally expelled from the city by Bishop Cyril (415).

Had those catastrophes not befallen the Jews of Alexandria, there is no telling how long the Jewish community there might have survived, on the basis of a Hellenized rationale of Judaism. The fact that such a rationale kept a person of great intellectual power and saintly character like Philo within the Jewish fold, and that his teaching was accepted by the Jews who filled the large and famous synagogue of Alexandria, points to the probability that, had the Jews been allowed to live in peace, the original Alexandrian community could have survived to this day.

It would be a mistake, however, to assume that what enabled Alexandrian Jews to find survival value in Philo's rationale for Judaism was the intrinsic validity of Hellenic philosophy. Philo himself contested its validity. When it came, for example, to the idea of God, he arrived at an idea of his own which was neither Scriptural, on the one hand, nor in keeping with the spirit of the dominant philosophy of his day, on the other. Neither Plato nor Aristotle found it necessary to conceive God as "unknowable." Likewise Scripture certainly stresses again and again that the survival of the People of Israel depends upon their knowing God. Jeremiah states expressly what it means to know God: "Let him that glorieth glory in this: that he understands and knows Me, that I am the Eternal who exercises mercy, justice and righteousness on the earth" (Jer. 9.32-33).

Through the use of the ideationist approach to the Bible, Philo misinterpreted its intent with regard to the idea of God. He also took issue with the philosophers, and, in the name of Judaism, introduced into theology one of the most obfuscating ideas concerning God. "The terms ineffable, unnamable and incomprehensible," writes Professor H. A.

Wolfson, "by which the unknowability of God is expressed by Philo, do not occur as a description of God in extant Greek philosophic literature before Philo, but once these terms were used by Philo, they begin to occur frequently in Greek philosophy" (*Philo,* vol. I, Harvard University Press, 1947, p. 6).

Ever since then the concept of "ineffability" has played havoc with speculative thinking, creating a mythology about inconceivable conceptions and unthinkable thoughts about "noumenal" existences. That same intent of Philo to emphasize the uniqueness of the God of Israel, by ascribing to Him a transcendence that rendered all contact with sensate experience demeaning, led him to assume the existence of an intermediary god, the Logos, who was the actual creator, or Demiurge, of the world. Thus what Philo had expected would serve as a philosophical rationale for the Judaism of his day turned out to be, before long, the basis of a rationale for Christianity. That is evident from the opening verse of the Gospel according to St. John, which, according to James Moffat's correct translation, reads: "The Logos existed in the very beginning" (John 1.1).

What rendered Philo's rationale an effective means in its day of making Judaism viable was not mainly the intrinsic validity of his idea of God. It was, rather, the fact that Philo made it possible for his idea of God to stimulate in his fellow-Jews of Alexandria the desire to identify themselves with the Jews of Eretz Yisrael and with their Torah as a way of life.

Philo lived in an age when the universal assumption of tribes, city-states and nations, that the laws which governed their lives were of divine origin, had begun to break down. Thus, Plato's claim, that the laws of Minos which obtained in Sparta and Crete had been dictated by oracles from Zeus, was no longer taken seriously by the time Philo lived to see the loss of Greek independence. In strong contrast, no matter where the Jews resided and whatever their political allegiance, the laws of Moses, in the words of Philo, "remained secure from the day they were first enacted till now" (Wolfson, *ibid.*, II, 191). The stability and immutability of the Torah was thus, for that day and age, an adequate rationale for Judaism. That can scarcely be the case nowadays when only a few of its ritual laws, and even fewer of its social laws, are all that have remained in force of the 613 commandments in the Mosaic Torah.

Philo's rationale thus derived its survival value not from its ideationist content, but from the kind of attitude and action it called for. It was accepted by those Jews of Alexandria who experienced, in terms of communal life, their involvement in the corporate body of the Jewish People. Above all, Philo's rationale called for an attitude marked by an unshakable faith in the divine origin of the Torah and in the divine sanction of the Temple in Jerusalem, then the two main *sancta* of the Jewish People. And finally it called for the observance of ritual practices which helped to maintain the solidarity of the Jewish People and to keep alive its spiritual and moral commitment.

"Jewish polities," writes H. A. Wolfson, "governed by the laws of Moses, as much as it was possible for these laws to be practiced outside of Palestine, existed throughout the Roman-Hellenistic world as well as throughout the Parthian world. How Philo looked upon these widespread Jewish polities in their relation to the Palestinian polity may be gathered indirectly from scattered passages in his writings. The Jews in the diaspora are described by him as colonies of the Jewish population in Judea, and these colonial Jews, while 'holding the Holy City where stands the sacred Temple of the most High God to be their mother city, still account each city in which they had been born and brought up as their native city, just as Jerusalem is the native city of the Jews born therein.' The Jews of Palestine and of all these colonies constituted to Philo one whole nation, of which the Jews in each locality were a part" (Wolfson, *ibid.,* II, p. 397).

"As in native Judaism," adds Wolfson, "so also in Philo, the Messianic Age is conceived not only as the age of national deliverance and national prosperity but also as an age during which Judaism will become a universal religion" (*ibid.,* p. 415). . . . "While the Mosaic Law will be universally accepted during the Messianic Age, there will still exist, as according to native Jewish tradition, many distinct national states" (*ibid.,* p. 425).

Philo's attempt at providing a rationale for Judaism other than the one implied in the Torah itself, proves that, for a rationale in terms of a non-Jewish philosophy to be valid for Judaism, it has to meet two requirements: first, it has to be based on what is regarded in its day as a rational conception of God; secondly, that rational conception of God has to be integrated into the commitment to maintain the unity and solidarity of the Jewish People and to retain its *sancta* as well as its Messianic ideal. The first of the above requirements indicates that the Jewish tradition may have to undergo change in its conception of God from time to time. The second requirement indicates the aspects of the tradition which have to provide the element of continuity. What is important, however, is that whatever changes the conception of God may undergo, it must function in the same way. It must continue to act as incentive to every Jew to cooperate with his fellow-Jews in their effort to become "a People in the Image of God."

If Jews would bear those facts in mind and act on them, they could afford to question frankly and unreservedly the historicity of supernatural events which figure in the tradition as the validation of the belief in God and in the Torah as the revelation of His will. If Judaism is to survive, it is in need of a rationale for those inquiring and open-minded Jews whose number is on the increase, and whose alienation from Jewish life is fatal to it. Such a rationale has not yet been formulated. We may rest assured, however, that it can be formulated, because to the average thinking Jew nowadays not ideation, but action, is the key to authenticity, nor is immutability an index of reality. The key to authenticity, or the index of reality or meaning of whatever exists, from an electron to Deity, is the continuity between antecedents and consequents in a changing context of events.

A rationale for Judaism to be valid in the dominant intellectual climate of our day has to be based on the association of authenticity not with that which is static and immutable, but rather with that which manages to evolve, without loss of its individuality. Such a rationale is certain to recognize in Judaism not merely a religion, but an evolving religious civilization. Philo and Maimonides, without being fully aware of it, actually operated with that conception of Judaism. Spinoza, on the other hand, insisted on taking every statement in the Bible, with its anthropomorphisms, literally. Having viewed all existence in "geometric fashion," only that which was static was authentic. A Bible that had to be reinterpreted, according to him, could not be authentic. That is why he broke with Judaism. Philo and Maimonides, however, assumed that reinterpretation was not only possible, but obligatory. That assumption enabled them to keep Judaism alive. The philosophy underlying that assumption, which is based on function as a sign of authenticity, was the very opposite of ideationist philosophy which they professed. It is the only philosophy, however, that can give modern-minded Jews the motivation which might enable them to be perfectly at home as Jews in the most rationally advanced climate of opinion of our day.

Chapter IV

MAIMONIDES' RATIONALE*

Judaism found itself a second time in search of a rationale some nine centuries after Philo. During the following five centuries the Jewish intellectual struggled to resolve the conflict between the teachings of traditional Judaism and those of Greek philosophy which was being mediated at the time by outstanding Arabic thinkers. In the twelfth century, Maimonides solved that predicament in his *Guide for the Perplexed* and in some of the introductory chapters to his *Commentary on the Mishnah.* This time it was Aristotle rather than Plato who dominated the intellectual atmosphere. As Philo had managed to come to terms with Plato, so did Maimonides manage to come to terms with Aristotle. As Philo had taken issue with Plato on an important theological doctrine, so did Maimonides take issue with Aristotle on another important theological doctrine. Thus they both vindicated the contribution which Judaism made to philosophy itself, thereby demonstrating Judaism's philosophical superiority. On the whole, however, it is philosophy in the name of reason which spells out the rationale for Judaism rather than the Jewish tradition itself.

In the first place, the conception of God throughout Scriptures is expressed in anthropomorphic terms which offend the philosophically trained mind. Consequently, Maimonides stresses most emphatically that we cannot arrive at a correct conception of Deity by studying merely the surface meaning of the text of the Torah, as most people naively suppose. Any

* Based on Chapter VI of the author's *Judaism in Transition* (Covici-Friede, N.Y., 1936).

one who accepts the simple and literal meaning of the Torah, as the only one, is guilty of heresy and forfeits his salvation, since he is bound to picture God as a magnified
human being and as having human traits. *Some training in
metaphysics as a means to the proper understanding of the
Torah is, according to Maimonides, as indispensable to salvation as conformity to the precepts of the Torah.* The symbolic or figurative meaning of the language of revelation is
by far more important than the literal, and only philosophic
discipline enables one to decipher it. These assumptions carry
the implication—which Maimonides himself would surely
have denied—that reason is superior to revelation. Reason,
which professedly is accorded a place co-ordinate with tradition or revelation, is actually set up as judge to determine
the true meaning of traditional teaching. If a traditional
teaching appears contrary to reason, it must be interpreted so
as to conform with reason. On the other hand, in no instance
is tradition, or revealed teaching, made the criterion for judg-
ing the truth arrived at by reason. Where there is a conflict
between them, we do not discard our rational conviction to
conform to revelation, but we change the meaning of revelation by a process of allegorical interpretation to conform to
the conclusions of reason.

*Exalted as is Maimonides' conception of God, it has mani-
festly more in common with the metaphysics of Aristotle than
with the God-idea of the prophets and sages of ancient Israel.* Not a single one of the biblical passages quoted by Maimonides in support of his conception of God means what he
reads into it. When Maimonides, in conformity with his conception of God, put the stamp of heresy on all who ascribed
anthropomorphic attributes to God, and when he declared
that they forfeited their share in the world to come, he
aroused the ire of his contemporary critic, Abraham ben
David (RaBaD) of Posquieres. "Better and greater men than
he conceived God anthropomorphically on the basis of their

interpretation of biblical passages, and even more by reason of the *agadot* that confused their minds" (*Hilkot Teshubah* 1:7). Evidently RaBaD, although he shared Maimonides' opinion concerning the interpretation to be given the anthropomorphic epithets for God, resented converting Greek philosophical concepts into Jewish religious dogmas.

Maimonides' rationalism brought him also into conflict with popular tradition on the question of miracles. Did the miracles recorded in the Bible actually occur? This was one of the most mooted problems of that day. From a consistently Aristotelian point of view, their occurrence is inconceivable. The average Jewish believer, who knew nothing about Aristotle, was not troubled by any intellectual difficulties with regard to miracles. But the Jews who came under the influence of Greek philosophy were skeptical about the miracles. Such skepticism was bound to undermine their loyalty to Judaism. In Jewish tradition, those miracles served as proof of God's special providence over Israel, and hence as a validation of Israel's claim that it possessed the true revelation of God's will and the true key to salvation. Maimonides was therefore unwilling to deny the historicity of those miracles, but he could not afford to ignore the problem to which the belief in their historicity gave rise. He had to find a way of reconciling that belief with his Aristotelian philosophy.

In attempting, however, to establish the rationality of the belief in miracles, Maimonides departed from Aristotelian conclusions, but not from the Aristotelian method. This was why he found it necessary to do two things which were uncalled for in the traditional idea of God. In the first place, he developed an elaborate argument to prove that the world was created out of nothing. Secondly, he explained miracles as exceptional arrangements in the order of nature, provided for at the time of creation. Although Maimonides seems to rally to the defense of tradition, the pragmatic implications of his interpretation of miracles are very different from those

of the naive faith in miracles on the part of the unphilo-
sophical traditionalist. The latter is convinced that through
prayer he can, in a crisis, influence God to intervene in his
behalf, even to the point of setting aside the laws of nature.
A disciple of Maimonides, to be consistent, would have to
consider such prayer as futile, since the miracle either could
not happen in answer to the prayer, or else was preordained
to happen from the very creation. In either case, such prayer,
being *tefillat shav,* would not be a legitimate act of worship.

Maimonides' conception of God diverges furthest from
Jewish tradition in regard to the question of divine providence. According to the Aristotelian conception, God could
not interest Himself in perishable objects. His providence
could, therefore, be exercised only over species, but not over
individuals. Before the discovery of the theory of evolution,
it was generally assumed that all species, and, indeed, all
general concepts, were eternal and unchangeable. They were
therefore spiritual "forms," not material bodies, and could
be objects in the eternal mind of God. God could know
them, but the particular transient individuals, being composed of matter as well as form, or—to use terms that were
almost synonymous in Aristotelian thought—of body as well
as spirit—such beings were beneath God's notice. Hence
God's providence could be conceived only as *hashgahah
kelalit,* providence over the genus, but not as *hashgahah
peratit,* providence over the individual. Jewish tradition, on
the other hand, assumes that God exercises His providence
over the most insignificant of beings, to say nothing of the
human individual.

Maimonides, though dominated by Aristotelian logic, was
too much of a Jew to accept its more radical implications. He
escaped the seemingly inevitable dilemma by an ingenious
compromise between the traditional and the Aristotelian
view. That compromise harmonized with his idea of the *sum-*

mum bonum as the philosophic contemplation of God. According to him, the Aristotelian view of divine providence is correct, as far as it applies to the lower animals. He finds it also acceptable with regard to the generality of mankind. Only those human beings who attain an intellectual conception of an infinite, eternal and wholly spiritual God are the objects of His direct providence. The rest, however, who fail to achieve that intellectual development, are under the dominion of natural law, which makes for the preservation of the species. It is evident that although the belief in divine providence is thus upheld by Maimonides, it is far from being in accord with Jewish tradition. So much for Maimonides' conception of God.

To provide Judaism with the kind of rationale which would satisfy the Jewish intellectuals of his day, Maimonides went to great lengths in his reinterpretation of Judaism. He gave it a different intention from that assigned to it by the ancient Tannaim and Amoraim, the architects of Rabbinic Judaism. He thus transformed, unconsciously no doubt, the entire pattern of traditional Judaism with its beliefs and practices. Just as with the same building-material we can construct either homes to live in or shops to work in, so with the same teachings and institutions we can construct radically different social and religious systems. It is the intention that creates the pattern. Maimonides injected into Jewish tradition a different intention from that given to it by the very authorities whose decisions, dicta and interpretations he organized into his great Code. That intention stemmed less from those authorities than from Aristotelianism, combined with some neo-Platonic elements, which he adopted from the philosophy of the Moslem philosopher, Avicenna.

The intention of a way of life, whether religious or philosophic, may be inferred from its conception of what constitutes for it salvation or fulfillment as human beings. With the same authoritative texts and rules of conduct it is possible to fashion diametrically opposed types of character, depending upon what one conceives as the ultimate goal of human endeavor, the fulfillment of life's highest potentialities, or the supreme good which should determine life's purposes. Both the rabbis and Maimonides use the term *ha-olam ha-ba* (the world to come) to designate "salvation," or the attainment of life's goal, but they use it in two such radically different senses that they seem to be moving in different universes of discourse. The type of human being that would result from the effort to attain *ha-olam ha-ba*, as the rabbis understood it, would resemble Hillel. The type of human being that would result from the effort to attain *ha-olam ha-ba*, as Maimonides understood it, would resemble Aristotle.

According to the rabbinic view, the world as originally created was perfect, but man corrupted it through his sin. In the future, however, God will re-create this world. It will, in effect, be a new world, "a new heaven and a new earth." In the meantime, the consequences of man's original sin bar his way to the "tree of life," the fruit of which might have rendered him immortal. As an additional punishment for his sin, man is doomed to a life of toil and travail. The time will come, however, when God will destroy death. Man will then enjoy immortal life in that new world, or the world-to-come.

Having a share in the world-to-come, in the sense of being entitled to a life in the hereafter, is traditionally conceived not as a reward of individual merit, but as intrinsically due to God's special grace which He confers on all who belong to Israel, His Chosen People, for having accepted the Torah. The particular share of the world-to-come that would fall to each individual Jew, or the nature of the bliss to be there enjoyed by him, might be commensurate with his personal merit in this world. However, non-Jews who have lived up to the seven cardinal ordinances God had given Noah and his descendants are also entitled to a share in the world-to-come.

Maimonides, however, transformed the foregoing doctrine of the world-to-come. After summarizing the traditional views current in his day (*Commentary on Mishnah,* Sanhedrin, ch. X), he warns the reader against taking literally any of the homiletic passages that describe the world-to-come. According to Maimonides, the world-to-come is the spiritual experience of the perfected individual soul after death, and cannot be apprehended by man so long as he is alive on earth. Here his soul, being attached to the body, is dependent upon the senses. We can no more conceive the bliss of the world-to-come, while we are alive, says Maimonides, than a fish can imagine what fire is. Our senses are bodily functions, and therefore cease to function when the body disintegrates. Man is corporeal, and all his organic functions minister to his physical organism which is inherently subject to change and ultimate destruction. Death is man's inevitable end, as it is that of all living beings. Only in one respect does man differ from them, and that is in his ability to contemplate the nature of God who is eternal, infinite and unchanging. This ability renders the individual soul one with God. Philosophically, the knower and the known are in reality one. By thus becoming one with God, the soul attains spiritual immortality. One has to be an ideationist to arrive at such a conclusion.

Such immortality is an achievement, and not a group privilege conferred on Jews. The assertion that all Jews have a portion in the world-to-come must not be construed, according to Maimonides, to mean that every individual Jew will actually, and in person, participate in this salvation. Its significance lies in the fact that God's revelation of the Torah to Israel, and to Israel alone, has given to the Jew possession of the main instrument of salvation. But to function as such an instrument, the Torah must not only be obeyed, but understood in terms of the most advanced intellectual development. It must convey those true concepts of God by which the individual can enter into communion with Him. Mere conformity to the commandments of the Torah, without appreciation of their deeper meanings, cannot bring salvation. In the last analysis, it is metaphysical thinking alone that can confer salvation. All the laws of the Torah are either symbols of metaphysical ideas, or are means of regulating the social life of the Jewish People, in order to make it possible for them to engage in intellectual pursuits leading to a metaphysical comprehension of God.

According to Maimonides, the resurrection of the dead does not mean, as it did in rabbinic Judaism, resurrection to an everlasting corporeal existence. It means that, by a divine miracle, those of Israel who in this world have led righteous lives, in accordance with the precepts of the Torah, will be brought back to life during the reign of the Messiah. They will then enjoy the tranquillity necessary for the study of the Torah, and thus attain spiritual perfection. In time, however, they will die again, since their bodies are necessarily subject to disintegration. Only their souls will live on forever, and enjoy that union with God which is man's supreme bliss.

It is thus apparent that Maimonides gave to the belief in the world-to-come a totally different meaning from that which it had for the rabbis. In doing so he set up a new goal for Jewish life, and a new hierarchy of spiritual values. Although he assumed, as had the ancient Sages, that the necessary means to earning a share in the world-to-come was obedience to the laws of the Torah, the function of that obedience necessarily assumed a different character from what it had for those Sages. It is therefore no exaggeration to state that Maimonides' version of traditional Judaism is a veritable transformation of it.

The adoption of the foregoing untraditional conception of salvation led Maimonides to depart from the traditional conception of Israel. In rabbinic teaching, the only individuals whose merits account for the superiority of Israel are the three Patriarchs. The election of Israel took place in accordance with the promise God had made to those Patriarchs. Israel is thus conceived as enjoying divine favor only through the merit of the Fathers. That is why God is addressed in the opening benediction of the *Amidah* as "the God of Abraham, the God of Isaac and the God of Jacob."

On the other hand, the People of Israel, in its collective capacity, is more important than its greatest spiritual leaders, including Moses. The gift of prophecy was vouchsafed to Moses only for the sake of Israel. This is the significance of the midrashic interpretation of the words, "And the Lord spoke unto Moses: 'Go, get thee down; for thy people, that thou has brought up out of the land of Egypt, have dealt corruptly' " (Ex. 32.7). The Sages represent Moses as replying: "Yesterday Thou didst say to me: 'Thou shalt come up, thou and Aaron with thee' (Ex. 19.24). Why then dost Thou tell me now: 'Go, get thee down'?" (Ex. 24.1). According to our Sages, God's answer to Moses was: "Not for thine own glory wert thou chosen as My messenger, but for the glory of the People of Israel." That is also implied in the passage which tells of Jacob's dream: "And behold the angels of God were ascending and descending on it" (Gen. 28.12). Jacob was given to understand that, if his descendants were righteous, both they and their messengers would achieve high rank in the world. But if they were not righteous, both they and their messengers would be degraded (Ex. R. XLII, 2).

Rabbinic Judaism does not regard a people as existing for its saints or prophets; on the contrary, a saint or prophet owes his distinction to the people he serves. Whatever mental or spiritual gifts a man possesses, he must use not only for himself, but mainly for the improvement of his people. The realization of the spiritual implications of life, according to rabbinic Judaism, requires group life, and the larger the group the greater is likely to be the manifestation of the divine. The habitat of the *Shekinah* is the *Kenesset Yisrael*, the *ecclesia* of Israel, and not any individual Jew however spiritually great.

For Maimonides, the reverse is true. He is dominated by the Hellenic aristocratic ideal. For him, the prophet, or saint, is the purpose of human existence. Israel's greatness, which he affirms no less zealously than the sages, consists, according to him, not in its collective functioning as a people living in accordance with God's laws, but in its ability to produce a great number of prophets and knowers of God. This is borne out by his interpretation of the belief in the Messiah. The only significance of the Messianic kingdom for Maimonides is the leisure it will afford the scholar, by reason of the tranquility which will then prevail, to achieve spiritual perfection through his intellectual pursuits. From the traditional point of view, however, the belief in the Messiah was the expression of hope for the return of Israel to its homeland and for the recovery of its ancient glory. The rabbis assumed that the greatness of Israel would then be so manifest to the nations that they would accept its spiritual hegemony, and come to worship its God as the only true God.

Similarly in regard to the conception of Torah, Maimonides deviated from the traditional assumption in his understanding of what constituted salvation and the goal of human existence. According to tradition, since the Torah is the word of God, those who study it and observe its behests, or *mitzvot*, come to possess a knowledge of God. This is true whether or not they understand the reasons for the *mitzvot*. But this was not the opinion of Maimonides. *Since, according to Maimonides, God can be known only through the medium of the intellect, the only way in which the Torah can function as a medium of the knowledge of God is to interpret its behests in the light of reason.*

Maimonides assigns two general purposes to the *mitzvot* of the Torah: the well-being of the soul, and the well-being of the body. According to him, only the right ideas concerning God, nature and man can confer well-being upon the soul. Under the term "well-being of the body," he includes all practical precepts, both mandatory and prohibitive, that have as their purpose the regulation of the civic life and the establishment of peaceful relations among men. These practical precepts are not an end in themselves, but a means to the well-being of the soul. Thus the perfection of the soul, which is attained through knowledge, is the purpose of human life.

When we survey the precepts which have as their purpose the well-being of the soul, we discover that they refer to ritual observances. Some of them, like the laws of the sacrificial cult, have the negative purpose of weaning the Israelites away from idolatrous and superstitious notions of God; others, like the laws pertaining to the Sabbath, the wearing of phylacteries, or the reciting of prayers, have the positive purpose of inculcating belief in the unity, eternity and incorporeality of God. If we fail to discover any significant purpose in the ritual observances, it is due either to some lack in our knowledge, or to some incapacity of our intellect. It is true that the Sages say of the *hukkim,* or statutes, which are assumed to refer mainly to ritual observances, and which seem to have no rational basis, that they are decreed by God, and that no one dare question their importance or binding character. According to Maimonides, however, what the Sages mean is not that it is forbidden to search for the underlying reason of those observances, but that we should not use our failure to find any valid reason for them as an excuse for disobeying them.

From that standpoint, the purpose even of ethical conduct is mainly to assure the tranquillity which is necessary for the contemplation of God. As to what constitutes ethical conduct, Maimonides accepts the Aristotelian doctrine of the

"Golden Mean." The criterion on which that doctrine is based is intrinsically esthetic rather than ethical. To quote from Aristotle himself, "We say of good works of art, 'It is not possible to take away or add anything,' implying that excess and defect destroy goodness in art. Virtue is more exact and better than any art" (*Nicom. Ethics* II, vi, 9). This conception of ethics as a fine art is worlds removed from the passion which breathes throughout the Bible for righteousness as the essence of Godhood and of God-likeness. Nevertheless, Maimonides, in his Introduction to the ethical treatise of the Mishnah known as *Abot,* avails himself of Aristotle's doctrine of the "Golden Mean" to interpret the ethics of our ancient Sages.

The foregoing instances of the difference between the rabbinic version of Judaism and Maimonides' version make it evident that Judaism, as expounded in his *Commentary on the Mishnah* and in his *Guide for the Perplexed,* virtually underwent a transformation at his hands. He subjected its theological beliefs, its national aspirations, its ritual observances, its social institutions and ethical ideals to revaluation in accordance with his philosophic conception of the world-to-come. That his reinterpretation came to be regarded as a classic expression of Jewish teaching is even more significant. If Judaism is capable of including Maimonides' *Commentary on the Mishnah,* his *Mishneh Torah* and his *Guide for the Perplexed* among its library of religious classics, it is because *Judaism is more than a specific philosophy of life; it is the ongoing life of a people intent upon keeping alive for the highest conceivable purpose, despite changes in the general climate of opinion.*

If we seek to account for the fact that Maimonides, notwithstanding his untraditional views, was accepted as a great religious authority in Israel, the answer is to be found in his devotion to the Jewish People and its civilization. His life was wholly consecrated to their service; their interests were his interests. His actual, if not always his theoretic, criterion of Jewishness is loyalty to Jewish interests, material and spiritual, rather than acquiescence in a particular creed. The Jews could forgive, or ignore Maimonides' heterodox views, because they appreciated his contribution toward the maintenance of their unity and solidarity. He may have reckoned with Jewish life from a novel viewpoint, a viewpoint that was located in alien thought; but he reckoned with Jewish life in its entirety. He was interested in every aspect of it, and devoted all his energies to the interpretation of its teachings in accordance with a consistent pattern that took account of everything which Jewish tradition held sacred—the Bible, the Talmud, Jewish fellowship, Jewish practice, and Jewish hopes.

The great importance that Maimonides attached to the principle "Separate not thyself from the community," is significant. "He who departs from the ways of the community, even though he commit no transgressions but only separates himself from the congregation of Israel, and performs no *mitzvot* in fellowship with them, and does not take part in their distress nor share their fasts, but goes his way as if he were a Gentile and not a Jew—such a person has no share in the world-to-come" (*Hilkot Teshubah* 3, 14). That is why those of the Jewish People who could not follow the metaphysical reasoning of the *Guide for the Perplexed* could revere Maimonides for his *Commentary on the Mishnah*, and above all for his great code, the *Mishneh Torah*. That is why ordinary Jews, who were not learned, were impressed by what they knew of Maimonides' saintly character and his selfless devotion to the Jewish People.

CHAPTER V

HERMANN COHEN'S RATIONALE

For the third time in its career Judaism is again in search of a rationale. An outstanding rationale which modern Judaism has produced is that of Hermann Cohen.

Hermann Cohen was born in 1842 in the small town of Coswig in one of the small North German dukedoms. His father, who was a cantor and a teacher, gave him a good Jewish training in the traditional subject matter, such as Bible and Talmud, and introduced him to the study of Maimonides' philosophical writings. The latter must have made a deep impression upon him, because his frequent references to Maimonides indicate a high regard for his interpretation of Judaism and a desire to emulate him in guiding the perplexed of our day. When the young Cohen completed his studies at the Gymnasium in the city of Dessau, he was admitted, in 1859, to the then recently established Jewish Theological Seminary of Breslau, which was headed by Zechariah Frankel, and on whose faculty were some of the most eminent founders of the Scientific Study of Judaism. At the same time he studied the Greek classics with Jacob Bernays at the Seminary, and by himself as an externe of the Breslau University. Apparently his interest in philosophy led him to leave the Seminary, without completing its rabbinical courses, and to make the study and teaching of philosophy his career.

At the age of thirty-one he finally succeeded in receiving an appointment as *Privatdozent* (instructor) at the Marburg University, which had not yet attained the reputation it later achieved through his role in it. The department of philosophy was then headed by Friedrich Albert Lange, the well-known author of the *Geschichte des Materialismus* (History of Materialism). Cohen wrote a work on Kant not long after he began teaching, and was soon thereafter recommended for the full professorship which materialized after three years, when Lange retired. The interview between Lange and him, on his original appointment, gives us at once an insight into his attitude toward Judaism in general, and toward religion in particular, which marked his religio-philosophic outlook. Lange had said to Cohen that, whereas philosophically they were at one with each other, they differed religiously. To that Cohen replied, "What you call Christianity, I term Prophetic Judaism." That so pleased Lange that he opened his Bible and pointed out the passages in the Prophetic Writings which he had marked.

Rosenzweig, in his introduction to the three volumes of Hermann Cohen's writings, calls attention to what it meant in those years for a Jew to receive an appointment as professor of philosophy in a German university. Germany was then intent upon developing a spirit of national unity with a sense of cultural mission. It expected the philosophy professors at the various universities to imbue their students with that selfless devotion to their fatherland which would enable it to exercise the cultural hegemony of mankind. The unprecedented succession of great thinkers, poets, and musicians, who had flourished since the middle of the eighteenth century, stimulated that ambition. For a Jew therefore to have been entrusted with the teaching of philosophy was not possible in a university like that of Berlin. At Marburg there happened to prevail a more liberal spirit, and Lange himself, to whom Cohen owed his appointment, was an advocate of democratic socialism. That explains how Cohen was entrusted with so responsible a position, and why he felt throughout his life that he owed the German nation a debt of loyalty and love which he had to pay in full. That, no doubt, influenced his attitude toward Judaism.

Hermann Cohen's role as interpreter of Judaism constitutes the attempt of a representative Jewish thinker in the Germany of the latter half of the nineteenth century to justify the effort of Jews to retain their Jewish individuality in the new life opened up to them by emancipation from their medieval disabilities. That emancipation was being granted them in dribs and drabs, and with strings attached. Professor Salo W. Baron describes the situation pointedly when he refers to "the vicissitudes in the protracted struggle for emancipation in Germany (including Austria) as that classical laboratory for the Jewish question in the nineteenth century" (*A Social and Religious History of the Jews,* vol. II, p. 239).

Though no longer aliens, the Jews in Germany were unwelcome fellow-citizens. They were kept out of positions of high rank in the government, the military and the academic world. Before long the new form of Jew-hatred, known as anti-Semitism, arose. The anti-Semites resented the Jews' efforts to assimilate to the cultural life of Germany, without renouncing their Jewish identity, even more than they resented the refusal of some Jews to assimilate. It became quite evident that the emancipation had been far from a wholehearted and unconditional grant. It was accompanied by a tacit expectation not only that the emancipated Jews would flock to the baptismal font, but also that they would become totally inconspicuous. As for actually playing an important role in the cultural and industrial life of Germany, that was not even to be considered.

What particularly irritated the political authorities in Germany was, in the first place, that the few who had converted to Christianity and had begun to play an important role in the cultural life of the nation were known, as in the case of Heine, to have treated their conversion as a mere formality. Secondly, Jews who refused to accept Christianity were assumed to have done so not out of any strong convictions about Judaism but out of a lack of patriotism.

The systematic and intensive campaign of the anti-Semitism to which nineteenth-century Germany gave birth was a new form of Jew-hatred. It was not due to the natural dislike for the unlike, but to the calculated search for a scapegoat on which to put the blame for national or personal frustration. One of the outstanding anti-Semites during the early part of Cohen's career was Henrich von Treitschke, a German who stemmed from a military Prussian family, and who was prevented by a physical handicap from achieving his military ambition. He possessed great talent as a historian and professor of political science, and he used it to educate the German people to look to military victories abroad rather than to political privileges at home.

It was Treitschke who may be said to have roused Hermann Cohen from his slumber as a Jew. In the 1879 edition of the *Preussiche Jahrbücher* which Treitschke edited, he published a dissertation entitled *Ein Wort über unser Judentum*. He argued that the Jews belonged to a different racial stock from the main body of the German nation, and that their religion was tribal and exclusive. Consequently, despite all their efforts to assimilate to the German nation, they were bound to remain a foreign body in it. Cohen had by that time virtually put Judaism out of his mind. He retained only a sentimental attachment to it, which expressed itself in visits to his father's home on the High Holidays and during the Passover festival. On the other hand, he considered a Jew's conversion to Christianity an act either of intellectual dishonesty or moral insensitivity. In later years, however, he made a point of stressing the fact that it was not the instinct of devotion to faith and race which guided his Jewish consciousness, but philosophical method and historical control (*Juedische Schriften,* I, p. 333). What could be more symptomatic of how little the fact of Jewish existence as such had counted in his thinking?

Treitschke's anti-Semitic assault on Judaism was a challenge which Cohen could not afford to ignore. He felt that he had to declare himself as a Jew and to prove that Judaism was a *universal* religion. To remain loyal to Judaism was in no way incompatible with wholehearted devotion to the unity and greatness of the German nation. Cohen considered himself as a *baal-teshuvah* (penitent) from that time on.

Most significant, however, for a description of Cohen's stance as a Jew is his reply to Treitschke, which Treitschke ignored and which Cohen himself published as a brochure entitled *Ein Bekentniss zur Judenfrage* (A Confession Pertaining to the Jewish Question). The following is a summary paraphrase of that "Confession" (*Juedische Schriften,* II, p. 70):

We Jews have been expecting to be integrated into the German nation, but now Treitschke again raises the problem of race. He maintains that Judaism is a national religion of a foreign tribe; we Jews are therefore unassimilable. That forces me to confess. I speak not as a Jewish theologian but as a professor of philosophy, who is an Israelite monotheist. (In his correspondence with Treitschke Cohen had asked him to use the term "Israelites" instead of "Jews".)

There may be different forms of religion, but religion is one, as is ethics. Each so-called religion is merely a particular vehicle of religion as such. *Actually there is no essential difference between Israelite monotheism and Protestant Christianity.* Judaism emphasizes the spiritual nature of God and the Messianic future of mankind. Jews accept the idea of religious humanism as formulated by Kant in his *Practical Reason,* without accepting the dogma of the Incarnation, though it substantially symbolizes the humanization of religion. With the liberalization of both Judaism and Christianity, the two religions will ultimately merge into the religion of the German nation, in which all its citizens will participate. I object to Lazarus' statement that there can be no German religion; I maintain that Jewish religion is just as German as is Christian religion. Actually we are on the way toward a German religion. Only the forms of worship at present divide Israelites from Christians. Even in that regard, Israelites have modified much, and in time, God willing, will modify more.

We love Germany as our fatherland and our mother country even when it does not live up to what it should be. In time we shall merge with the German race. That, however, need in no way compromise the Israelite religion.

The Palestinian party (Zionists) has no roots in German *Kultur*. Graetz's Israelite nationalism is perverse. Lazarus' assumption that true culture must allow for differences is entirely mistaken. It is a moral duty to foster cultural unity. Israelites have only one permanent task, namely, to preserve monotheism until a "purified Christianity" also adopts it.

If Israelites will be treated as equals in all respects, their national assimilation through social adaptation and intermarriage will make headway. When, however, the State shows partiality toward Jewish converts to Christianity, it acts immorally and leads to religious retrogression among the Israelites themselves. If we are to become part of the German nation for which a common religion is necessary, we Israelites must foster the religious education of our youth, in order that we may contribute our monotheism to the German religion.

Our modern Israelite religion is, indeed, an adaptation to modern Protestantism. Both have already given up much of their old ways of thinking: we the Talmud, and they their Church tradition. Even for our modern idea of Messianism we are indebted to Luther, of blessed [*sic!*] memory. *

---

* "It is difficult to understand the behavior of most German Protestants in the first Nazi years," writes William L. Shirer, "unless one is aware of two things: their history and the influence of Martin Luther. The great founder of Protestantism was both a passionate anti-Semite and a ferocious believer in absolute obedience to political authority. He wanted Germany rid of the Jews, and when they would be sent away he advised that they be deprived of

When we read Cohen's reply to Treitschke, together with some other statements published by Cohen during that year, particularly the supplementary one which deals with the problem of the Sabbath (vol. II, p. 66), it is evident that Judaism was to him essentially a *religious philosophy*—ethical monotheism—and that Jews were a kind of religio-philosophical society. Since their integration into the life of the general community made the observance of a Saturday Sabbath infeasible, he concluded that it would not affect their Judaism if they observed the Sabbath on Sunday.

In that same year (1880) Cohen wrote, in his supplement to a statement on the Sabbath he had written in 1869, what, in a way, sums up his entire approach to the problem of Judaism: "I can prove that the religion of Kant, yea, even of Lessing, in many important respects, resembles our own living religion more than that of our own dear benefactor Mendelssohn."

Hermann Cohen's *Religion der Vernunft,* which represents his final formulation of what he regarded as the rational and viable element in Judaism, spells out in specific terms the ethical monotheism which, with some additional elimination of the traditional Jewish ritual, he believed would ultimately become the religion of the entire German nation. Needless to say, subsequent events in the world at large and in Germany in particular have proved his blueprint for Judaism's future good only for some visionary air-castle, without the least foundation in reality. He idealized the Incarnation myth as centering the attention of religion upon the condition of man. He glorified Luther who, as events have since demonstrated, may be accounted the evil genius of Germany.

'all their cash and jewels and silver and gold' and furthermore 'that their synagogues or schools be set on fire, that their houses be broken up and destroyed . . . and they be put under a roof or stable, like the gypsies . . . in misery and captivity as they incessantly lament and complain to God against us,' advice that was literally followed four centuries later by Hitler, Goering and Himmler" (*The Rise and Fall of the Third Reich,* Crest Book, pp. 326-327).

He regarded Protestantism as akin to Prophetic Judaism. He was blind to the rising tide of anti-Semitism which was to sweep away all hopes of the Jews that they would enjoy the blessings of the emancipation. He assumed as late as 1879, long after anti-Semitism had achieved official recognition, that he was still living in the Germany of Kant, Herder, and Lessing, instead of that of Fichte who had advised that Jews should be deprived of all rights and deported to Palestine, and of Hegel who glorified war and considered it a moral necessity. All these misconceptions betray either a naivete, or a mental astigmatism, which prevented Cohen from sensing the realities of the situation in which he found himself. A physician whose diagnosis is undependable is barely qualified to make the proper prognosis. Why then do we concern ourselves in knowing what Cohen had to say about Judaism?

Hermann Cohen deserves to be better known than he is for a number of reasons. In the first place, his *Religion der Vernunft* is meant to be more than a Jewish theology, like Kaufmann Kohler's work by that name. It claims to be a presentation of Judaism, not from its own standpoint, but from that of objective universal reason. The title of the book *Religion der Vernunft,* and the subsequent elimination from the original title of the definite article *Die,* indicates that its subject is not Judaism or Jewish religion, but religion in general. Judaism is utilized merely as an illustration; hence, the use of its source-material as illustrative of rational religion as such. It is only incidentally and indirectly, and for that reason perhaps more effectively, used as a *rationale* to convince the Jew who wishes to act as a rational human being, that he ought to remain loyal to the Jewish religion.

If we are interested in knowing how the Jews have been reacting to the new condition created by their enfranchisement and desegregation, we cannot afford to ignore Hermann Cohen and his *Religion der Vernunft.* It was evidently in-

tended for the many intellectual Jews in Germany who
were eager to become thoroughly Germanized, because they
saw in the German version of democratic socialism a more
relevant and meaningful ideal than in Jewish Messianism,
but who could not conscientiously adopt Christianity as their
religion.

Franz Rosenzweig, in his introduction to Cohen's *Jewish
Writings,* points out what acted in his career as a bridge by
which he returned to Judaism after having virtually abandoned it. It was Cohen's faith in ethical socialism (I, XXIII).
Cohen, by virtue of the unconscious pull which Judaism exercised on him, read into the socialist critique of the social
order the main burden of the prophetic message to the Jewish
People and into Messianism the fulfillment of the socialist
ideal. That fact gives us an insight into what must have convinced Cohen that *Judaism, as a religion, possessed the most
rational basis for the belief in God.*

He must have arrived at that conclusion through the following line of reasoning: Pure ethics addresses itself to the
individual; it provides the individual with a basis for his
loyalty to the state and to the laws by which it enables him to
fulfill himself, though not completely; the state constitutes
the frame for the functioning of the individual, in relation to
his fellow individuals; for complete fulfillment, the individual needs to *transcend* the state; he has to relate himself
to mankind as a whole, he has to be a citizen of the world,
as Stoicism taught long ago; for mankind to constitute the
all-inclusive frame for the self-fulfillment of the individual,
he needs a concept like monotheism: "the rise of monotheism
in Israel is an inexplicable mystery; but equally so is Messianism which the prophets in Israel first clearly articulated as
the universal destiny of mankind" *(ibid.,* I, ch. XIII). By thus
seeing a rational connection between Jewish monotheism
and Messianism, and by equating Messianism with socialism,
Cohen returned to Judaism.

How little attention Cohen paid to the problem of Jewish existence is evident from his open avowal, during his years at the Marburg University, of assimilationist hopes. He went as far as to advocate intermarriage of Jews with non-Jews. This probably explains why the spokesmen for the Reform movement have not included him among their number, despite the fact that his rationale for Judaism has much in common with theirs. On the other hand, Kaufmann Kohler, the most authoritative spokesman of the Reform movement, has written as follows:

"Yet, just because of this universalistic Messianic hope of Judaism, it is still imperative, as it has been throughout the past, that the Jewish people must continue its separateness as 'a Kingdom of priests and a holy nation' and for the sake of its world mission avoid intermarrying with members of other sects, unless they espouse the Jewish faith. Israel's particularism, says Professor Lazarus, has its univeralism as its motive and aim" (*Jewish Theology,* New York, pp. 445-446).

It is, indeed, difficult to say which of the two rationales for Judaism is less objectionable—Cohen's, with a workable conception of Messianism and acceptance of intermarriage, or Kohler's prohibition of intermarriage, with the reduction of Messianism to pulpit oratory.

To be able to evaluate properly a modern rationale for Judaism, it is essential to keep in mind the fact that the present predicament of Jewish life is the consequence of the rise of modern nationalism which, incidentally, led to the Jewish emancipation, and to the spread of modern naturalism, which is identified as the Enlightenment. Modern naturalism challenges all traditional religions, including the Jewish religion with its traditional version of the purpose and meaning of Jewish existence. Modern naturalism, as a challenge to the religious tradition of the Jews, is in a sense, only a modern version of the philosophies which were current in pre-modern times. If Judaism managed to counter the challenge of the philosophies of Plato and Aristotle, why should it not be able to counter the challenge of the philosophy of Kant? This is virtually what Hermann Cohen tried to prove with his treatise on *Rational Religion*—and succeeded eminently.

Nevertheless, Cohen failed to reckon with the challenge of emancipation to Jewish existence. Before the emancipation, the Jews actually existed as a nation, despite their lack of a state and their being in exile. Kant himself referred to them as a Palestinian nation, although in comparison with their status as an *ecclesia,* their nationhood was dormant. With the acceptance by the Jews of the citizenship of other nations, their existence as a group could no longer continue under the status of Jewish nationhood. The only status under which their existence as a group might have continued was that of an *ecclesia,* had all Jews subscribed, as they had done in the past, to the Written and Oral Law. Since that was no longer feasible, the problem of Jewish existence under the unprecedented conditions of our day should have engaged the minds of the Jewish scholars and thinkers. Instead, the Jewish scholars confined themselves to reconstructing the Jewish existence of the *past,* and the Jewish thinkers confined themselves to articulating the *rationale* for Judaism as a religion. Neither the one nor the other considered it necessary to concentrate on the specific form and the objective validation of Jewish *existence* in our day.

Even so great a philospher as Hermann Cohen dealt with the problem of Jewish existence in *ad hoc* and empirical fashion, as can be learned from his *Juedische Schriften,* published with a highly informative Introduction by his disciple Franz Rosenzweig. Thus it seems that throughout the years of his professorship at the Marburg University Cohen gave little thought to the collective life of the Jews. On the other hand, during the years he taught at the Akademie fuer die Wissenschaft des Judentums, he attached spiritual significance to the need for Jews to maintain their communal separateness. That is very strongly reflected in some of the chapters of his *Religion der Vernunft*.

A second reason for becoming acquainted with Hermann Cohen's rationale for Judaism is to get at the root of what must be wrong with the kind of general philosophy which could have misled so great a thinker. He not only developed a blind spot for what was happening around him; he also envisaged the destiny of Judaism as a kind of Nirvana. He deprecated in the strongest terms any tendency to resurrect the corporate life of the Jewish People through Zionism, and interpreted Jewish Messianism as the transformation of Judaism into a universal religion, with each of the modern nations, particularly Germany, adopting it and giving it its own national expression.

What could have led Hermann Cohen to arrive at so bizarre a conception of Judaism? There can be no doubt that his preoccupation with philosophy as such, and particularly with the classic ideationist philosophy, accounts for his having regarded Judaism itself as a philosophy and the Jewish People as its vessel. It was Kant who had emphasized the fact that religion is one, and the various religions are merely different vessels which impress their internal shape upon religion (*J. Sch.*, II, 75). Accordingly, religion as such is essentially philosophy. Most German philosophers considered religion as a primitive stage of philosophy. Schlegel, on the other hand, regarded religion as evolutionary and therefore destined also to be the "consummation of philosophy." That was apparently also Cohen's view of Judaism.

It is conceivable that a philosophy might function as a unifying factor of a school, or of a social group for a considerable period of time; it cannot, however, by itself, form out of the one or the other an organic social body, with an urge to self-perpetuation. The carrier unit of a philosophy is essentially an individual person. By treating religion as a philosophy, the ideationist philosophers had ultimately to resort to the device of adopting certain ideas as dogmas, and of making the acceptance of those dogmas a prerequisite to membership in the corporate body, whether church or nation, which became the vessel of religion.

Comparing religion to the liquid content of a vessel and the corporate body that fosters it to a vessel is a fallacy which could have arisen only from the dualistic thought pattern of the classical ideationist philosophy, beginning with Plato and culminating with Hegel. The vessel—and in this case the Jewish People—was not conceived by Cohen as intrinsic to, and inseparable from, the substance of the Jewish religion itself, as the human body is intrinsic to, and inseparable from, its life and mind. In ideationist philosophy, body and mind are not two aspects of the same reality, but two separable realities. Likewise, a people and its religion, according to ideationist philosophy, are two separable realities. The very title, *Rational Religion, in the Light of the Source Material of Judaism*, indicates that Judaism was to Cohen a philosophical religion. Since he conceived both philosophy and religion in purely ideationist terms, he came to think of Judaism as a religious philosophy, and therefore as transferrable from the Jewish People to the German people. By the time that happens, the Jewish People will have become so integrated into the German people that the survival of Judaism will no longer be a problem, since there will no longer be any Jews.

To be properly oriented to the problem of religion, we have to realize that religion is only a general and abstract term, like the term "language." Just as language exists only as languages, so religion exists only as religions. Each religion functions as a means of fostering in the individual members of a clan, tribe, city, state or nation an awareness of mutual responsibility for enabling each of them to make the most of his life, or in theological terms, to achieve salvation. Each religion identifies as holy or divine whatever it regards as enabling the members of the group, or the group as a whole, to make the most of life. From that standpoint, *Judaism is the civilization of the Jewish People, and Jewish religion is that aspect of Judaism which identifies as holy or divine whatever in the cosmos impels and enables the Jewish People, individually and collectively, to make the most of life ethically and spiritually.*

To realize what Cohen means by the term "rational religion" it is necessary to have a clear idea of his conception of reason, as part of his philosophic system. To say, as some do, that his "system is a consistent extreme idealism which teaches that being is wholly rooted in reason," is merely to put him in the same class with Hegel. It is true that, as the founder of Neo-Kantianism, he also taught that "being is wholly rooted in reason." His conception, however, of the function of reason was radically different from that of Hegel. To Hegel, reason was so absolutely self-sufficient that, as the spider exudes its own cobweb, so reason was assumed to exude from itself whatever was real. The principle of "thesis, antithesis and synthesis" could dispense with the data of experience.

Cohen, to be sure, reckoned with the data of experience almost as little as did his master Kant; however, he took issue with Kant on the way reason functioned. According to Kant, reason imposes, once and for all, the categories of space and time, together with its logical categories, on the data of the senses, which Kant conceived as emanating from the mysterious and unknowable "thing-in-itself." On the other hand, Cohen maintained that reason was not a kind of mental faculty which, with its fixed set of *a priori* categories, immediately exhausts all that is to be known about anything. Reason was to him a *continuous process* of searching for the authentic in the data of experience. According to Cohen, no data of experience necessarily remain identically the same after each renewed application of reason to them. On the

contrary, they tend to change. As reason proceeds with its
search, the data of experience become different with each
step in the progress of reason's search. Reason is not a static,
but a dynamic, function. The authentic, therefore, is not a
final and absolute fact, but a goal that is progressively being
striven for, though never actually achieved.

The only idea a child, for example, can have of time is in
terms of days and nights, of the seasons of the year, of the fact
that he grows older every day, week, month and year. For the
physicist in the laboratory, the idea of time is in terms of the
clock by which he regulates his experiments. For the theoretical physicist, time is the independent variable in the dif-
ferential equation of motion. For Kant, time is a built-in
category of the mind by which it measures the data of the
senses. Each foregoing conception of time is a rational one.
There is, however, a greater approximation with each conception to the authentic nature of time. Neo-Kantianism, of
which Cohen was the founder, maintained that even Kant's
idea of time is not yet the absolutely authentic one. Further
contemplation, which experience or experiment might stimulate, might elicit an even more authentic idea of time.

Cohen applied the same method of reasoning to the idea
of God. It must be remembered that he was very much impressed by the results of Wellhausen's scientific study of the
Bible, the outcome of which was the evolutionary conception
of Jewish religion. He therefore accepted as a fact that the
Jewish idea of God has evolved from a less rational to a more
rational one. However, *it started out being rational,* in that
it was the first idea that intuitively sought to identify as God
the only being that was authentically such. Authenticity in
the idea of God meant for ancient Israel what authenticity
meant for the Greek philosophers: permanence and immutability, as well as eternity (cf. Ps. 90.2; 102.27, 103.11). No
other religion made that a criterion for godhood. Hence the
uniqueness of Israel's idea of God.

Being rational, however, does not mean that the idea itself is static. On the contrary, with experience, it deepens and comes nearer to being absolutely authentic, though it never gets there. Thus Israel's idea of God evolved from being national in its scope, to being universal. Later, it evolved from being anthropomorphic to being entirely spiritual. In our own day, according to Cohen, the idea of God has to evolve *pari passu* with the idea of ideal humanity, of which the idea of God is a correlate.

The point in all this is that, by giving this new direction to classic ideationism, Cohen advocated, in theory, the need for consulting the data of experience (*Religion der Vernunft*, ch. XIII, 279-280). He himself, however, did not always live up to this rule. That explains why Cohen, in practice, continues to view life from the ivory tower of classical ideationism, and never gets rid of his blindspot for some of the most obtrusive and strident realities. He moves from one hypothesis to the next, without testing each hypothesis by observing carefully the data of experience to see whether they verify it. New data of experience are dealt with cavalierly by him. He depends on the process of reason to progress, automatically as it were, from one generalization to the next, as a result of its inherent power to mature.

That is why, until aroused by Treitschke, Cohen was under the delusion that he belonged to a nation dominated by the rational good will of a Kant and a Herder. That accounts for his mistakenly assuming that, as a Jew, he belonged to a historical religio-philosophical society, instead of to what had been a nation in exile and one in need of a new status. With two such unrealistic assumptions as data of experience, his neo-Kantian hypothesis concerning the role of ideas could scarcely prove of much help in the formulation of a rationale for the modern Jew. The trouble with Cohen's rationalism is that it is a kind of half-way station between ideationist and functional rationalism.

Nevertheless, there is much in what Cohen says about the Jewish religion that those who are in search of a rationale for Judaism cannot afford to ignore. Here and there, Cohen is carried away, despite his own contention to the contrary, by his love for Judaism as a way of life, which was implanted in him by his father. He gives expression to many a valid insight which renders the reader oblivious to what is sterile in his ideationism. In fact, those insights betray unconscious trespasses on his part into *functional* rationalism.

The most seminal of Cohen's ideas on religion is that the prophets paved the way for the principle in monotheism that religion should have as its chief concern man and not God. With that conception of the ethical function of religion, Cohen arrives at his second seminal idea, that God is the correlate of man. In other words, Divinity is to be conceived as that aspect of nature which impels and helps man to transcend his animal nature. Man in the image of God cannot find his fulfillment in the pursuit of power and pleasure. God as "the Power that makes for righteousness" is the Power that makes for the salvation of men and nations. At one point he states the matter bluntly when he says: "The God concept can be recognized only in the concept of the moral law" (*Religion der Vernunft,* p. 417).

The comments on the text of the Epitome of Cohen's *opus magnum* are intended to help the reader find the numerous seminal truths which are valid within any rationalist frame of reference. It is a work on religion, which is Judaism's first full-size response to the emancipation of the Jews from the political, intellectual and spiritual thraldom of the Middle Ages.

PART TWO

Epitome of Hermann Cohen's

RATIONAL RELIGION

In the Light of the Source-Material of Judaism

———

INTRODUCTION[1]

Explanation of the title of the book and the nature of its project: A descriptive study of the various religions is not enough; it does not convey a real understanding of what a religion really is, or ought to be. What is needed is a normative, or rational, concept of religion as such. That calls, first, for a statement of what in a religion constitutes rationality, and secondly, for a statement of what is the specific content of rational religion.

A. REASON[2]

Religion,[3] man's distinctive trait, cannot have its source in sensate experience, which man shares with the subhuman. Neither can it originate in the elemental instincts, or subrational impulses, which lead man either to struggle against brute power, or to cringe before it.[4]

---

1. Cohen's approach to the problem of religion in general, and Jewish religion in particular, is unique. As a philosopher he assumes the primacy of reason, and formulates in this introduction what a rational religion ought to be like. He then proceeds to name the sources of Jewish religion, which he expects to analyze for the purpose of noting to what extent it conforms to his norm for a rational religion.

2. What constitutes rationality in a religion?

3. Rational religion.

4. They are manifestations of power and cannot of themselves generate the moral principles in accordance with which man must use whatever power he possesses. Rational religion is essentially ethics based on belief in God.

Whatever is related to desire cannot be the source of religion.[5] Rational religion deprecates all manifestations of egoism, hedonism and materialism, which are rooted in sensate experience.[6]

The theory that religion results from the accidental working of social forces contradicts reason.[7] The same applies to the theory that religion is the invention of the privileged classes, such as priests or rulers, with vested interests.

Religion is neither a substitute, nor a compensation, for the limitations of man's understanding.[8]

---

5. Of rational religion.

6. All of which are sources of power in man, but not of rational religion, which prevents that power from being misused.

7. Since to Cohen, God is synonymous with the rational order of the world, and religion is the affirmation of the rational order, or of God as manifest in the human will, therefore, to say that religion is the product of the accidental working of social forces would contradict his original assumption concerning God.

To Cohen, religion is essentially an individual experience. This is consistent with his assumption that it is an expression of ideationist rationalism. From the standpoint of functional rationalism, however, religion is the product of society, as well as the expression of personal experience and reflection. In actual life, religion is the combination of two strands: the societal strand which takes the form of worship and ritual, and the individual strand which takes the form of ethics and philosophy. Later on, however, in dealing with Jewish religion, Cohen states that religion began as myth and legend which have their source in the imagination and not in reason. This is an instance of inconsistency in his ideationism, in that a datum of experience is permitted to influence it.

8. In this statement Cohen deprecates the mystical assumption that the function of religion is essentially to have man reckon with the incomprehensible, unknowable, ineffable or mysterious

Nor is it intended to compensate for the ignorance of science and philosophy on the part of the masses.[9]

From the standpoint of reason, religion is a function of human consciousness.[10] Human consciousness unfolds itself through the wealth of national experience,[11] though rational religion does not attain its consummation in the consciousness of any particular nation.[12]

Rational religion is as much a creation of the human mind

---

aspect of reality, and that to fail to reckon with that aspect of reality is to remain either disoriented or devoid of authentic religious experience. That conception of religion is a hangover from its primitive stage, when man, knowing next to nothing about the world, lived in a state of "holy terror." In that state of mind, "holy" meant untouchable or taboo. In course of time, when the light of reason began to dawn on the human mind, the sense of the holy gradually came to associate itself with whatever gives a sense of purpose and meaning to human life.

9. In this statement Cohen deprecates the theory that primitive religion, with its magic, was a forerunner of science, and with its ideas about gods, was a forerunner of the philosophic conception of God. Those who subscribe to that theory point to the masses, who fail to comprehend the achievements of science and philosophy, as still practicing primitive religion.

10. This statement negates the supernatural or revelational origin of religion. It implies that religion is a normal function of human consciousness.

11. This leads the reader to expect that Cohen will not limit his discussion of religion to some metaphysical idea of God. Insofar as he recognizes the societal factor as contributing to the unfolding of human consciousness, and religion as a function of human consciousness, he is bound to reckon with religion not merely as the idea of God, but also as a societal phenomenon.

12. By rational religion he means specifically a rational conception of God. He is therefore correct in maintaining that such a conception of God is not the product of collective consciousness,

as are science and philosophy.[13] It exists among all people that are capable of developing and possessing science or philosophy. This attests to its universal human character.

The Greeks were as original in science and philosophy as were the Jews in religion.[14] The Jews accepted certain concepts of Greek philosophy, but not Greek science,[15] because Judaism [16] is inherently philosophic.

Reason in religion stresses the unreliability of sensate ex-

---

or, as he puts it: "does not attain its consummation, etc. . . ."

13. Here, too, he speaks of the rational idea of God. He means to say that such an idea of God is the product of natural human experience, as are science and philosophy, and not of supernatural revelation.

14. Just as science and philosophy were not the creation of the collective consciousness of the Greeks, but only of a few outstanding intellectual geniuses, so the rational conception of God was not the creation of the collective consciousness of the Jews, but only of a few outstanding spiritual geniuses. Moreover, just as philosophic truth is experienced by individuals, so is religious truth, according to Cohen, experienced by individuals. He thus ignores the fact that religion is essentially a social phenomenon which is individuated.

15. To understand this statement it is necessary to know Cohen's estimate of Plato and Aristotle, which is different from the conventional one. To him Plato was the philosopher *par excellence* of ancient times, and Aristotle was the scientist *par excellence* of ancient times. Both philosophy and rational religion —which, for Cohen, had to be based on a rational conception of God—had a bearing on ethics, on what we *ought to do,* whereas science had a bearing only on knowledge as such, on what we *ought to know.* That is why the Jews, in Bible times, were not interested in Greek science.

16. He uses the term "Judaism" as synonymous, and coextensive only with Jewish religion, both as the idea of God and

perience and emotion and affirms the dominion of law. Reason is the foundation of Law.[17]

Wherever law obtains, we are sure to find reason at work.

---

as a manifestation of the Jewish collective life. From a functional standpoint, it is more helpful to define Judaism as the dynamic religious civilization of the Jewish People, and Jewish religion as that phase of Judaism which is concerned with the idea of God in terms of belief and practice. Moreover, we note here the conception of religion as philosophy, which differs from Greek philosophy in that its central theme is not man or the world but God (see above, p. 14).

17. He refers to ideationist rationalism, insofar as it leads to the good life (cf. above, p. 50). In terms of functional rationalism, that is the case insofar as it leads to a life of moral responsibility in action. Whether ideationist or functional, reason demands of religion that it be spelled out in laws of human behavior and the regulation of human relations. Hence Cohen's affirmation: Reason is the foundation of Law.

According to Cohen, (pure) ethics is to jurisprudence what (pure) logic is to the sciences. That represents, on Cohen's part, a deviation from Kant. According to Kant, law is the antithesis of morality. In law, a person acts because of outer pressure. That makes conduct a case of heteronomy. In morals, on the other hand, a person acts because of inner conviction, which makes conduct autonomous. It may well be that Kant was influenced in this antithesis of law and ethics by St. Paul, while Cohen was influenced by the spirit of Jewish tradition.

The inevitable conclusion to which Cohen's thinking must lead is that politics should be ethical, and the state should be an object of religion to its citizens (cf. ch. V, pp. 47-48). In other words, the state should be the embodiment of law, which should itself be the embodiment of ethics. Since ethics is intrinsically based on a rational conception of God, politics should be permeated by the spirit of rational religion, and the state should

B. RELIGION[18]

What is the relation of religion to ethics?

Ethics, in its effort to counteract the isolation and apotheosis of the individual, posits individual man as integrally a part of humanity.[19] In ethics, the individual is fundamentally a member of humanity.

The individual, however, transcends his empirical ego not only as a member of humanity, but also as a member of the state,[20] which is the connecting link between the individual and humanity.

---

constitute the church of a religion that is national. Cohen expected that both Judaism and Christianity would ultimately be rid of their particularistic aims, and that they would converge upon the purpose of transforming Germany into that kind of religious state.

What is most significant, however, is that Cohen openly avowed that he regarded Judaism as owing its survival to the fact that it was dedicated to the idea of the universality of the Messianic unity of mankind. Such Messianic unity presupposed that all the states which were to be united were themselves inherently ethico-religious in character (cf. ch. XVIII on The Virtues).

18. What is the specific content of rational religion? When is an idea of God rational? The answer which is implied in what follows is the following: When its subject matter is what *man* ought to be. Hence, rational religion and ethics are related to each other as substance and purpose.

19. By that Cohen means that ethics, or in functional terms, moral responsibility, is that which distinguishes the human from the sub-human species, or that which makes man man.

20. Cohen has in mind here the state as defined by Kant in *The Science of Right,* Part II, where we read: "The state [is] constituted by the common interest of all to live in a juridical

The institution of law, which points to the achievement of international law in a coming Union of States, connects the individual with humanity.[21] Ethically the state is thus the medium through which the individual realizes himself, as a member of a superpersonal community.

The individual, however, recognizes in every other indi-

---

union. . . . Viewed in relation to the supposed hereditary unity of the people composing it, the state constitutes a nation *(gens).*" Hence, to be fully human, the individual has to be a member of an organic society. That implies that a person cannot really be ethical unless he functions as a member of an organic society. This is only another way of stating the well-known principle of Aristotle that man is *zoön politikon,* a state-building animal. Once again we note that Cohen sees religion not only as an idea of God, but also as a social phenomenon. Moreover, the ethical implication for him of the idea of God calls for participation in an organic society. Unlike Hegel, Cohen recognized the indispensability of the data of experience for reason to organize.

21. If the state is to serve the individual as the medium through which he is to live up to the ethical implications of the rational idea of God, it itself has to be governed by laws which articulate what is ethical and which enable it to act ethically in relation to all other states. Hence Cohen concludes that the rational idea of God must lead to universal peace and a United States of the World.

Kant preceded Cohen in the advocacy of such a Union. Thus, in his *The Science of the Right,* Part II, we read: "Further, as the surface of the earth is not unlimited in extent, but is circumscribed into a unity, national right and international right culminate in the idea of a universal right of mankind, which may be called *Cosmopolitical Right (jus cosmopoliticum).* And national, international and cosmopolitical right are so interconnected that, if any of the three possible forms of the juridical relation fails to embody the essential principles that ought to regulate external freedom by law, the structure of legislation reared by the others will also be undermined, and the whole sys-

vidual a person like himself—a "fellow-man." In this recognition, there are meanings not implied in the ethical relation of the individual to humanity as a whole.[22]

What those meanings are can be stated only by religion.

---

tem would at last fall to pieces." Thus what Kant arrives at from practical considerations, Cohen arrives at from ideationist considerations.

22. There is a gap at this point in Cohen's argument. He passes over from the individual, in his relation to humanity, to the individual in his relation to a fellow-individual, by a leap of faith. He might, however, have easily bridged the gap between the one relationship and the other by identifying the ethical, or law of the good life, with the functioning of moral responsibility (see below, p. 295). As subject to the polarity of individuation and of interaction, the human being experiences his selfhood or independence as well as his otherhood or interdependence. As the infant gains in self-consciousness, he experiences his dependence before he asserts his independence. When he begins to assert his independence, he does so aggressively. That means he does not recognize the presence of independence in those against whom he asserts his own independence. Only as he begins to mature does he recognize the need for independence on the part of those with whom he interacts. It is only then that he begins to see in them *fellowmen*. For that development of the ethical principle of moral responsibility one has to be a member of a nation. Cohen had in mind the German nation for the Jews of Germany. In other words, the principle of moral responsibility does not function in a vacuum, nor in humanity as a whole. It functions only, to begin with, among human beings who, belonging to the same nation, have occasion to interact with those nearest to them.

Now we can understand why only religion could elicit the recognition by the individual person of a "fellow-man" in every other individual. The religion which Cohen regards here as accountable for this fellow-feeling, for which even the Stoics with their high ethical sense, and Spinoza with his pantheism had no

Religion is needed to supplement ethics.[23] Ethics deals with man's relation to the totality of mankind; religion, with man's relation to his fellow-man.

Personality, which I recognize in my neighbor, makes of him a person like myself, a "fellow-man," and not merely a member of mankind. This awareness of personality as essentially "fellow-man" we owe to religion.

A classic illustration of the need of supplementing ethics with religion is the Stoic attitude toward suffering.[24] Stoicism advocates apathy as an ethical duty. But suffering must not be a matter of indifference, especially when it strikes a fellow-human.

Nevertheless, from a purely ethical standpoint, there seems to be no value to sympathy. In fact, it may be argued that we only delude ourselves when we think that we suffer *with*

---

place in their thinking, is not the rational idea of God, but the social experience which is the product of the nation-state with its collective consciousness.

23. Here we come upon the most enigmatic fact in Cohen's philosophic career. Virtually through all the years at Marburg University he did not find it necessary to assign to religion, or to the idea of God, a function which was not fulfilled in ethics. See above, p. 50 for an attempt to explain this radical change from the assumption that religion is properly conceived when it can be dissolved into ethics, to the reasoning whereby religion is assigned a distinctive role in human life. In any event, it is an inconsistency such as this in Cohen's ideationist rationalism which brings his thinking closer to functional rationalism and, therefore, makes it more relevant to the kind of rationale Judaism needs today.

24. Stoicism saw the universally human differentia in the individual human being only in the operation of reason. It made a point of identifying in the individual that which was common to all human beings, regardless of what state or nation they be-

someone else. Actually, what we suffer is only our own pain. This has been pointed out by Schopenhauer. Spinoza goes so far as to put sympathy in the same class with envy. He deprecates it, as he does all other emotions.

It is only religion that can justify sympathy. Sympathy, in making us *aware* of our suffering, transforms our fellow-man for us from a mere object of cognition to one who, like ourselves, possesses a personality of his own.

In ethics, duty is deduced from the intrinsic laws of reason, regardless of consequences. Religion, however, refuses to accept this indifference to consequences. The religious ideal must make for life. Hence it culminates in Messianism.[25]

Plato (in *Theaetetus*) maintains that there can be no end

---

longed to. Hence it saw no ethical value in the emotion of sympathy, which could not serve as a rational common denominator among all human beings. Feeling only interfered with the equanimity essential to the normal functioning of reason. Spinoza likewise regarded sympathy as outside the scope of reason.

According to Cohen, the role of emotion in human life is to enable the individual to project himself into his fellow-man, and thereby to experience his own individuality all the more as one pole of the polarity that spells moral responsibility. That is not stated clearly in what he writes, but is implied in the fact that he ascribed to religion a refusal to accept the indifference to consequences such as was advocated by abstract ethicists like the Stoics or Spinoza. The duty to reckon with the consequences even of an ethical action derives from the identification of its ethical character with moral responsibility.

25. There can be no clearer affirmation of functional rationalism than the statement that religion (rational) refuses to remain indifferent to consequences, and that Jewish religion is the application of functional rationalism, insofar as the Jewish concep-

to evil, since it is necessary as a foil to goodness.[26] Judaism, however, in teaching that God is the creator of good and evil, implies that He will ultimately eliminate evil. This is the essential teaching of Messianism.

It is a mistake to assume that the Messiah will come after injustice will have come to an end. To have faith in his coming essentially means to have faith that wrong will ultimately be defeated by right.

This faith, being in a category by itself, cannot be shaken by any appeal to psychology, philosophy or so-called realism.

The Messianic concept of God is religion's contribution to pure ethics.

Depending upon our orientation, when we resort to introspection we may discover, as Ezekiel did, the origin of religion, or as Socrates did, the origin of ethics.[27]

---

tion of God is such as to lead inevitably not only to philosophic ethics but to Messianic ethics.

Messianism is conceived by Cohen as the culmination of the religious ideal insofar as it makes for the advancement of human life. It is quite evident that the life which the religious ideal aims to achieve is the life of the nation. When that life is governed by reason as he conceives it, i.e., by the law of righteousness, it helps to bring mankind nearer to the fulfillment of the Messianic ideal of the prophets.

26. Although Cohen accepts Plato's idea of the Good in its cosmic implications as being the rational meaning, or goal of existence as a whole, he prefers, as a Jew and out of loyalty to Jewish religion, to follow it in its emphasis upon God's absolute uniqueness, rather than agree with Plato in his assumption of the ultimate dualism of Good and Evil. Messianism is thus not only identical with the ethical perfection of mankind, but also affirms its own philosophical conception of God.

27. The point here is that the origin of ethical religion, as well as of ethics as such, is not the collective consciousness, but the in-

In contrast with mythological religion,[28] which regards a man's ancestors as responsible for his sin, Jewish, or rational, religion regards the individual as responsible for his own sin. This is Ezekiel's discovery.

By studying introspectively the problem of sin, I get to know myself.[29]

I cannot know any man's sin as well as my own.[30] I should

---

dividual conscience, and not the nation, but reason as it functions in the individual person. This is consistent with ideationist rationalism.

28. Cohen refers to Christian religion with its dogma of original sin from which man can be redeemed only through faith in Christ and in his crucifixion as an atonement for that sin. From the standpoint of functional rationalism, the idea that an individual is responsible for the sins of his ancestors carries the idea of nationhood to an absurd conclusion, in that it nullifies the individual pole in the polarity of human responsibility. Historically, of course, Jewish religion in its first stage did emphasize the inclusion of descendants in the reward for the merit and retribution for the sins of the fathers, as is evident from the statement in the Ten Commandments. Cohen would probably have described that stage as mythological, and have dated *Jewish* religion from the Babylonian Captivity.

29. By studying introspectively the problem of sin, as, according to Cohen, the prophet Ezekiel must have done, a person comes to realize that he might have resisted the temptation to commit it. He thereby discovers in himself that freedom to choose between good and evil which is the pole of independence in the polarity of moral responsibility.

30. It is impossible so to know another person as to be able to know how strong the temptation which caused him to sin or how much of freedom to choose he possessed to withstand the temptation. Sympathy applies only to suffering, but not to sin.

not judge anybody as sinful; he is a "fellow" in suffering, and I should sympathize with him as such.

All measuring and weighing of man's inner worth in terms of his fate on earth is useless and misleading. Judaism answers the old question, "Why do the righteous suffer?" in a manner which could not have occurred to Plato.[31]

The Prophets were not philosophers. They were statesmen, and, as such, more consistent in their idealism than Plato. With all their national patriotism, they were also world-citizens. Their own nation was, for them, the stepping-stone to a United States of Mankind.

---

31. To understand the rest of this section, it is necessary to realize that Cohen displays here an intuitive insight into the nature of Jewish religion, which is generally missed. He senses the fact that the Jewish conception of God is rational and social. It is rational, in that the function of that conception is to set forth the primacy of the Good in the cosmos, and of the good life for man. It is also social in that it serves as a symbol of the organic character of the nation which is a product of natural forces set in motion by the intercommunication and interaction of those who belong to it.

Cohen regarded the prophets as the only correct interpreters of Jewish religion, because they alone synthesized in their idea of God both the rational and the social version of it. They therefore did not need to account for the suffering of the righteous in terms only of the rational conception of God. Limited to that conception, which is that of Plato, the prophets would have had either to attribute the suffering of the righteous to some sin committed by them, or to the inability of God to prevent the evil powers from having their way. But the prophets realized that if the righteousness which an individual lives by is to bring him happiness, the nation to which he belongs has to be based on social justice, i.e., a just distribution of the goods and services which the nation has at its command. They would therefore be inclined to attribute the suffering of the righteous person to the injustice of the social order of the nation to which he belongs.

They considered the internal danger which arose from the caste system. That system, which divided the rich from the poor, constituted a greater danger to the state than the external one. The poor became for them the symbol of human suffering. When, therefore, the God of Messianism abolishes suffering through the establishment of moral goodness, He will enable man to overcome the evil of poverty which is the source of human misery.

Thus the God of the Prophets is the God of the poor. They regarded poverty as the sickness of the state and of society as a whole. This practical view turned their attention away from the eschatology of paganism and from the attempt to conquer death by means of magic.

Because of its social orientation and program, Prophetic Religion occupies a special place in the realization of moral goodness.

THE SOURCES OF JUDAISM[32]

The Jewish national institutions and their distinctive and original values grow from the soil of the Sacred Scriptures. This has given Judaism its national spirit.[33]

The literature of the Jews is a national literature. Its originality, however, lies in its unique idea of God. The spirit of ancient Israel derived its distinctive character from its God concept.

---

32. Read: *The Sources of Jewish Religion.*

33. The discussion of Jewish religion, from the standpoint of what Cohen calls its "national institutions" which give it "its national spirit," is a far cry from his philosophically rational approach to the conception of God. This discussion involves the reader in Jewish religion as a manifestation of the life of the Jewish people with its "long history." Here Cohen writes not as the

Evidence for this is the long history of the Jewish people.

Deuteronomy bases the worth of the new doctrine concerning God mainly on the "statutes and judgments," or on the legal norms for social and individual morality to which that doctrine gives rise. These laws are expected to call forth the admiration of the other peoples for the wisdom of Israel. This synthesis of theory and practice became a characteristic trait of Judaism.

The Pentateuch as a whole is of this two-fold character. It is the source both of the ideas which generated the national spirit and of the practical measures which that spirit evolved.[34] In Deuteronomy, for example, the statutes and judgments are followed by a statement of the general principles underlying them.

The scope of the sources becomes wider as we proceed to the other books of the Bible. Although it begins with myths and legends, the national history gradually assumes political character. This was due to the influence of the Prophets. Prophetism is the spiritual nucleus of Jewish creativity. Its source is the history of the nation, and its basic principle is the indivisibility of politics and religion. Prophetism was a function of the political life of the Jewish nation.[35]

---

philosopher, but as the sociologist of Jewish religion, even though he ascribes to that religion "a unique idea of God," and to ancient Israel "a distinctive character" by virtue of that unique idea of God.

34. Here Cohen notes the reciprocal action of the rational and the symbolic conception of God. "The statutes and judgments" in Deuteronomy reflect the rational conception of God, and the general principles in Deuteronomy reflect the symbolic or national conception of God as the correlate of ancient Israel.

35. The national history of the Jewish People begins, as Cohen puts it, with myths and legends. In their very nature they reflect the national conception of God. Due to the influence of

Other factors of a genuinely national character also played a role. An additional source of Jewish religion is the lyric poetry of the Bible. The Psalms, which grew from the same roots and were nourished by the Prophetic writings, unfold the unity of Jewish nationhood and religion. Such unity exists neither in the Babylonian psalms nor in the lyrics of Pindar.[36]

The Psalms lead naturally to the wisdom of Proverbs. The

---

the prophets, the history of the People of Israel becomes more factual. It is viewed from the standpoint of the rational conception of God as lawgiver who demands justice in the political and economic life of Israel. The indivisibility of politics and religion to which Cohen refers has nothing in common with the indivisibility of church and state. The church is the embodiment of group religion and a source of corruption when united with the state. The religion which the prophets sought to unite with politics was national and ethical.

36. The religious teachings of the great prophets of Israel have not yet become integrated into the conscious will of the Jewish People and still wait with their embodiment into public policy for the Messianic era. Nevertheless, they do form an integral part of the collective sub-conscious of the Jewish People. This is evident from the role of the Psalms in the ritual routine of Jewish life, a role which is second only to that of the Pentateuchal Torah. It is the main source of the religious liturgy of the Jewish and Christian religion. No matter how dulled by repetition the mind of the worshipper may be, it could not altogether escape the unique synthesis in the biblical Psalms, as Cohen expresses it, of "nationhood and religion," of the rational and the societal conceptions of God. One of the main problems which engages the biblical exegete is: Who is the "I" in the Psalms? Is it the poetic author, speaking for himself as an individual, or does he represent himself as the spokesman for the People of Israel? Such religious synthesis is not to be found either in the Babylonian psalms or in the lyrics of Pindar.

wisdom of Koheleth rises to a higher level in the Song of Songs, and the truth sounded in Proverbs strikes a profounder chord in Job.[37] The reason ancient Hebrew poetry did not create dramatic tragedies is that the Prophets themselves beheld much tragedy in actual life.[38]

---

37. A possible solution of the problem as to the "I" of the Psalms is that when his theme is sin, the author speaks of his personal experiences, and when his theme is enemies, he speaks in behalf of the House of Israel. Cohen evidently regards the theme of sin as the characteristic one. That is why he considers the book of Proverbs as a natural sequel to the Psalms, for the awareness of sin is naturally followed by a desire to know how to avoid it and how to discern and follow the path of virtue, which is the theme of Proverbs.

It is not altogether clear how Cohen arrived at the notion that the Song of Songs is a higher form of wisdom than Koheleth. He evidently accepts the traditional designation of the third part of the Bible as "Wisdom," and the traditional interpretation of the Song of Songs as a metaphorical version of the love between God and Israel. Consequently, though the wisdom of Koheleth consists of the conclusion that the way to overcome religious doubts and questionings is to obey implicitly the law of God, it is far inferior to the wisdom which forestalls such doubts and questionings by advising the Jew to share the experience of his people as a consequence of the love between it and God.

"The truth sounded in Proverbs is that virtue brings its reward and vice its punishment." That, however is only partially true. The question of why the righteous suffer is ignored in that "truth," which has to be qualified in the light of actual experience as set forth in Job.

38. A far simpler explanation seems to be the fact that the main theme of Greek tragedy is man's helplessness vis-à-vis Fate. The author of Koheleth was evidently a Jew who had been deeply influenced by the spirit of fatalism which marked Greek tragedy. There are plenty of themes that could have been worked up into literary tragedy. But he would have had no audience for it, be-

The entire Jewish tradition,[39] beginning with Moses and
the Prophets, had a dual character, which was later crystal-
lized in the written and the oral law, in Talmud and Midrash,
in Babli and Yerushalmi, and in Eretz Yisrael and Diaspora.[40]

In Deuteronomy as well as in the Books of Ezekiel and
Ezra there is the dialectic of the prophets who deprecate animal sacrifices and the priests who advocate them.[41]

---

cause Jewish religion abhors the idea of Fate as much as it does
idolatry, since Fate negates moral responsibility. The only reason
the book of Koheleth was admitted into the canon is that it was
interpreted to mean that to view human life, from a standpoint
that is this-wordly or "under the sun," one cannot but come to
the wrong conclusions concerning God and man. The only alternative is to view human life in terms of otherworldliness, or
"above the sun" (cf. *Midrash Rabbah* on Koheleth, ch. 1:3).

39. The main point from here to the end of this section is that
the Jewish tradition reflects the synthesis which Jewish religion
succeeded in achieving. It was both rational and national religion. It was the first religion to have succeeded in that endeavor
mainly through the passionate and divinely inspired teachings
of the great prophets. Hence the dual character of the Jewish
tradition.

Cohen then proceeds to itemize a list of dualities which illus-
trate the foregoing assumption. As in all such *a priori schemata,*
facts are made to conform to the *a priori* scheme into which they
are forced. What follows is mere surmise as to what Cohen really
had in mind.

40. The written law probably represented to Cohen rational,
and the oral law, national religion. The Talmud was rational,
the Midrash national. Talmud Babli was rational and Yerusalmi
national. Eretz Yisrael spelled national religion; and Diaspora,
rational religion. This might explain his negative attitude to
Zionism.

41. The prophets represented rational religion, and the priests
national religion.

In all these sources prose and poetry are commingled. *Halakah* and *Aggadah* form a unity, like branches of the same tree. *Halakah* includes civil, sacrificial and ritual laws. The civil laws are based on a number of logical principles.

Already in Deuteronomy "teachings" and "judgments" possess a distinctly ethical character. Likewise, *Aggadah* "embroiders" the *Halakah* in the Torah itself.[42]

Another characteristic of the Jewish national literature is its oral aspect, which endows it with permanent creativeness.[43]

---

42. The prose writings of the Bible are for the most part rational in spirit, whereas the poetic writings are national in spirit. That contradicts his conception of the prophets, whose writings are mainly poetry, as eminently the spokesmen of rational religion. On the other hand, one can understand why *Halakah*, which means law, should be identified with rational, and Aggadah with national, religion.

43. Here Cohen inadvertently abandons ideationist reason and follows the line of thought suggested by functional reason (see above, pp. 55-56). Creativity does not comport with ideationist reason. From the standpoint of ideationist reason there can be "nothing new under the sun." What looks like evolution of something new is assumed to be present in latent or potential form in the initial Idea, or Absolute, and is merely an unfolding, but not a new creation. By contrast, functional reason does not try to explain away the fact of creativity, which is implied in all change that is not entropy, or a dissipation of energy. On the contrary, it views creativity as an ongoing process in the cosmos. When deliberately activated by man, creativity contributes to his growth and progress and to his approximating fulfillment or salvation. That is part of man's God-likeness. Cohen did not seem to be fully aware of the importance of creativity as a characteristic of Jewish religion, or he would have said much more about it.

The Torah is not confined to the revelation of Sinai, but is a continuing tradition of teachings of successive generations.

In all its styles and forms, however, the tradition is permeated by a uniform type of rational thought.

Talmudic interpretations of the Bible consist of ideas and practices which are by derivation read into the biblical text.

Additional source material is to be found in the medieval philosophical, ethical and exegetical texts.

Medieval poetry, which is a continuation of the Psalms, reflects the suffering of our people and the history of our religion.

From all these sources there emerges a clear idea of Judaism.[44]

The Jewish folk-spirit, which created this religion, is not based on racial unity,[45] but on the uniformity of spirit which pervades this entire religious literature.[46]

---

44. As a religion, is what Cohen implies. Actually, what emerges is Judaism as a religious civilization.

45. Cohen wants to make sure that even the national element in Jewish religion is not the product of *race* unity, because, as a German Jew, he was aware of the menace of race consciousness to civilization in general and to the Jews in particular.

46. The Jewish folk-spirit is rational because it is based on a religion which is rational, in contrast to the folk-spirit of the German nation which is based on blood kinship, and is therefore irrational.

That assumption, however, has to be qualified in the light of the prohibition against admitting members of certain races into "the community of the Lord" (cf. Deut. 23.4 ff.) and the purgation of the Jewish families carried out by Nehemiah and Ezra.

In the workaday activities of the Jews, the influence of other peoples played a part, but their religion, which united them, remained their own national creation,[47] despite occasional inner conflicts, as those between prophets and priests, rationalists and mystics.

The principle of Israel's uniqueness is stated in the formula: "Hear, O Israel, the Eternal is our God, the Eternal is unique." That stresses the uniqueness of God as well as of Israel. The idea of Israel's uniqueness was later expanded into the concept of the uniqueness of mankind.[48]

Ethics and religion are separate disciplines only when methodologically considered. Their content, however, is the same. Thus, in the enumerated Jewish sources, we meet with ideas concerning man in the discussion of religion, and with ideas concerning God in the discussion of moral goodness.

In the teachings concerning man, God is represented as determining the life of men and nations. There is unity in God, in mankind and in each individual. The Jewish consciousness knows no distinction between religion and moral

---

47. Cohen has in mind only the ethical or prophetic strand. As far as the national strand of Judaism is concerned, biblical science and archaeological discoveries have identified considerable borrowings from other religions. The conflicts between prophets and priests, between rationalists and mystics are to a large extent the conflicts between national religion and rational religion. Those conflicts have not been entirely resolved. They will be ultimately resolved when the national strand in Jewish religion is entirely rationalized and ethicized. That will happen when the national strand comes to be viewed as the functioning of the cosmic law of organicity of which the ethical manifestation is loyalty.

48. In the sense of being an organism, despite apparent contradictions and inner conflicts. The same is true of mankind.

goodness. Only those Jews who are pantheists at heart deem it necessary to salvage the ethical element in Judaism.[49] The individual, however, who has come under the influence of monistic thinking, or of the poetic idolatry of nature, gains nothing from this religionless Jewish ethics.

Religion is either intrinsically ethical teaching, or it is not religion. Only philosophical ethics[50] can be independent of religion.

This identity of religion[51] with ethics is the inevitable product of the original and unique character of the Jewish spirit, which is expressed in the teaching that only God is true being.

The Jewish God concept does not minimize the worth of this-worldly life. Based on reason, it unifies God and man, religion and ethics.[52]

---

49. In this and the following paragraphs we become further acquainted with Cohen's conception of religion and ethics as identical in their subject matter, which is the Good, in the Platonic sense of the term, as the purpose or meaning of the cosmos as a whole, as well as of Israel and mankind. By the "pantheists at heart" he refers to followers of Spinoza. From their viewpoint, functionally speaking, the world is nothing more than a congeries of blind purposeless mechanical forces. If they happen to be Jews, they feel impelled to justify their Jewish identification by the claim of the Jewish contribution to the domain of ethics which is entirely religionless.

50. He probably refers to Aristotelian ethics.

51. Both national and rational religion can be identical with ethics. In that sense, the identity of religion and ethics may unqualifiedly be said to be the product of the Jewish spirit.

52. National religion is possible only in this-worldly life. If even national religion can prove to be rational, then the God concept on which it is based is no mere symbol of group unity and consciousness, but the living God of the universe.

In drawing upon reason as a source of religion, we can identify both the particularist and the universal elements in religion.[53] At the same time we arrive at the element which is conducive to bringing religions into the domain of reason.

Judaism is not the only rational religion. Other monotheistic religions,[54] too, are rational, although they are not as consistent and original as Judaism. Originality is itself an advantage in a rational religion. It is a sign of creative reason which has emancipated itself from the allure of misleading notions. Originality carries with it the stamp of purity.

Chapter 1
THE UNIQUENESS OF GOD

Monotheism emphasizes not the oneness, but the uniqueness of God.[1] In polytheism it is not the number of gods that matters, but the identity of a god with the world and with its natural forces.

---

53. At this point it is quite apparent that Cohen has moved away from ideationist rationalism and has begun to draw upon functional rationalism in his conception of religion. Functionally, religion is both particularist, as when it objectifies the group consciousness of nations, cities and churches, and universalist, as when it identifies in the cosmos that which gives purpose and meaning to human life in general.

54. He evidently refers to the religion of Islam which, in theory, is strictly monotheistic. However, in not being original in its monotheism, Islam retains vestiges of idolatry, such as the worship of the Kaaba Stone.

1. The main point Cohen makes in this chapter is that the term "god," in the rationally ethical religion of the Jews, has none

Monotheism conceives nature as a manifold force in which God manifests Himself. But He is not identical with any part of it.

The doctrine of God's uniqueness, or incomparableness, is of a philosophical nature. This is contrary to what we expect, since religion is not philosophy. Nevertheless, the God Idea, in so far as it is rational, is rooted also in philosophy.

---

of the denotations or connotations that it has in polytheism. The difference is the following: whereas in polytheism a god is identified with a part of the world and its natural forces, and in pantheism, with the world as a whole, the God of monotheism has nothing in common with either. He is totally different.

Cohen realizes that his affirmation of God's uniqueness is a highly abstract idea and is out of character with religion as such, and particularly with the mentality of ancient Israel. That fact does not faze him. He merely answers one riddle by posing another riddle—the inexplicable one of artistic genius. He ascribes so inconceivable an idea as a God who has nothing in common with anything within the range of human experience to "the collective mind of the Jewish people." "We should have to sum up," he adds, "the entire history of that people in some basic formula, if we were to explain the origin of monotheism. Even then we should not succeed."

The main point, however, which Cohen wishes to convey is correct and highly significant: A true religion must have a true idea of God. The spiritual history of the Jewish People is the history of a progressive approximation toward a true idea of God, because it began with a unique intuition as to what makes a god *God*. The other peoples assumed that what makes a god *God* was the possession of some superhuman power, and the ability to share some of it with his loyal worshippers without diminishing any of his own. The Israelites (not collectively, but through the guidance of a spiritual genius like Moses), on the other hand, clung to one God by the name YHWH, to whom they ascribed not only supreme power but also a supreme sense of justice. They

Civilization, however primitive, requires the activity of reason. But this is not enough to account for the rise of monotheism, an ineluctable historical riddle.

The individuality of the artistic genius, which underlies the work of art, is inexplicable; much more so the genius of a people.

Monotheism is not the product of an individual mind, but of the collective mind of the Jewish people. We should have to sum up the entire history of that people in some basic formula, if we wished to explain the origin of monotheism. Even then, we would not succeed.

Historical fact alone does not explain the rise of monotheism. Monotheism arose as a reaction of ancient Israel against polytheism in Canaan and Egypt. Although the part played by the sojourn in Egypt and the Exodus in the development of monotheism is quite evident, it does not account for the idea itself—the idea of a God who is altogether

---

also assumed that YHWH expected of his worshippers, if He was to share some of His power with them, the exercise of justice.

On the basis of that conception of YHWH, the Israelites assumed that what we term "forces of nature" were lesser gods who acted as YHWH's messengers. Possessing no will of their own, they could exercise the power entrusted to them only in the way YHWH Himself would use it. On the other hand, human beings, who had a will of their own, had to resist the temptation of using unjustly and violently the power entrusted to them. Therein lay the uniqueness of their conception of YHWH, who from being at first a national god soon came to be regarded as the only god who was really God, and therefore the God of all mankind.

Thus was it possible for the ancient Israelites, with the help of Moses and the great prophets, to arrive at a unique conception of God, with the uniqueness as being *within* the range of human experience instead of being beyond it.

different,[2] and who is related to nature in a different way from that ascribed to other gods.

It is significant that polytheism is interpreted by means of representational art, while monotheism is interpreted by the word; for art depicts physical nature, while the word expresses man's inner nature.[3]

The sources of Judaism derive from older traditions which were reworked and reinterpreted to conform to the national spirit in its evolution.[4]

Take, for example, the term "Elohim," which is allegedly a polytheist survival. What is noteworthy about it is that it is almost always used with a singular adjective and verb. This indicates how firmly the monotheistic idea was rooted in the consciousness of ancient Israel, so much so that there was no apprehension that the plural form "Elohim" might be misunderstood as implying the existence of more than one God.

---

2. The point he makes about the uniqueness should not be confused or identified with what modern theologians attempt to express by the term "otherness." Otherness has a metaphysical connotation similar to that implied in the terms "unknowable" and "ineffable." On the other hand, Cohen's term "uniqueness" implies that God is knowable, but in a way different from that which the pagan gods were known by their worshippers.

3. Instead of "physical nature," and "inner nature," read "sensate experience" and "inner experience."

4. A factual observation which enables one to grasp the dynamic aspect of Judaism as an evolving religious civilization. The term "Elohim," as the God of Israel, though generally understood throughout Scriptures as a singular noun despite its plural form, is probably intended to express the idea of Divinity as such. The ancient Hebrew was lacking in the capacity to express abstract concepts.

Without doubt both the Yahwistic and the Elohistic sources take monotheism for granted.

Another ancient name for God is *Shaddai*. It was a collective term for all the demons that were opposed to Yahweh. Later, it became a synonym for God as the Almighty, who is both "destroyer" as well as "creator." [5]

The name YHWH was evidently intended to express the relationship of God to the world. The name was derived from the root *haya*, "to be," which points to an integral connection between the God of monotheism and the concept of being.[6] In Greek philosophy also, the three concepts of "unity," of "being," and of "God" were treated by the Eleatics (Xenophanes) as interrelated. The Eleatics emphasized being and unity as contrasted with the aspect of change which the world presents to the senses.

The Eleatics connected the reciprocal relationship of being and unity with a third concept, namely, God. But they considered God and the world as identical. Pantheism [7] was present in Greek philosophy from its very start.

Pantheism overplays the idea of unity, by identifying the unity of God with the unity of the world.

Monotheism negates not only polytheism, but also pantheism.

The difference between the Jewish idea of God and that of

---

5. An original interpretation of the divine term "Shaddai."

6. This interpretation of the name *Ehye Asher Ehye* suggests a common objective to the origin of Israel's idea of God as unique and to the cosmological philosophy of the Greeks. That objective was authenticity. For Israel, it was the authentic God, and for the philosophers it was the authentic world.

7. Cohen's *bête noire*.

Greek philosophy is evident especially in the exaltation of the concept of being in Judaism, which conceives of God as an entity, or being as such (essence), not as *a* being.

This is why the struggle against anthropomorphism and mythology is contemporaneous with the rise of the Israelite idea of God.[8]

The meaning of *I am that I am* is that God is being, in the sense of ever-existing and unchanging.[9]

The meaning of the second commandment is "Thou shalt regard no other forms of being as gods."

The uniqueness of God consists in His being incomparable (Isa. 40.25) not only with all *personal* beings, but with *all forms* of being.

Uniqueness of God also implies a distinction between essence [10] and existence. This confirms the superiority which monotheism attaches to reason. Reason is the instrument

---

8. Not true. The struggle against anthropomorphism and mythology was carried on only by Jewish thinkers who came under the influence of Greek philosophy, first, in the beginning of the Common Era, and later, in the early Middle Ages.

9. Latest J.P.S. translation states: "Meaning of Hebrew uncertain" (footnote to Exod. 3.14).

10. This idea, which is basic to Kant's *Critique of Pure Reason,* is the main hypothesis of classic ideationism. Its full implication is realized when we bear in mind that this hypothesis has been the source of two misleading principles in classic philosophy: 1) that there is an unbridgable gap between essence and existence, and 2) that essence alone is authentic, which is not the case with existence.

Cohen, like Kant, starts with that same hypothesis. He deviates, however, from Kant in denying that the essence of any being or existing thing is capable of being grasped or identified finally or absolutely by any idea of it. He recognizes the indispensability of

which identifies essence, in contrast with the senses which identify existence.

Reason also exposes the fallacy of the ontological argument, which confuses essence with existence.

Uniqueness is not identical with oneness. God's uniqueness implies that He has no connection with any form of material entity.

Pantheism, as compared with monotheism, is actually a variety of anthropomorphism.[11]

There is another Hebrew term for God, *Shekinah,* denoting that He transcends space. It describes God as "abiding," i.e., that God does not change.[12] Monotheism affirms that "God is *Shekinah.*" The abiding is the eternal origin of motion.[13]

---

scientific method whereby the idea of the essence of things has to be continually revised. In that way the idea progressively approximates the truth concerning the essence, though it never finally attains absolute truth.

Insofar however as Cohen operated with the basic hypothesis of classic ideationism, he did not rid himself of the dichotomies of reason and experience, mind and body, God and the cosmos, Jewish religion and the Jewish People, and from the tendency to regard reason, mind, God and Jewish religion as self-sufficient for an understanding of rational religion. That accounts for some of the highly questionable conclusions he arrived at concerning what Jews should *do* with their Judaism.

11. Questionable. It is certainly not true either of Stoic, or of Spinoza's, pantheism.

12. Not true, and out of historical context. In ideationist thinking, the criterion of authenticity is immutability, unchangingness, abidingness. That criterion which virtually all thinkers, whether religious or philosophical, regarded as absolute, has proved to be a Pandora's box of all kinds of fallacies.

13. An echo of Aristotle's "Unmoved Mover."

God also transcends the limitations of time (Isa. 46.10; 48.8.)

"I am that I am," implies that the *being* of God is altogether self-contained and self-sufficient, unlike a substance involved in the movement of matter.[14]

Judaism [15] ignores nature and natural man [16] by grounding ethics in the knowledge of the good.

Opposition to hedonism is rooted in monotheism.

Change cannot be ascribed to God. The Psalmist, like the Prophet, sees in change evidence of non-being and transience (Ps. 73).

With its religion so permeated by reason, the Jewish people was uniquely prepared to develop the scientific approach.[17] However, its spirit negated all reality but God.[18] This metaphysical conception of God gave rise to the idea of a unique God of ethics.[19] Only the conception of God as the creator of nature, implying the dependence of nature, is compatible with the idea of a moral order of life.[20]

---

14. See Note 10.

15. Jewish religion.

16. Not true of the Pentateuchal Torah, where earthly well-being is promised as reward for obedience to the laws of God and earthly suffering threatened as punishment for disobedience (Lev. 26.3 ff.), nor of the prophetic writings (Isa. 1.19-20).

17. The approach of ideationist rationalism.

18. God alone is eternal and immutable; therefore, He alone is authentic being. Cohen overshoots the mark. YHWH was assumed to be the only authentic *god*.

19. See Note 1.

20. Only the conception of God as the aspect of creativity in nature, implying its dependence upon God as "the Power that makes for righteousness," is compatible with the ideal of a moral

The idea of God's uniqueness has had to withstand many onslaughts. One of them was that of dualism, during the Persian period.[21]

There was a time when reason itself was arrayed against monotheism. This was the case in Alexandria when Jews attempted to synthesize the idea of God with imperfect nature. As a substitute for dualism, they projected the concept of the *Logos* as a kind of lesser god who mediated between God and nature.

Reason,[22] however, can recognize only *being* as absolute, and, therefore, only One God and no mediator between God and nature. Trinitarianism is no more rational than dualism.

In the final analysis, the basic Jewish idea is that both nature and man possess *being,* or essential reality, only as they derive it from God, who is the essence, or *being,* of all temporal being.

On the other hand, the Logos concept arises from the misapprehension of the reality of nature and man. The same

order of life. That is how functional rationalism interprets God as Creator.

21. It must be remembered that the term "uniqueness" as applied to God means that God is not *a* being, but being or essence, and therefore idea. In the capacity of idea, God is a correlate of the unity of mankind and its Messianic fulfillment. That enables us to understand in what way both Persian dualism and Christian trinitarianism are regarded by Cohen as antagonistic to monotheism. Persian religious dualism was merely the reduction of the many gods of polytheism to two gods. There is nothing unique about Ahura Mazda or Ahriman. The case with trinitarianism is different. It was arrived at by way of Platonic rationalism. That does not mean that it is necessarily logical or correct. Authenticity, or God, can be only one, as the following paragraph points out.

22. Ideationist rationalism.

misapprehension is responsible for the notion of immortality, as though the human soul [23] were on a par with God.

The Jewish concept of immortality merely amounts to saying that the spirit returns to God who gave it.[24] Human immortality, however, should not serve as a pretext for likening the *being* of God, which is underived, to what is spiritual in man, which is derived.

The destiny of the individual has nothing to do with the concept of Messianism, which is the fulfillment of humanity.

Human worth derives not from one's individual existence, but from humanity as a whole.

No pictorial representation can express either the idea of humanity or that of God's uniqueness; it was, therefore, prohibited.[25]

---

23. The human soul, from the standpoint of reason, both ideationist and functional—and the same is true of the human person—is the individual human being, insofar as he is not satisfied with the gratification of his physical hungers, or with the release of his physiological tensions. A man's striving to act rationally, ethically and creatively is his soul. The soul is therefore the correlate of a living person on earth. When he is no longer alive, it is meaningless to speak of his soul.

24. That way of referring to immortality is merely an admission of ignorance as to what it means. It makes sense, however, if understood in the light of what has been said of the soul in the previous note.

25. Both this and the preceding paragraph seem to imply that individual immortality is of no concern to rational religion. The main concern of rational religion is the future of mankind as a whole. That being the case, rational religion cannot make use of pictorial representations to symbolize its ideas or aspirations.

Chapter 2

THE WORSHIP OF IMAGES

Love is the self-emancipation of reason from theory and its transformation into ethical conduct. Man's relationship to the God, whom we come to know through reason, must, therefore, be actualized through love.[1]

To know God means to acknowledge Him. Acknowledgment is an act of will.

Were God merely an object of knowledge, He would not be an only God, because knowledge is knowledge of anything as a member of a class.[2]

Therefore, the relationship must be based on love.

Love for God means much more than knowing Him. It means the awakening consciousness of a new power.[3]

But since love involves the will, there are false, as well as true, manifestations of the love for God.

---

1. In speaking of reason as emancipating itself from theory and transforming itself into action, Cohen actually deviates from strict ideationist rationalism and invades the domain of functional rationalism. He is, in this respect, consistent with his own deviation from strict Kantian ideationism. He equates ethical conduct with love for God.

2. That is the Aristotelian conception of knowledge.

3. Consciousness of "a power that makes for righteousness" and for the salvation of mankind.

The recognition of inauthentic criteria of love for God leads us to infer what constitutes authentic love for Him.

Polytheism stems from love for the manifold phenomena of nature.

Multiplicity is inherently appealing, though man wants to find some underlying unity in that multiplicity. Hence, love for God, as defined by philosophy, is knowledge of Him. In monotheism, however, love for God transcends the merely knowable.

"Reverence" for God means "to serve," *avad,* or "to be a slave," because it demands the whole man. Even the Messiah is a "servant of God."

The two prerequisites of loving the Only God are acknowledgment and self-surrender.

Total self-surrender presupposes one master.[4] This is why monotheism cannot tolerate polytheism.

Not to realize the absolute necessity of exterminating idolatry, and to consider it merely a form of pantheism, is not to grasp the true meaning of monotheism.

The love for God cannot remain passive. The truth about God must be established and maintained actively.

There can be no tolerance with respect to polytheism, even at the cost of human life.[5] Except for idolaters, however, all

---

4. And therefore the integration of one's personality.

5. Socrates was an idolater. "He said that he who knew by what signs the gods give indication to men respecting human affairs would never fail of obtaining counsel from the gods" (Xenophon's *Memorabilia,* Book IV, ch. 8). It is almost incredible that Cohen would not have the prohibition of genocide apply to idolators. If that is what he does imply, we have unmistakable

men are our brothers (Deut. 23).[6]

The opposition of monotheism to polytheism is not only a matter of numbers, but is motivated by the impropriety of representing God by an image.

The Prophets' antagonism to art was motivated by fear that it might culminate, as it generally did, in a pictorial representation of God.

How could the Jews resist the universal trend of linking religion to art?[7] And yet, with all their opposition to *plastic* art, they managed to foster *poetic* art.

We shall find the answer, when we deal with the concept of the human being as defined by monotheism.

With respect to God, however, Judaism[8] maintains that God, as authentic being, has no image. In Christianity, the making of icons was a burning issue.

---

evidence of the dangerous consequences to which ideationist rationalism is apt to lead. What Cohen says about tolerance as inapplicable to idolaters, "even at the cost of human life," confirms the fact that ideationist rationalism has been the main source of dogmatism. The genocide, which the Torah regards as having been commanded by God against the "seven nations" of Canaan, is a rationalization that belongs to the primitive stage of Israelite religion. That is why it is so important to point out which parts of the Pentateuch represent only the *first* stage of the Jewish religion. Since then, Jewish religion has passed through two stages in its development, and is now on the threshold of a third stage.

6. That leaves very few brothers.

7. They didn't. The cherubim, and the oxen on which the huge laver in Solomon's temple rested, were part of the ancient way of linking religion to plastic art.

8. Jewish religion.

The very reference to Jesus as the "Son of God" was already a retreat from pure monotheism.

In the same way as man is differentiated from the rest of creation, so must God be differentiated from nature as a whole, and from everything in nature.[9] This is the fundamental difference between monotheism and pantheism.

The struggle against the artistic representation of God could only have been waged by men who were themselves great artists in the art of poetry (cf. Isa. 44).

The Atonement hymn *veye'etayu* reads: "Let them be ashamed of their idols, because they are nothing but illusions, and their worshippers are self-deceivers."

That those who worshipped idols really worshipped the ideas symbolized by them is no valid excuse for idolatry. Monotheism teaches that God cannot be represented by any symbol, since He is the archetype of all symbols, of all thought, and of all being.

It is significant that neither architecture nor poetry was included in the biblical ban against art, although even man may not be represented by a plastic symbol, according to monotheism.

The lyric poetry of the Psalms would not have arisen, had plastic symbols of God been permitted.[10]

---

9. Can he possibly imply that man, in relation to the rest of creation, is totally different, as he would have us conceive God as totally different?

10. A rather naive assumption. The discovered Ugarite texts refute that assumption (cf. *Kitve Ugarit,* ed. by Dr. H. L. Ginsberg).

The theme of this poetry is the rare relationship between God and man, which plastic art cannot express.

Chapter 3
CREATION

The uniqueness of God does not denote merely that God is apart from the world. It also has the positive significance of supplying the static and unchanging element behind the continual flux of the world. In that regard, it is like the concept of substance, with which science and philosophy operate, and which has to be assumed as underlying the process of causation manifest as change, or becoming.[1]

This makes it possible to define the uniqueness of God affirmatively as the logical ground of causation.[2]

Science deals with causation in nature, but the Religion of Reason supplies the logical ground of causation and of man. To *understand* human nature we use the causal approach, but to *improve* human nature we have to posit God as its logical ground.[3]

---

1. That is true Spinozist doctrine. Why then does he rage against Spinoza?

2. The entire approach in Spinoza's ethics is *more geometrico,* which is another way of saying "on logical grounds" or "on the basis of logical, versus experimental, reasoning."

3. Really to understand human nature, from the standpoint of functional rationalism, we have to deal with it as a problem of improving it. This is where Cohen breaks with Kantian ideationism, and arrives at a half-way station in his advance toward functional rationalism (cf. above, p. 57).

The doctrine of God as creator means that God is the *logical* ground of existence.[4] This is His very essence and His characteristic attribute. "Becoming" is thus *logically* included in God's "being."

The concept of creation posits the fundamental distinction between pantheism and monotheism. Pantheism, which accounts for the world by assuming emanation, assumes that God is immanent in the world, in a materialistic sense. Monotheism, on the other hand, posits that God is only the logical, not the material, cause of existence.[5]

According to Genesis, Chapter 1, chaos does not mark the beginning of the world. It was the state of the earth after it was created.[6] No material stuff is posited as the beginning of the world, only a point in time. There is no need to assume a pre-existing chaos, since the Being of God logically implies creation. The term "chaos" used in the Bible denotes not infinite, but inchoate or formless, matter.

Nature and becoming derive *logically* from being. Thus

---

4. This is a radical denial of the traditional conception of *creatio ex nihilo,* and at the same time a deliberate reinterpretation of it from a functional point of view.

5. In this paragraph, Cohen makes clear his deviation from Spinoza's conception of God. To Spinoza, God is the substance operating in parallel fashion through two of a possible infinite number of attributes, namely, extension and thought. To Cohen, thought alone is authentic being. Extension, like Kant's thing-in-itself, is merely a continuing challenge to thought to become more authentic.

6. Here Cohen misunderstands the meaning of the Hebrew *hayeta* in Genesis 1.2. It is used there in the *pluperfect* sense, implying that the earth had been null and void before creation set in.

the creation of the world is to be inferred logically from the Being of God.

Creativity is the basic attribute of God, identical with His uniqueness.

If God were not the Creator, being would be identical with becoming, thus making God and nature synonymous.[7]

The main significance of the monotheistic concept of creation is in ethics rather than in science and philosophy. This "creation" had been replaced in Jewish tradition by "renewal" (*hiddush*), indicating that God is manifest in the constant renewal of nature, that is, in its continual "becoming." [8]

The finite must be constantly renewed; it has no autono-

---

7. Which is the reason Spinoza has no place in his *Ethics* for the conception of creation.

8. From the standpoint of functional rationalism, the traditional conception of creation out of nothing, as an event in time, is meaningless. Kant, too, has put a final quietus on that conception. The human mind, he stated, cannot conceive the universe as having begun at a particular point in time, nor as having had no beginning. Consequently, if the idea of creation is to function in our day, it has to be reinterpreted as the creativity that is part of nature. Creativity is the dynamic or ever-changing aspect of the cosmos. It is that in the cosmos which prevents its entropy from having the last word. From the standpoint of human life, creativity is man's capacity to adapt himself to new conditions, to grow, to progress, to approximate the goal of perfection.

It is not true that the concept *hiddush,* or renewal, replaces the traditional conception of "creation." *Hiddush,* in the liturgical phrase "he reneweth daily the work of creation," refers to the fact that the world would deteriorate had not God renewed it with each new day.

mous creativity. The daily renewal of the world builds a bridge between the finite and the infinite. As for the problem of the world's beginning, that is left to pre-logical myth and is no concern of Judaism.[9]

Chapter 4
REVELATION

What is the place of human reason in the drama of "becoming?"[1]

It is the instrument of God's revelation to man.

Revelation is not a manifestation of God in the world or *in* man; it is the communication of God *to* man. This is why the pantheistic notion of revelation as the explication of what is implicit in nature is untenable.[2]

---

9. It is an exaggeration to say that Jewish religion treats the story of creation as a pre-logical myth, which it does not take seriously. Every time the Jew recites the Sabbath *Kiddush*, he refers to the Sabbath as commemorating the original divine act of creation.

1. That question, spelled out in terms of Cohen's own perspective on reason as that which organizes and gives direction and purpose to sensate experience and to our inner drives and hungers, might read thus: "Whence does reason derive its logic, its esthetics and its ethics? It certainly does not spin them out of itself." His answer is: "From God, who communicates to man the principles by which reason operates in the world of human experience," which to Cohen is the "drama of 'becoming.'"

2. Cohen could not state more clearly than he does here the difference between the ideationist and the functional concep-

Reason is basic not merely to the knowledge of nature, but also to the knowledge of the ethical; [3] its origin is in God.

The danger of conceiving God and His relation to man in concrete terms is greater in the concept of revelation than in that of creation.[4]

---

tion of reason. According to either conception, reason is God's revelation to man. There is a difference, however, in the content of the revelation. According to the functional conception of reason, reason is an instrument of *God's self-revelation* to man, an instrument whereby polarity, for example, which is inherent in the cosmos, becomes responsibility and a means to man's salvation. Cohen is right in designating that as pantheism, but wrong in condemning pantheism out of hand. According to his own ideationist conception of reason, reason is an instrument of revelation, through which God merely communicates his will, namely, the *laws* of logic and ethics.

3. Reason, as knowledge of what we have to know, is "logic"; as knowledge of what we have to do, it is "ethics." As either, it derives its principles neither from social convention nor from empirical experience, but from God.

4. To conceive God's relation to man "in concrete terms" means identifying some actual experiences as a manifestation of God. That constitutes thinking in pantheistic terms. That, according to Cohen, is a danger we are more liable to incur with regard to the concept of "revelation" than with the concept of "creation." In other words, we are more likely to assume that we experience God's self-revelation to us, when we choose to live up to some moral responsibility, than when we hit upon some new idea or invent some new device. In the latter case, we are more likely to attribute the new idea or the invention to our own cleverness; in the case of moral responsibility, we feel impelled by an extraneous force which enables us to overcome some inner resistance and therefore are likely to identify that as a self-revelation of God.

According to pantheism, human reason is part of divine reason—not so according to monotheism.

Revelation is not related to ethical reason in the direct manner that cause is to effect, but as a premise is to a conclusion. There is no direct communion between the mind of God and the mind of man.

Revelation is a philosophical postulate, not a factual experience.[5]

Deuteronomy, in summarizing the preceding books of the Pentateuch, reckons with all doubts and questions concerning the original account of the manner in which the nation came to have its religion.[6] It concerns itself especially with the problem of the incorporeality of God.

Revelation, as a historical event, is limited by some to the Ten Commandments. Others include not only the Torah but

---

Had Cohen not been under the domination of an *idée fixe* against pantheism, he would have had to explain just what is wrong with identifying an experience like the exercise of moral responsibility as the self-revelation of God. Such an explanation, however, would have to contradict his basic assumption that to be God, He has to be absolute idea, free from all taint of matter, change or becoming.

5. Revelation as factual experience is compatible only with pantheism. As an ideationist postulate, "revelation" means that the laws of logic and ethics cannot be derived from experience. They are imposed upon the raw material of experience. Their only source can therefore be God who reveals them to man.

6. No Jew before the age of modern biblical science ever suspected that which Cohen ascribes to Deuteronomy. That the author of Deuteronomy could have dealt with "all doubts and questions concerning the story of the divine revelations as described in the Book of Exodus," is nothing less than an anachronism.

also the rabbinic teachings under the rubric of revelation.

The Deuteronomist realized the misconceptions to which the story of the theophany in Exodus might give rise. He, therefore, found it necessary to explain them away (Deut. 4.13,15,16). Even the reference to God's "voice" is interpreted in Deuteronomy as the inner voice of the people.

The Deuteronomist seeks to prove that monotheism constitutes the deepest meaning and truest worth of the people of Israel. The national consciousness of Israel is aroused in Deuteronomy, by the synoptic view of its history, to stress the establishment of monotheism as its mission in the world.[7]

---

7. All that Cohen says about the Deuteronomist is allegorical reinterpretation. The Deuteronomist was not an ideationist rationalist, and could not actually have meant all that Cohen ascribes to him. What Cohen does in this chapter is to give to the traditional dogma of revelation another than the literal account of it recorded in Exodus. Traditional Jewish religion, according to Joseph Albo, the author of *Ikkarim*, is based on the following three dogmas: 1) that God exists, 2) that the Torah was supernaturally revealed by God, and 3) that He rewards and punishes every human being according to what he deserves.

To Cohen, the Jewish religion, being a rational religion, is in no need of dogma. It is in need, however, of its tradition in which those three dogmas figured too prominently to be explained away. The only way to maintain the continuity of its tradition is to reinterpret that tradition in the light of reason. But then the question arises: What is reason?

In ch. V, p. 55, we have noted that modern thinkers have been divided on what constitutes reason. The ideationist thinkers, to whom Cohen belongs, identify reason as the intuitive, or *a priori,* axioms by means of which the mind organizes whatever it receives from the outer or inner senses. That renders reason, according to what Cohen says above (page 100), the instrument

7. (*continued*)

of revelation through which God makes known His will, or His laws, to man. At this point he carries forward that version of reason, and, in the light of it, interprets the contents of Deuteronomy.

According to Cohen, the message of Deuteronomy is that the People of Israel is the people of revelation because, in its obsession with justice as embodied in "statutes and judgments," it reveals the operation of ideationist reason, which is the *instrument* of revelation. Cohen carries through consistently this allegorical reinterpretation in a more radical fashion even than Philo, leaving nothing of the traditional conception of the supernatural description of the revelation as a historical event. What is more, he even ascribes the denial of its historicity to the seventh century B.C.E. In any event, Cohen succeeds in reinterpreting the traditional doctrine of revelation in the light of his conception of reason.

For those to whom reason means understanding any thing or event in terms of its functioning in various contexts, and to whom the dogma of divine revelation as the historic event described in Exodus is incredible, a type of reinterpretation of Deuteronomy is necessary which, though it may differ in some important respects from Cohen's, is likely to have much in common with it. Any reinterpretation, whether functional or ideationist, treats the content of the tradition itself as indispensable to Jewish religion. That means that what has come down from the past of Jewish religion must figure in the consciousness of the modern Jew who wishes to identify himself as a Jew. Secondly, any reinterpretation is based on the assumption that the literal statement of a tradition need not, if it cannot, be accepted or integrated into one's world outlook. Thirdly, from the standpoint of either method of reinterpretation, to be an adherent of Jewish religion, one must share the collective and historical consciousness of the Jewish People and be inspired by it to live an ethical life.

That is why, even those who have a functional conception of reason can find much they can learn from Cohen's *Religion der Vernunft*. As long, however, as his reinterpretation of the dogma

God, as interpreted in Judaism, reveals Himself only spiritually.[8] A physical theophany could take place only through a medium that is not itself conscious of the meaning of godhood.[9] A spiritual theophany, however, requires a human being who is himself spiritually endowed. Such a one was Moses, who represented his people. He was both the apostle [10] and the teacher of monotheism.

Moses' role as mediator between God and Israel does not minimize the role of the people of Israel as a whole in the

---

of revelation falls short of meeting with their approval, it is necessary to propose for them an alternative reinterpretation. What follows is an attempt at one that is in keeping with the functional conception of reason.

In the first place, it is a generally accepted historical fact that the discovery of the book of Deuteronomy brought about the religious revolution in Judea in 621 B.C.E., thirty-five years before the destruction of the First Temple and the second transportation of Judeans into Babylonian captivity. Deuteronomy therefore played a role in intensifying the religious consciousness of the Jewish People. It limited the sacrificial cult to the one Temple in Jerusalem. That limitation enabled the Jewish religion to survive the suspension of the sacrificial cult. Moreover, it represents an ideal synthesis of the two functions of religion: the cultic function, which utilizes the belief in God to fortify the solidarity of the people and the individual's loyalty to it; and the ethical function, which utilizes the belief in God to stress the primacy of justice in all human relations. The fact that some passages in Deuteronomy conflict with our sense of what is just does not detract from the fact that, in its day, it represented the most advanced effort to articulate the primacy of justice as man's duty to God.

8. Spiritually here means through human reason.

9. Like the theophany in the burning bush.

10. He arrived at monotheism, according to Cohen, through his own reason.

origination of monotheism. The Torah stresses that his contemporaries too were partners in the covenant with God.[11]
All this tends to make the revelation of God to Israel more
an inner experience of the nation in its continuity than a
concrete experience of one particular generation.

Moses' role as mediator led by necessity to his tragic fate.
Otherwise, he would have been deified and the people of Israel would have fallen away from monotheism.

Moses' death, and the denial of a usual grave to him,
helped focus attention upon God as the Creator of the nation
that was to be dedicated to monotheism.

The breaking of the two Tables of the Covenant, too, is
intended to detract from the importance of the theophany.

Another instance of the same spiritualizing tendency is the
characterization of the "statutes and judgments" of the Torah as "wisdom."

These "statutes and judgments" do not refer to the cult,
but to the moral, social and civil legislation of the Torah.

The purpose of the Deuteronomist was to stress the divine
character of the laws of the nation, rather than the miracle
of the theophany at Sinai. It is as the teacher of these laws
(as Rabbenu) that Moses figures in Jewish tradition.

The "statutes and judgments" bespeak God's nearness to
Israel. Their justice and wisdom are valid for all time. Thus

---

11. Cohen tries hard to reinterpret the traditional account of
the Sinaitic theophany and of the role of Moses as intermediary
between God and the people of Israel. He does that in order to
make out a case for Judaism as a rational religion, which, unlike
Christianity, does not have to be validated by miracles.

revelation should be interpreted as wisdom and reason.

The people of Israel is repeatedly reminded that it was called into being for the purpose of observing the divine "statutes and judgments" [12] (Deut. 6.20-24).

Among them is the commandment to love God [13] (Deut. 11.1).

The Deuteronomist evaluated the laws of the Torah from the standpoint of their wisdom and thus ascribed spiritual meaning to the theophany.

Revelation, like the creation, is consummated in the human spirit. Man as a rational being, not any particular people, not even Moses, is the true correlate of the God of revelation.[14]

---

12. For once Cohen realizes that the uniqueness of Judaism reflects the uniqueness of the People of Israel as a self-perpetuating nation. What he fails to realize, however, is that for it to be such a nation it needs most of all a homeland of its own.

13. By loving reason.

14. Cohen's version of the God idea as a correlative one is, no doubt, his most original and important contribution to the vitalization of religion. It inhibits the mind from the tendency to hypostatize, or to personify, Divinity, and turns our attention to the only true source of a genuine understanding of what we should mean by God. That source is, as Cohen reminds us frequently, rational man. By identifying that in man which makes him rational or fully human, Cohen assumes, we arrive at the cosmic idea which spells God. Human speech abounds in correlate terms. "Parent" is a correlate of "child," "teacher" of "pupil," "king" of "people," etc. In his concept of correlation Cohen deviates from ideationist rationalism. That concept calls to mind sensate experiences of which the idea is a correlate. Here again we find Cohen in the half-way station between ideationist and functional rationalism.

Elsewhere in Deuteronomy, we encounter again the unmistakable effort to shift the emphasis from the theophany to the rational basis for the laws (cf. 30.11-14 and Jer. 31.30-33).

In this frame of reference, Jeremiah speaks of "a new covenant," Isaiah of "a new spirit," and Ezekiel of "a new heart."

This tendency to interpret revelation spiritually and as ongoing is the logical consequence of the definition of God as the only true being, precluding also all sensate experience in relation to God.[15]

Revelation, as a rational concept, denotes the relationship of Divine reason and man's reason.

We should, therefore, regard as the logical development of monotheism the medieval thesis that revelation is compatible with reason, and the more or less clearly enunciated principle that revelation has its origin in reason.

The very term "first principles of reason," *muskkalot rishonot,* which is used for the fundamental principles of Jewish religion, shows the extent to which reason was assumed to be the basis of religion.

It is characteristic of all spiritual-ethical cultures that they place a high value on the eternal in contrast with the ephemeral.

The basic laws of social life existed at first as unwritten laws, to which later all written laws had to conform. They constituted the body of natural law in contrast with conventional law. What the Greeks called "unwritten laws," the Jews found

---

15. In true ideationist fashion, true being, according to Cohen, cannot be associated with sensate experience, because of its evanescence.

in the written Torah. The Jews wanted the future to be continuous with the past. By attaching high value to the written law, they were able to use it as a means of fortifying the authority of the oral law which was bound to evolve in the course of time. The Greeks, on the other hand, were mainly interested in using their ancient law as a means of deriving from it general principles by which to evaluate the laws of their own day.

Eternality, which is a characteristic of the rational, is for the Jew a trait of revelation.

"Revelation" is not really a traditional term. Tradition speaks of the "giving of the Torah." That does not imply the existence of some mystery which has to be "revealed." God "gives" the Torah as He "gives" life, sustenance, death.

Revelation testifies to reason, which is not merely biological or sensate experience. It comes from God and helps establish the correlation of man and God.

The philosophical terms *a priori* and *a posteriori* correspond to the Torah terms "the face" and "the back of God." [16]

A priori is that which is a precondition to sensate experience. In philosophy, the principle of development presupposes something static and unchanging. Similarly, in religion, we need some element which is not merely the contribution of Moses or of the Patriarchs, but which issues directly from the idea of God.

The history of Israel no sooner refers to the recognition

---

16. He refers to the story told in Exodus 33.12-23, where Moses asks God to show Himself to him, and where God responds by permitting Moses to see Him after He has passed him by. This is allegorization after the manner of Philo.

of those static principles as "theophany" than its rational spirit asserts itself and transfers Sinai to the heart of man.

History is not the logical source of reason, but reason is the logical source of history.[17]

Chapter 5
THE CREATION OF MAN
VIEWED RATIONALLY

The opening chapters in Genesis give two different accounts of man.

The first account is altogether mythological, referring to man as created in God's image, unless God's image be interpreted as a metaphor. Being, or God, has meaning only as a presupposition for the *becoming* of the world.[1] Within the process of *becoming,* man occupies a central position by virtue of his knowledge. That knowledge brings God into relation with man.

Being, or God, is the logical basis of man's knowledge, especially ethical knowledge of the distinction between good and evil. The creation of man must, therefore, refer to the creation of human reason.

---

17. The paragraphs not commented on make sense from the standpoint of either ideationist or functional reason.

1. The fact is that "being" and "becoming" are mutually correlate; neither means anything without the other. As little as God means anything apart from the world, so does the world have no meaning apart from God.

Zechariah (12.1) associates the conception of God as creator of the world with His role as the creator of man's spirit (cf. Job, 33.4 and 32.8). Knowledge, art and wisdom[2] stem from God.

There is an intimate relationship between the spirit of the People of Israel and the Spirit of God (Num. 11.29). Isaiah also foresaw the time when all mankind would be filled with the knowledge of God (11.9).

Man is not only an organism; he is also a rational being. Through reason he enters into relation with God.

Reason is the divine prerequisite for man's relationship with God; reason is the common bond between God and man.

Spirit is altogether different from matter. The postulate that God alone is absolute *being* implies that He is spirit. The recognition of this truth leads to the negation of polytheism.

The spirit of man,[3] however, is not part of the Spirit of God. It is only the instrument of the relationship into which God enters with man.

This interpretation of spirit also explains the emphasis which the Deuteronomist and all the Prophets placed on the knowledge of God and, especially, on the love for God.

Love means intimacy of relationship. Only knowledge can clarify the character of this relationship[4] (Deut. 4.39).

---

2. Logic, esthetics and ethics. That is the thesis of his *Der Begriff der Religion im System der Philosophie,* Giessen, 1915.

3. Reason (cf. above, p. 100).

4. This sounds like an echo of Spinoza's intellectual love of God.

The prophets reinforced the demand for knowledge because monotheism rests its case upon reason; they believed that the spread of monotheism depended upon reason. Only through knowledge, and in knowledge, does God enter into relation with man.

Our liturgy, too, recognizes this dependence upon knowledge of God in the benediction "Thou graciously bestowest knowledge upon man." [5]

Monotheism arose in a spiritual climate which was averse to the scientific spirit.[6] It nevertheless called for the exercise of reason, especially in the domain of ethics. Though it does not approach that domain with scientific logic, it does emphasize reason as its basis.

Reason saves monotheism from the allure of mysticism,[7] which has frequently grown out of the soil of science and philosophy.

According to the Talmud, after man dies and comes before God to be judged, he is asked: "Did you fix special times for study? Did you pursue your studies wisely?" (Shab. 31a). This indicates how highly the rabbis valued the proper method of reasoning in study. So did Plato, who identified knowledge with correct reasoning (*logon didonai*), while in medieval Jewish philosophy the *muskalot* indicate that objective

---

5. It is the first of the thirteen petitional prayers recited thrice daily during weekdays.

6. The scientific spirit to Cohen is represented by Aristotle, who bases his ethics on the fact of man's striving for happiness and not on ideationist reason, as does Plato. According to Plato the Good, which he identifies as the supreme idea, or as God, is that toward which all creation, including man, is tending.

7. That is part of his objection to pantheism, in that it identifies God with nature.

reasoning was regarded as a prerequisite to a knowledge of religion.

Medieval Jewish philosophy was the product no less of Islam than of Jewish monotheism.

In prophetism proper there is an unmistakable basis for rationalism. Reason is indispensable to monotheism, not because it enables us to perceive causal relations,[8] but because it helps us to discern purpose and meaning.

Nothing really would be gained from understanding the *cause* of creation and revelation, but we stand to gain much by knowing their *purpose*.

Chapter 6
GOD'S ATTRIBUTES AS MANIFEST IN HIS DEEDS

A rabbinic story, told in Berakot 33b, argues that the recital of God's attributes be limited to those mentioned in Exodus 34.6, which may be reduced to two: love and justice. They are attributes, not of God's being,[1] but of God's functioning.

Instead of attributes of static *being*, such as uniqueness, omnipotence and omniscience, Judaism stresses those of func-

---

8. Which is the function of science.

1. The essence, or being, of God is idea, which is devoid of attributes. It is only in human experience that God is manifest in various ways. Those are His attributes.

tion; [2] and instead of being causation-centred, Judaism is purpose-oriented.

What does purpose mean when applied to God?

It means the way God manifests Himself in human experience [3] and in the purposes of man's life. These divine attributes are therefore patterns or norms for human behavior.

Other parts of Scripture enumerate holiness and goodness [4] as divine attributes. The Holiness Code (Lev. 19) stresses the former; Deuteronomy, and especially Psalms, the latter.

Holiness originally had a mythological connotation.[5] By the time, however, it was embodied in the precept: "You shall be holy" (Lev. 19.1), it came to mean the relationship between God and man, because the demand that man be holy follows from the fact that God is holy. Thus "holy" came to mean being ethical.

God *is* holy; man has to *become* holy. While holiness is God's essence, it is man's task or purpose, without which he cannot be human.

---

2. Which should prove that Jewish religion can be best understood and makes most sense from the perspective of *functional* reason.

3. What Cohen states is that to see a divine purpose in the world means to see purpose in the trend of human events and experiences, by identifying in them that which may serve as a source of guidance for human conduct.

4. Holiness refers to the God of group, or cultic, religion; goodness refers to the God of ethical religion. In the Bible, both conceptions of God are mutually integrated.

5. Holiness was at first *limited* to group religion in which myth played an important role, because it articulated the collective consciousness of the group.

Holiness is not a metaphysical attribute. It means that God's spirituality should be man's ethical life pattern.

Modern biblical scholarship fails to grasp the ethical significance of holiness as a *functioning* concept in monotheism. Historical insight into the development of monotheism does not necessarily lead to an understanding of its true meaning.

Although holiness was first associated with the sacrificial cult, it outgrew cultism and came to be applied to moral conduct.[6]

We see this development of the concept of holiness in the Prophet Isaiah's designation of God as "the Holy One of Israel" (Isa. 47.4; 29.19).

Isaiah humbly referred to himself as a "man of unclean lips," and Moses spoke of himself as "of uncircumcised lips." [7] Isaiah had keener sensitivity, due perhaps to his more intense experience of God's holiness.

Many passages in Isaiah and elsewhere in the Hebrew Bible point to the spiritualization of the concept of holiness. Holiness thus came to mean moral perfection, instead of aloofness from that which is impure.

Holiness also embraces love and justice, and attaches equal importance to both of them.

Thus did the Deuteronomic teaching concerning "statutes and judgments" serve as the norm for the prophets.

Although the concept of holiness retained some vestiges

---

6. See Mordecai M. Kaplan, *Meaning of God in Modern Jewish Religion,* p. 150 ff.

7. The real reason is that Moses thought he would have to speak to Pharaoh.

of its older meaning—the sacrificial cult, for example, was based on the older notion of holiness—Jewish religion evolved from spiritual holiness to ethical holiness. The new concept evolved out of the old, without entirely eliminating it.

Chapter 7
THE SPIRIT OF HOLINESS

The spirit of man,[1] as an instrument of holiness,[2] activates his correlation with God.

This spirit was illegitimately personified as *Logos*.[3] Such personification was unwarranted, because God, man and the *Logos* are wrongly conceived as constituting a partnership, in which each has a special function. Holiness is thus regarded as the special function of the *Logos*.[4] In monotheism, however, holiness mediates the relationship between God and man.

It is noteworthy that the Bible generally associates the "spirit of holiness" with man and not with God. Its association with God occurs only three times, twice in Isaiah and once in Psalms.

In Isaiah 63.10, "spirit" is used as a synonym for God. "Spirit" here has the same meaning as in the following verse:

---

1. Reason.
2. Ethics.
3. Cf. above, p. 91.
4. The reference is to the Holy Ghost, one of the three persons in the Trinity.

"And He formeth the spirit of man within Him." In Zechariah 12.1 there is reference to the people into whom God places His spirit.

Of no prophet nor of the Messiah is it ever said that God put His spirit *into Him*.[5]

The term "Thy spirit of holiness" in Psalms 51.13 focuses attention upon its connection with ethics. "To thee alone have I sinned," expresses the awareness that all sins against one's fellow-men *are* sins against God (Ps. 51.6).

This psalm makes clear the real meaning of "spirit," namely, man's power of renewal—self-renewal—by which sin is overcome.

The spirit of holiness belongs to God and man in common. It protects man against the power of sin. Sin can never altogether destroy the spirit of holiness in man.[6]

It does not refer, as Kautszch maintained, to the spirit of prophecy, but to the divine element implanted in man by God.

Through the spirit of holiness the call is extended to every person to be holy. This is the meaning of the verse which speaks of God as being sanctified through man (Lev. 22.32).

In sanctifying God, man becomes holy (Lev. 11.44).

---

5. Since holiness, or the spirit of holiness, is manifest in ethical conduct, it cannot be ascribed to an individual *qua* individual. It can be manifest only in the interaction among individuals of a people.

6. As long as a human being interacts with others, he is bound to have some sense of moral responsibility.

The spirit [7] is the creation of God,[8] and as such is subject to renewal. Its constant renewal renders it holy.

The negation of all intermediaries between God and man emphasizes the uniqueness of God. Were the holy spirit to be personified, the relationship between God and man would cease.

God and man remain distinct in the correlation: man sanctifies God and God sanctifies man. Common to both is the process of sanctification.

Christianity, pantheism and mysticism accuse Judaism [9] of negating all union between God and man. The truth is that the union of God and man in Judaism refers to their logical interdependence,[10] not to their mystical union.

The "spirit of holiness" as described in Psalm 51, limits the union of God and man to holiness. The effect of this limitation is to render holiness synonymous with ethical goodness.

Critical ideationism, too, differentiates between scientific and ethical knowledge, whereas other philosophic systems, such as those of Descartes and Spinoza, make no such distinction.

Without resorting to philosophy, the logic of monotheism is carried through consistently in the Bible. While in the Pentateuch holiness is said to be realized through "statutes and judgments," in the Prophets and Psalms the "spirit of

---

7. The sense of moral responsibility.

8. The sense of moral responsibility is a manifestation of divine creativity.

9. Jewish religion.

10. Their mutual correlation.

holiness" refers to the ethical spirit or, in Kantian terms, to "practical reason." [11]

Due to the spirit of holiness, man emerges as an individual. Not spirit,[12] but the spirit of holiness makes man man; only ethical reason, not reason [13] as such, has this catalytic power. Monotheism differentiates the human from the non-human as the special concern of ethical reason.

This self-limitation of human knowledge was surmised by Greek philosophy, when it evolved the idea of the Good, which it identified with God. Lacking the concept of the "spirit of holiness," it needed some other connecting link between God and man. When Philo followed Plato in evolving his *Logos* concept, instead of remaining true to the concepts of his own people, he abolished pure monotheism.[14]

Philo was not the only one to be seduced by the charms of pantheism and half-understood Platonism. In the Middle Ages, even so pious a thinker as Solomon Gabirol wrestled with the ambiguities of pantheism.

Only the monotheistic posing of the ethical problem was sufficiently potent to close the door to all mysticism. Only conduct determines whether one is worthy of the spirit of holiness. There is no other criterion. No amount of rational [15]

---

11. To Cohen, as a neo-Kantian, "Practical Reason" is that conception of reason which conceives itself as inherently and logically leading to the idea of God, and not by the *tour de force* argument used by Kant himself in his *Critique of Practical Reason*.

12. As used in the term "the Holy Ghost."

13. In the Aristotelian, or the scientific, sense of the term.

14. Because the *Logos* concept led to the idea of God as Trinity.

15. No amount of science or philosophy as such.

knowledge can elicit man's inherent spirit of holiness to the extent which his correlation with God enables him to manifest.

In the hierarchy of the virtues, the Talmud [16] enumerates the acquisition of the spirit of holiness, not as the cause, but as the result of "holiness." Although "resurrection" comes after the "spirit of holiness" the statement is qualified by the saying that "loving-kindness excels all other virtues."

The concept of the "spirit of holiness" is free from all association with mysticism.[17]

The most important inference from the proper understanding of the concept of "spirit of holiness" is that to know God metaphysically is unimportant, but to know Him ethically [18] is of supreme importance. All notions of holiness, whether theoretical, mystical or cultic, other than the one which identifies it with human conduct, have a nimbus of idolatry. In monotheism, holiness is essentially a human attribute.

Both mysticism and pantheism believe in the possibility of actual union between God and man. Neither recognizes the fundamental difference between conduct and knowledge.

These problems form the content of theoretical ethics and the practical content of man's self-education, understood as religion, if by religion we mean the divine education of man.

---

16. Abodah Zarah, 20b.

17. Mysticism is a purely individual experience, whereas holiness which, to Cohen, is synonymous with ethical conduct, involves inter-personal relations.

18. That follows more directly and more emphatically from the perspective of functional, than from ideationist, reason, because in functional reason, action rather than knowledge is the seat of authenticity.

Isaiah would not have us infer from the holiness of God that God transcends man's comprehension (Isa. 5.16). When man sanctifies himself through righteousness, or just conduct, he perceives God's holiness (Lev. 11.44; 22.32; Isa. 8.13).

The Torah deprecates the notion that it is possible to become holy by mastering the divine mysteries, or by performing actions which enable one to acquire divinity (Exod. 31.13; Lev. 20.8; 21.8.). The Torah negates all forms of mystagogy and ascetic practices as a means to attaining holiness.

If you want to be holy, show it by your humility and humane behavior. That takes time. But if you think that you are holy because you possess deeper spiritual insight, you merely prove that you do not begin to understand the nature of holiness. Only when you realize the endless nature of the task involved in being holy can you understand what is meant by man's correlation with God.

The holiness of man consists in self-sanctification, which has no limit and, therefore, cannot be static; it is ceaseless striving and growth.

We fail to note the interaction between ethical holiness and the spirit of holiness, if we regard the spirit of holiness as a separate entity. God does not suffer the spirit of holiness to act as intermediary between Him and man. Man should not permit himself to worship the spirit of holiness as though it were a deity.[19]

No human being can be holy except by virtue of the holiness of his behavior toward his fellow-man.

"Holiness" and "spirit" supplement each other. "Holiness"

---

19. The Holy Ghost.

helps us to realize that "spirit" is an aspect of conduct, and "spirit" helps us to realize that "holiness" is an aspect of ethical reason.

Chapter 8
THE DISCOVERY OF MAN AS FELLOW-MAN

It is a mistake to assume that we naturally discern the human in our fellow-man. Only that which is ethical in us enables us to see the human in others.[1]

The correlation between man and God is predicated on the correlation between man and man. Only when we are

---

1. It is difficult to grasp the thought of this chapter if we read it in the light of ideationist rationalism. What Cohen tries to say here is more understandable in the light of functional rationalism. According to the latter, moral responsibility is a function of reason. Moral responsibility is an *ethical* principle, because it dictates what man must do to fulfill his role as man. It is also a *religious* principle, because it derives from cosmic polarity which, when it operates in man, enables him to achieve his role as man. That polarity is the synthesis of individuation and interaction with the environment.

Cohen discusses in this chapter how a human being discerns in another human being a person like himself. His explanation, translated into terms of functional reason, is that, insofar as a person experiences a sense of moral responsibility, he recognizes a fellow-man in his neighbor. A human being has a sense of moral responsibility to a cat or a dog, only to the extent that he discerns in it a degree of human-like loyalty. That is the point of this first paragraph.

aware of our neighbor as a fellow-man are we fit to enter into correlation with God.[2]

The Jewish national consciousness expressed in the literature of monotheism addresses itself mainly to ancient Israel. An ancient Israelite knew himself as being a descendant of Adam as well as a descendant of Abraham.[3]

Originally only the members of one's own people were recognized as fellow-men. This, however, was true when those who belonged to other peoples or states were Israel's enemies. Since Israel was covenanted to the only true God, and since the other nations were regarded as the enemies of that God, they were also the enemies of Israel. This attitude toward other nations, however, could not last, since it would have put an end to monotheism, by precluding any relation to God on the part of "the nations." Monotheism, therefore, has provided a concept which ultimately enables all mankind to be included within the scope of "fellow-men."

The term in the Bible which negates any distinction between Israelite and non-Israelite, is "sojourner."

The natural process of inter-communication among peoples gave rise to a special regard for the stranger, although

---

2. This paragraph also becomes understandable when, instead of thinking in terms of ethical reason in the abstract, we think of it functionally as moral responsibility, integrity, loyalty and creativity. Those ethical traits have their source in nature.

3. The question he deals with here is the following: to what extent did the ancient Israelites really experience a sense of moral responsibility to others besides fellow-Israelites? His answer, which is elaborated in the rest of the chapter, is that monotheism brought them ultimately to see a fellow-man in every human being, because monotheism spelled moral responsibility, or reason, in Cohen's terms.

his status was inferior to that accorded in the Bible to the sojourner.

The rabbinic concept of "Noahide" goes further even than the biblical concept of "sojourner" in bridging the gulf between Israelite and non-Israelite.

The significance of monotheism for the concept "Noah-ide" is implied in the story of the Deluge. To Noah as the symbol of mankind God promised to sustain man forever. This is God's covenant with every individual human being, whether or not he belongs to Israel.

Noah was saved because he was righteous. Righteousness cannot become entirely extinct; therefore, the human race cannot be destroyed.

The Pentateuchal text assigns to Abraham the destiny of being the source of blessing to all "the families of the earth." [4]

Ben Azai's opinion [5] that the cardinal principle of the Torah is the one which represents man as having been created in the image of God, is more rational than that of Rabbi Akiba who maintains that the teaching which makes all men equal is "Thou shalt love thy neighbor as thyself." [6]

To limit the concept of "neighbor" to members of one's own people implies disregard for *all* human beings as persons.

The love for one's fellow-man should derive from the

---

4. This is a misinterpretation of the text in Gen. 12.3. Its correct meaning is that the nations will bless one another by saying: "May you be as fortunate as Abraham."

5. Ben Azai's conception seems to imply, according to Cohen, that the idea of God is the correlate of the ideal humanity.

6. Rabbi Akiba, on the other hand, seems to agree with Cohen on the place of sympathy in human life.

recognition that he too is God's creature. It should not be based on mere sentiment. In monotheism's account of man's origin, no distinction is made between those who do, and those who do not, profess monotheism.

The Jew is a descendant of Noah, even before being a descendant of Abraham, and even as a descendant of Abraham, his being blessed depends upon having the other nations bless him. He is, like all other human beings, a creature of God and a bearer of His image.

Monotheism made the extermination of the idolatrous nations inevitable. No theodicy is required [7] to justify that which in its own day was a matter of necessity.

On the other hand, we do have such behests as those which permit Edomites and Egyptians of the third generation to become part of the people of Israel (Deut. 23. 8-9).

Before long, however, the concept of "fellow-man" was extended to include also the foreigner (cf. I Kings 8.41, 43). Solomon's prayer at the dedication of the Temple does not discriminate between an Israelite and a non-Israelite. The Messianic prophecy of Isaiah (56.7) refers to a time when all nations will join in the worship of God.

Idolatry was not merely a matter of cult; it was associated with moral degradation. The Talmud says that the Jews would have renounced idolatry long before they actually did, were it not for the licentiousness which rendered it alluring (Sanhed. 63b).

Maimonides added another basic concept: "the pious Gentiles."

---

7. Actually possible, in terms of either conception or reason.

The "pious Gentiles" belong to the category of Noahides, who have to obey the seven Noahidic precepts. Those are purely ethical laws, except for the Noahidic prohibition of idolatry. The aim of that prohibition is to prevent the Gentile "sojourner," who does not acknowledge the God of Israel, from introducing idolatry into Eretz Yisrael.

The concept "Noahide" is the source of the natural rights of man and of freedom of conscience. It proves that the meaning of theocracy is not unity of religion and state, but unity of ethics and state.

Johann Selden, in his *De jure naturali et gentium juxta disciplinam Ebraeorum* (London, 1640), points out the importance of Jewish law for world justice (*pro jure mundi*). Andreas George Waehner, in his *Antiquitates Ebraeorum,* (I., p. 601) and Hugo Grotius praise the Noahidic laws.

Most significant, however, is the political and civic recognition of the rights of the sojourner. Johan David Michaelis long ago pointed to Mosaic justice "as the first to treat the sojourner as a neighbor" (3 Auf. 1793, Teil 2, 8, 445).

Leviticus 24.22 derives the right of the sojourner from the belief in one God. Note the appeal in that verse in the name of "your God." (Deut. I. 16; 24.17-18).

In Leviticus 25.35 ff., the sojourning-stranger is called "brother."

The equality accorded to the sojourner is such that a Jew may be sold to him as a slave [8] (Lev. 25.47).

---

8. How does slavery comport with equality? Later we read that the Romans had a bad conscience, on account of their slave economy (see p. 132). On the basis of Cohen's reasoning in this chapter, the Romans seemed to have had a keener awareness than

The sojourner is even granted a share in the Land (Ezek. 47.22).

The reasons for the duty to love the sojourner, which apply to fellow-men in general, are given in Leviticus 19.33-34; Exodus 22.20; Deuteronomy 10.18-20.

The ancient theocracy of Israel throws light on the historical functioning of monotheism. The union of religion and state had disadvantages, but it also had advantages. The fact that the priests were civil servants made it necessary for the prophets to be statesmen. This enabled the prophets to develop the religion so as to meet the challenge inherent in the conflicts between the state and social justice. Not only the rights of the native, but also those of the sojourner, called forth the intervention of the prophets.

In fact, the problem of who is one's neighbor emerges mainly from the class struggle between rich and poor, which obstructs the unity and the equality of human beings.[9]

---

the Jews of other human beings as their fellow-men.

9. We have here an attempt at an alternative theory to the one proposed by Karl Marx concerning the exploitation of one class —the laborers with their poverty, by another class—the owners of property and instruments of production. Cohen's theory is entirely naive. Moreover, it points to no concrete method of changing that condition. If translated, however, into terms of a concrete manifestation of functional reason like moral responsibility, the alternative theory at least does not sound too naive. What that theory amounts to is that the tendency of the owning class to exploit those who have nothing to sell but their labor power is due to a lack of a sense of moral responsibility on the part of the exploiters. A person who owns slaves does not recognize them as fellow-humans, because he does not experience a sense of moral responsibility toward them. That is what the proph-

How can we reconcile the idea of God, as the only creator of all human beings, with the gross inequality that exists among them? In Deuteronomy, we have, on the one hand, the statement that there should be no poor and, on the other, that the poor are always bound to be with us.

How can God permit this chasm to exist between the rich and the poor? And this difference is not the only one differentiating human beings. Yet, the differences in spiritual and esthetic endowments would not be a sufficient basis for questioning God's justice, nor would differences in physical power or prowess.

The story of Cain and Abel proves that the inability to comprehend God's justice in bestowing gifts and blessings is no justification for envy or hatred. The fact that God favors one human being more than another should in no way affect their attitude to one another.

Human beings, however, must reckon with those differences which are part of the social order they themselves establish.

---

ets recognized as wrong with the economic life of their people.

The trouble with Marxism is that it fails to see the moral aspect of the class struggle. It's appeal to the exploited classes to organize and seize power from the exploiters is an appeal to envy and hatred. So far it has proved to be an effective method of bringing about a change which only transfers the power to exploit from one class to another. The exploited certainly do not acquire a sense of moral responsibility to the defeated exploiters. The prophets appealed to the exploiters to realize that the poor who are their victims are fellow-humans for whose well-being they were morally responsible. Unfortunately, however, seldom have prophets' appeals proved anything but voices crying in the wilderness.

It is noteworthy that according to monotheism, man's first sin was bloodshed. Also, the one murdered was the brother of the murderer. Mere blood kinship, therefore, is unreliable as a means of preventing murder. Equally so is the fear of retribution.

Polytheism has no norm whereby ethics may set religion right. Monotheism, however, thanks to its unitary God has also a unitary ethics. The oneness of God renders the concept of man unitary, and every infraction of his unitary character is a moral transgression.

Social differences are the principal cause for questioning God's justice. They are not only objectionable in themselves, but are a hindrance to the spiritual and ethical development of human beings. The question why some are rich and some are poor is, therefore, a problem from the viewpoint of monotheism.

The problem grows more complex as the religious consciousness takes note that the wicked often prosper, while the righteous suffer.

How does monotheistic religion answer this age-old question? Is it enough to say that God knows what He does? Is it only we who cannot know? That may be an adequate answer, as far as the prosperity of the wicked is concerned, since on reflection, we might treat it with contempt.[10] But as far as the suffering of the righteous is concerned, a more satisfying answer is needed. We cannot question the value of their righteousness, since that might lead to questioning God's righteousness.

Shall we take the Stoical attitude and declare the problem of suffering irrelevant? The interdependence of the religious

---

10. Only on the "sour-grapes" theory.

consciousness with political and moral conditions prevents us from resorting to such an evasion. We may ignore our own ills,[11] but we have no right to ignore the ills of others, especially of good people.

Prophecy, in which monotheism attained its highest development, does not permit the problem of evil to be separated from the moral problem. The prophets were equally concerned to remedy the social order and to understand the cosmic order, because the human condition is a phase of the correlation between God and man. The prophets saw the problem of good and evil neither in the congenital differences, nor in the natural evils of sickness and death, but in the social contrasts among human beings.[12]

The social-economic complications cannot be treated as alien to the correlation between man and God. That is the main theme of prophetism. It does not shut its eyes to the ethical corruption that brings about social distinctions. Prosperity and suffering cannot be accepted as marks of divine approval or disapproval.

Death has no bearing on this problem. Death is a subject for mystics. But it is not within the purview of ethics, or true religion. Sickness is part of the problem of religion, insofar as it may be the result of social injustice.[13] The typically man-made evil, and one which is by no means unavoidable, is poverty.

---

11. Not true. We are responsible to ourselves for our well-being as well as for our well-doing.

12. The prophets were, as Cohen himself said before, statesmen. Statesmen and social reformers are not concerned with the problem of good and evil, mainly from a theological standpoint.

13. Job's being a sick man was not the result of social injustice, but as Job himself claimed, the result of divine injustice. It was, therefore, very definitely a religious problem.

There is another form of human travail which is a matter of social concern as part of religion, namely, mental suffering. This suffering is conditioned by the physical and psychological aspects of human life. However, only its social aspect, which is the result of poverty, is properly a problem of rational or ethical religion.[14]

The Psalmist too recognized that poverty represents the tragedy of mankind, and constitutes the great question mark for Divine Providence.

Throughout human history, poverty has been the main evil of the human race. It is not the physical aspect, but the psychological and social aspects of poverty that render it a distinctively human evil.

In poverty, the tragedy of civilization is compounded. This establishes the fellowship of the poor with their more fortunate brethren.

Shall we blame God for man's social ills?

The prophets paved the way for the principle in monotheism that religion should have man as its chief concern, and not God.[15]

What really matters is not whether God is just, but whether men are just in their social relations. The need of bringing this about is the ultimate goal of society.

Anxiety, as the result of poverty, is not a scientific but a social problem.

---

14. Why may not very good people, who suffer from a nervous breakdown through no fault of their own, nor as a result of poverty, be a problem for religion, as in the classic case of Job?

15. In section summarized in this and the following paragraphs Cohen is at his best.

When religion resorts to using anxiety as a means toward discovering our common humanity, it avails itself of our tendency to feel with others, or to sympathize with them in their anxiety.

To the Stoics, sympathy was suspect. To them, the goal of ethics was apathy. Yet, Stoicism extended the principle of dealing humanely to slaves as well as to foreigners.

But it was typically Roman in the way it translated its ethics into law. It lacked the free inwardness of Hellenism, and thus sympathy for the suffering languished. The Romans tried to appease their bad consciences,[16] caused by their slave economy, by means of the Saturnalia, the festival in which the slaves played master. This shows the impractical character of Stoic ethics.

According to Stoicism, the ideal wise man may be a slave. Slavery, therefore, need not be a source of misery. Man is essentially spirit; all else is incidental. The wise man does not suffer, because he is not supposed to have any feelings. How then can my sympathy reach him, or how can he regard his neighbor as a person like himself?

Sympathy, like all other human emotions, has its roots in the lower part of our nerve structure. By itself, therefore, it cannot act as a lever to raise the ethical consciousness. It must, therefore, be combined with the social idea.

Spinoza followed the Stoic line. Thus he regarded sympathy as originating from the same source as envy.

Envy arises from the awareness that others are better off than we are. It is natural for the poor to be envious of the rich and, of course, it is thus the very opposite of sympathy.

---

16. See note 8 above.

Spinoza refused to acknowledge this. He did not trust sympathy, because it is subjective. Like the Stoics, he had no social appreciation for feeling. The masses, he held, are incapable of ethical perfection.[17]

Schopenhauer regarded sympathy as an extension of self-pity, because the ego can never be completely merged with another "I" and its concerns.

Knowledge alone cannot fully reveal the individuality of my neighbor. But this is where sympathy, which is more than knowledge, enters the picture because "sympathy" is "feeling with" the sufferer.

Sympathy was for Schopenhauer a mediating concept for the metaphysical recognition of man. But this does not lead to awareness of what is human in one's neighbor. Moreover, according to Schopenhauer, all a human being amounts to is a "phenomenon" or illusion.

According to Schopenhauer, that which is authentically human is not limited to man; it pervades the entire universe. The "will" which is active in man is also active in the gravity of the stone. Thus there is no room for ethics in his system of *Die Welt als Wille und Vorstellung,* and no place for sympathy as an ethical trait.

In sum: Sympathy must be more than reaction to suffering; it must take on idea and action.[18] It must also direct us toward the community where the action is to take place and where

---

17. Not because the masses have no feelings, but because, according to Spinoza, in order to be ethical, we have to cultivate the power of reason. Since the masses are unable to think rationally, they lack the capacity to be deliberately ethical.

18. It would all become clear, if Cohen had added: "in the form of moral responsibility."

alone we can discover our humanity. Sympathy is thus not only the expression of the will as such, but also the lever of the moral consciousness.[19] It is that fundamental power in the moral universe which enables us to discover that our neighbor is as human as we are.

Ethics, which finds expression in law and politics, ignores the fundamental connection between poverty and brotherhood. Even Socrates had no interest in the problem of poverty.

Socrates declared that virtue is a fruit of knowledge. The problem whether the poor are in a position to achieve the knowledge necessary for being virtuous did not concern him.

The prophets were not theoretical ethicists. They did not differentiate between theory and practice. For them, the correlation between God and man spelled the correlation between man and man.[20] They could not evade, therefore, the question of how sympathizing with the poor might lead to the discovery of our common humanity.

Here, then, is a major and real difference between polytheism and monotheism. Polytheism permitted its mythology, even in the form of tragic drama, to ignore sympathy.

Perhaps this explains why there was no dramatic art in ancient Israel.[21] The Hebrew genius regarded it as important that suffering be alleviated rather than be given dramatic form to move the spectators to pity. The prophet was a prac-

---

19. He evidently identifies sympathy with a sense of moral responsibility.

20. Stated in terms of functional reason, this sentence would read: To the prophets, the fact that moral responsibility was rooted in the very nature of the cosmos gave to moral responsibility its imperative force.

21. It is not only "perhaps"; it is entirely far-fetched.

tical ethicist, statesman and jurist; thus his concern was to put an end to suffering. He was also a psychologist, in that he used sympathy as a means of proving that the very idea of man is deduced from the fellowship in the common human fate.

Chapter 9
RELIGIOUS LOVE

Love for God and for fellow-man is not given *a priori*. It cannot be taken for granted.[1]

Love for fellow-man is an integral characteristic of monotheism.[2]

That religion is a function of reason may be inferred from the fact that only in the framework of religion can reason evoke the universal love of fellow-man, and not in the framework of pure ethics.[3]

---

1. Neither the love for God nor for fellow-man can be an *a priori* assumption or taken for granted, because the knowledge neither of God nor of fellow-man is an *a priori* assumption. The knowledge of their existence is the product of the moral consciousness which requires "the wealth of national experience" to unfold itself (cf. above, p. 63).

In terms of functional reason, love is loyalty, and loyalty is that manifestation of moral responsibility which results from the awareness of belonging to a social organism, whether husband and wife, family, clan, tribe, nation or mankind.

2. Love for fellow-man, in terms of functional reason, spells loyalty to the one God whose existence makes of mankind one organism.

3. He has in mind Aristotles' ethics, which is based on the as-

In mythology, a god loves only the hero; man is not expected to love his god.

According to Spinoza, man is capable of love for God, but he must not expect God to love him. To love God is, for Spinoza, the same as to know God *(amor dei intellectualis).*

In religion, however, love is not synonymous with knowledge or ethics.

We might expect monotheism to teach that God loves man and that, therefore, man should love his fellow-man, thus imitating God. Actually man must first love his fellow-man.[4]

From the biblical laws concerning the stranger, it is evident that monotheism begins with love of man for man. Man has first to discover the common humanity in his fellow-man. Sympathy is directed first toward the stranger, regardless of his moral or religious qualifications. This sympathy is the basis for the discovery of "fellow-man" in our neighbors.

We are commanded to love the stranger, because God loves him. By loving the stranger we discover that God loves him.[5] The main function of religion is to help man discover that his neighbor is a brother.

---

sumption that happiness is the goal of ethical conduct. In functional rationalism, love is loyalty, which is a human manifestation of the cosmic principle of organicity. The love for God is a correlate of the love for one's people or for humanity.

4. That is in accord with the "principle in monotheism that religion should have man as its chief concern and not God" (cf. above, p. 131).

5. The term "love" in the statement: "God loves the stranger," has a different connotation from what it has in the statement "man should love God." There it means that inherent in the cosmos is polarity, which in man gives rise to moral responsibility and organicity. These traits give rise to loyalty, through which

Thus God is twice the creator.[6] After having created man He creates the brotherhood of fellow-men. This is what religion learns through reason.

After learning to love our fellow-man, we are reminded that God loves man and is especially gracious to the poor and the stranger. Together with the stranger, the Bible always mentions the orphan and the widow. They are typical of those who are poor.

With the growth of social conscience, the prophets became more insistent on inveighing against wealth and luxury. Their social sensitiveness grew more politically realistic, and by the same token, more deeply religious.[7]

Thus even worship came to be identified with helping the poor (Isa. 58). The poor, as flesh of our flesh, have a claim on our care, and thus help us realize the meaning of God's love.

To God, all men are poor.[8]

God's love is unlimited. It grows until it embraces the whole of mankind. This is the meaning of Messianism.

Messianism places the consummation of God's love in the

---

human beings become fully human. This is another instance where it takes functional reason to render an affirmation of ideationist reason understandable.

6. See chapter 3 on *Creation* and commentary.

7. That is understandable in the light of *functional* reason, which insists upon understanding any object, event, person or principle as part of a context, and moral principles as part of a social, economic or political context, and which notes the way it functions there.

8. That means that all human beings lack something which should elicit from us a sense of moral responsibility for seeing to it that it be made good.

distant future. In the meantime, the people of Israel is singled out as the object of His love. The prophets and the historians, however, during the troubled days of their people's decline, saw the People of Israel endure great suffering. They must have concluded that God loved Israel for the same reason that He loved the poor.[9]

The idea of Israel's election figures most prominently in those parts of Deuteronomy which describe Israel's sufferings.[10]

Suffering attains its maximum religious significance in the vicarious suffering of the innocent for the guilty. Even Messianism culminates in the Messiah who suffers for the sins of others.[11]

God's love for Israel does not detract from His love for

---

9. The homelessness and the statelessness of the Jews put them in the class of the poor, whose misery should awaken in the hearts of sensitive non-Jews a feeling of sympathy, and in their minds an awareness of moral responsibility for the sufferings of the Jews.

10. The analogy of the Jews to the poor breaks down at this point. Whereas the misery of the poor, according to Cohen, is the result of the social injustice on the part of those who are well off, the sufferings of the Israelites described in Deuteronomy are unmistakably punishment for their *own* sins.

11. Cohen attempts to refute the claim of the Christian theologians who see in the fifty-third chapter of Isaiah a prophecy of the advent of Christ. Cohen interprets that chapter correctly as a description of the way the nations have dealt with the People of Israel. The influence of his Christological environment, however, makes itself felt in his placing the crown of vicarious suffering on the head of the Jewish People and the sceptre of Messianism in its pierced hands.

mankind, neither does He love Israel differently from the way He loves other peoples.[12] The reason Israel is singled out as object of His love is that Israel is the Priest-People, the champion of monotheism, and, as such, representative of mankind. The People of Israel, moreover, is homeless, and without a state. It is "poor," and God's love for Israel is thus part of His love for the poor. It does not confer a privilege, but is a symbolic confirmation of God's universal love.[13]

The affirmation that God created the world and maintains it implies that He exercises His providence over the world of mankind.

Various human relationships are used for describing God's love for Israel, which symbolizes His love for mankind: such as those between bridegroom and bride, husband and wife, shepherd and flock. But none of them describes it as well as the term "compassion." That is the feeling "with" the victims of poverty, the evil which is the main obstacle to human brotherhood and equality.

The Hebrew language knows the indigent person as a "poor man," not as a "beggar." Helping the poor is not alms-giving, but "justice" *(zedakah)*. It is a mistake to assume that the agricultural background of these laws for the poor implies that they are of limited scope. On the contrary, their economic origin has led to the development of their ethical character.

---

12. This lends itself to the cynical remark: "except that the other peoples are not homeless and have states of their own."

13. Is not being a Priest-People a privilege? And does not the people owe that privilege to God's grace, and not to any merit of its own? Being representative of mankind and a symbolic confirmation of God's universal love is enough of a privilege.

In the Torah, property rights are limited to the satisfaction of one's needs [14] (Deut. 23.25).

The giving of tithes every third year to Levites and strangers is also a limitation on absolute property rights. The same is true of the offering of first fruits, as evident from the prayer prescribed for it (Deut. 26.5 ff.). The term "holy" in this prayer has definite reference to the *social* function of the law with regard to the "first fruits."

A further limitation of property rights is implied in the laws concerning the gleanings of the field, the forgotten sheaves, the corners of the field (Deut. 24.19), as well as in those concerning the Sabbatical Year, and the Jubilee Year (Lev. 25.4).

The institution of the Jubilee Year was not utopian. This is evident from its association with the remission of debts in the Sabbatical years. This remission, which applied also to the sojourners, is motivated by the desire to prevent pauperism: "So that there be no poor among you" (Deut. 15.4).

A further limitation to property rights is implied in the laws pertaining to the taking of a pledge (Deut. 24.10 ff; Ex. 22.25).

The law concerning the slave shows that the slave has to be treated as a human being, not as a chattel,[15] for God is the

---

14. But are everybody's needs alike or equal? However, the main point is that the underlying purpose of the social laws in Deuteronomy is to emphasize the moral responsibility for the relief of poverty and for the public maintenance of the servitors of the Temple who were not permitted, according to ancient law, to own land.

15. When a human being can be bought and sold, he is treated

creator of both master and slave (Job 31.13-15, 44; Prov. 14.31).

The law against exploiting a laborer stresses consideration for his soul (Deut. 24.15),[16] thus implying a connection between justice and man's relation to God.

The Sabbath symbolizes the essence of the monotheistic ethical teaching. Christianity did not only transfer it to Sunday in order to break with Judaism, but also divested the Sabbath of its socio-ethical significance.[17]

The Babylonian prototype of our Sabbath had no socio-ethical significance.

The reasons for the Sabbath given in the two versions of the Decalogue point to its ethical significance. They emphasize the equality of all men regardless of differences in their social status. This proves the basically ethical character and origin of monotheism.

These social practices are an expression of the national spirit of Israel permeated by the idea of God.[18]

The Sabbath, as a symbol of the acme of God's love for man, has become a universal institution of all Western nations.

---

as a chattel. Taking care of a vase or a dog does not make it human.

16. The "soul" here refers to one's life impulses which, according to Cohen, cannot be the source of religious experience (see above, pp. 61-62). The new Jewish Publication Society translation of that text reads: "for he is needy and urgently depends on it."

17. A very significant point.

18. Thus we have in the religion of Israel the synthesis, or integration, of the two functions of religion—to unite its adherents into an organic body in commitment to some transcendent purpose, and to ethicize the individual adherent.

By means of it, God manifests His compassion with man who, driven from Paradise, must toil for his livelihood. Even the laborer is free on the Sabbath.

The Jew experienced, on the Sabbath, God's love, which restored his human dignity to him.

Christian scholars seek to attribute the survival of the Jewish People to its adherence to formal law. They disregard the spiritual inwardness which comes into play on the Sabbath.

What is the meaning of God's love? Compassion with the poor, which God awakens in us. This type of monotheism offers solace for the checkered history of man.

Man's love for God, as set forth in the *Shema,* embraces the entire human person. It does not denote reverence for God and devotion to Him, as if He were a personal being. This is how Christ is loved by his followers. Jewish philosophy, however, tries to purge the God idea of all anthropomorphism.

But how is it possible to love an idea? The answer is: what we really love in a person is our idea of him.[19] Even in physical love, the person we love has to be idealized, that is, viewed as idea.

The God idea is the idea of the Holy God who is the spirit of holiness, or of moral goodness, which enters the Kingdom of Reality only when translated into action.[20]

Pure love springs from devotion which permeates one's whole being and activates one's mind, heart and will. It can be directed only toward ideals which serve as patterns for ethical conduct.

---

19. This is on the basis of ideationist rationalism.

20. This is an unconscious acceptance, on Cohen's part, of functional rationalism.

Man's love for God derives from love of fellow-man. The universal God is the source of human dignity and brotherhood—not of beauty, as in pantheism.

Religious love is in the love for the ethical ideal itself and not for any realization of it.[21] An ideal cannot be grasped unless it is loved. To be loved, it has to be known and practiced.

Jewish thinkers interpret the attributes of God by projecting them onto human conduct.[22] "God is merciful," means that man *ought* to be merciful. "God is holy" means that God represents the *ideal* of human behavior.

Love for God is based on knowledge. Knowledge has to culminate in love, if it is to be more than theoretical knowing.

Maimonides' intellectualism is of a different order from that of Aristotle, because it includes love. His rationalism is ethical rationalism.

Man's love for God is the theme of the Book of Psalms. We find there a full description of the yearning heart of man, not of the Divine Being yearned for. Only God's goodness is mentioned, but no other attribute.

The Psalmist's longing is for nearness to God (Ps. 73.28). This is the purest expression of religious piety. In mythologi-

---

21. Religious love, though achievable only *through* the realization of the ethical ideal, is not for the realization itself. This is quite a fine point in Cohen's ideationist rationalism; it is at least understandable and consistent with what is said later in the same paragraph. According to *functional* rationalism, however, the fact is that, for an ethical ideal to be loved, it has to be *practiced*.

22. Such reinterpretations are made possible by *functional* rationalism.

cal religion man yearns for identification with God, not merely for nearness to Him.

The Deuteronomist emphasizes the same idea (4.7). Jeremiah (23.23) finds it necessary to add that God "is not from afar." Remoteness, when ascribed to God, refers to His omnipotence, and nearness implies His entering into relationship with man. "Nearness to God" precludes mystical union.

Drawing near to God through ethical conduct is an end in itself; it is in fact the true love for God, and it negates mysticism and its passivity.

In equating love for the ethical with the love for God, we state that the ethical is not motivated by any ulterior motive.[23]

Chapter 10
THE INDIVIDUAL AS A RESPONSIBLE PERSON

We have explored the implications of the assumption that man is a rational being, and that through his correlation with God he becomes aware of being related to his neighbor by the common bond of humanity.

However, this does not necessarily mean that I am fully aware of my neighbor as possessing responsible selfhood. The I- Thou relationship is not sufficient to prove the existence of responsible selfhood in my neighbor, because it is something

---

23. This is a dig at Aristotle's ethics.

more than the product of social interaction. At this point, religion has to come to our aid.[1]

Only the correlation between man and God can lead to the recognition of *responsible* selfhood in our fellow-men.

---

1. If Hermann Cohen had anything to do with the role of the I-Thou relationship in the thinking of Martin Buber, we can note here wherein Buber deviated from Cohen. To Buber, apparently, that relationship is *sufficient* to establish the fact that "selfhood in my neighbor is something more than the product of social interaction." According to Buber such selfhood does lead directly to the belief in God. According to Cohen, however, I may have a keen sense of responsibility without knowing that my neighbor has it as well, unless I resort to ideationist reasoning and with Plato conclude that my neighbor, like the rest of Reality, aims at the Good, and like myself, experiences a sense of moral responsibility. Buber, on the other hand, seems to assume that I cannot help concluding intuitively that my neighbor, too, is a person and, therefore, I do not have to arrive by the indirect route of Plato's idea of the Good, at the inference that he, my neighbor, also experiences a sense of moral responsibility.

Functional rationalism does not have to resort to this fine-spun verbalization either for the assumption that my neighbor, too, is a person and has a sense of moral responsibility, or that moral responsibility is "more than the product of social interaction." In functional rationalism, we make sure of identifying the process of moral responsibility by the way it functions or operates. We note that it functions in the manner of polarity, or the synthesis of individuation and interaction, which is what makes of the universe a universe, of nature nature, and of man man. Insofar as that polarity or synthesis makes of man man, insofar as it gives rise to responsibility, I am sure that my neighbor is also dominated by that principle. And insofar as it enables me and my neighbor to fulfill ourselves as human beings, it is divine or holy. Due to the mental need for hypostatization, we give that divine process a name and call it God.

Insofar as the individual cannot divest himself of individual responsibility without divesting himself of his very humanity, ethics necessarily refers us to religion and to the correlation between man and God. Whether we are actually responsible or not, cannot be determined by abstract ethics. Only by experiencing the relationship with God can we vouch for the responsibility of selfhood.

Only religion can impart this meaning to ethics. As for mythology, it must fail in this respect because it does not treat the human being as a responsible person, but as the bearer of ancestral guilt.[2]

In declaring that punishment extends to the third or fourth generation, the Torah, too, is not quite free from the belief in the possibility of ancestral guilt.[3]

Aeschylus represents Athena as substituting a law-court for the Erynies. Orestes is freed from guilt because he is assumed to have sinned under the influence of an ancestral curse.

Only when man realizes that he himself has sinned and that he is not merely acting under the sway of a power outside himself, does he achieve moral progress.

Sacrifices are the oldest mythical symbol of the correlation between God and man. They were meant to appease the gods

---

2. This is a reference to the Christian dogma of "original sin."

3. The doctrine of inherited sin plays a role also in Jewish theology. If that doctrine is as irrational as that of original sin, at least the means of emancipating oneself from inherited sin, according to rabbinic theology, is far more rational than in Christianity. Instead of having to resort to implicit faith in the myth of vicarious redemption through the sacrifice of the Son of God, Jewish religion affirms the need for living a life of moral responsibility, as spelled out in the Torah, as a means of freeing oneself from the momentum of inherited sin.

and later came to be associated with relieving the feeling of guilt.

Animal sacrifice, basically a substitute for human sacrifice, has no ethical value, because it does not expiate sin through the effort of the sinner, but by means of a material offering.

It is remarkable that in an age when sacrifices were in vogue, the prophets recognized in the sacrificial cult the root of idolatry.

The prophet's denunciation of sacrifice, however, did not extend to worship as such.

Isaiah did not merely condemn the sacrificial cult which accompanied ethical wrongdoing; his entire outlook implies the complete rejection of that cult.

Amos and Jeremiah declared that the sacrificial cult was not part of Mosaic legislation.

The rejection of the sacrificial cult was a revolutionary step implied in the ethics of prophetic religion.

Did the prophets consider worship as an expression of individual piety exclusively, or did they also approve of community worship?

Was there an alternative to the abolition of the sacrificial cult? Was it possible to maintain it and do away with its abuses?

Those questions can be answered only on the basis of what actually happened, and not on the basis of theory.

Ezekiel actually did suggest the alternative of eliminating the abuse of the sacrificial cult by transforming its very character.

It is possible to tranform the character of an institution by infusing it with new meanings.

Modern biblical scholarship fails to reckon with the fact that social reformers and idealists have always had to operate within the framework of existing institutions. This fact enables us to understand the compromises in the book of Deuteronomy.

True progress depends on continuity in change, not on the preservation of dogmatic principles.

The prophets transformed the culture of their day by supplementing the social fabric of religion and ethics with the idea of individual responsibility. That led to the reinterpretation of traditional teaching.[4]

Chapter 11
ATONEMENT

Social ethics, as delineated in the books of the Prophets and in Deuteronomy, assumes that the "I" results from the "thou."

The "thou," however, only provides the basis of the "I," but does not supply it with creativity.

Ethics aims to integrate the individual into the group first, then into the state, and finally into mankind. In the begin-

---

4. The foregoing description of the historical development which took place in Jewish religion, under the impact of prophetic teaching, is an indispensable help to the proper understanding of Jewish religion, from the standpoint also of *functional* rationalism.

ning, however, there is the individual. The ideal state, too, consists of individuals.

When Isaiah (2.22) urged "cease trusting man," he referred to the sin of the individual.

The prophets regarded sin as the action of the individual directed against himself and against God.

Modern sociology tends to impute sin to the group, whereas theology reckons with man only as an individual. It is necessary, however, to combine both orientations [1] in order to arrive at the concept of the religious individual.

Ezekiel should be credited with the discovery that the source of sin resides in the individual. From the standpoint of the social prophets, this was, however, a retreat.

The social prophets freed the concept of sin from the mythological association with inherited guilt, but did not advance to the understanding of the significance of sin as originating in the individual.

The theory of ethics [2] deals only with the will to goodness; it does not reckon with the ambivalence of the human will.

That "the nature of man's heart is evil" (Gen. 8.21) does not rule out that man's heart may also have other qualities, such as the spirit of holiness.

Since God is his Creator, man cannot be inherently sinful. Sociology has no solution for the problem of sin.[3]

---

1. This proves that Cohen realized that Jewish religion was an organic synthesis of group and individual religion.

2. In ideationist, but not in functional, rationalism.

3. Because, to sociology, the individual is the product of social interaction. As such we miss in the individual that pole of moral responsibility which is the source of selfhood, namely, independ-

Ezekiel, in discovering the individual as the source of sin, interpreted sin as an offense not against fellow-man but against God.

Ethics stresses that sin presupposes freedom. Freedom cannot be understood in terms of cause, but only in terms of purpose.[4]

What is the difference between sinning against God and sinning against man? Is not sinning against God a fiction or an illusion?

The idea of sinning against God gives new meaning to the idea of man, first, by singling out the individual from the mass of humanity, and secondly, by extending our horizon beyond man.

In analyzing the causes of the World War [the reference is to World War I] we trace the economic and cultural factors. The individual has no place in such considerations.

However, when we call the individual to account, we appeal to his conscience. What is conscience? Is it a demon? "Conscience" is basically a sterile concept. It should be replaced by the concept of God as judge. Of course, we must take care not to vulgarize that concept by identifying it with ecclesiastical notions, such as a judgment-throne.

What constitutes sinning against God? Committing an act

---

ence and, therefore, the freedom to choose among alternatives of action.

4. That is why purpose, or the final cause, as a genuine factor in its own right for the understanding of human life and finding meaning in it, is an indispensable assumption in ethics and religion. To treat purpose, or final cause, as an illusion, as some of the positivist thinkers do, is to reduce human life to the blind and meaningless operation of mechanical forces.

for which a person must call his rational self to account.[5]

He who thinks of himself as a responsible person apart from the multitude, is reborn into a new life. That constitutes repentance.[6]

The true self in us emerges only when we endeavor to free ourselves from sin.[7] This self-emancipation transcends the moral law of the social order.

---

5. This is a striking application of functional rationalism. Cohen takes the concept "sinning against God," and asks himself how does that concept actually function in one's thinking? His answer: "committing an act for which man must call his rational self to account" sounds abstract. It is, however, perfectly intelligible, because it is a common psychological experience, and therefore entirely communicable.

6. This account of repentance also corresponds to a common psychological experience. What is particularly interesting in Cohen's description of sin and repentance is the fact that they both grow out of the experience of responsibility, the religious significance of which consists in its being *cosmic* in origin and *salvational* in its consequences. The luminous ideas of this chapter belong to the reference frame of functional, rather than ideationist, rationalism.

7. It will help us to follow Cohen's argument if we apply the method of functional rationalism and try to translate the main concepts with which he operates into functional terms. The concept of sin might well be identified as the failure to live up to the demands of conscience for the exercise of moral responsibility, authenticity, loyalty or love and creativity. To free ourselves from sin would then mean to free ourselves from the temptations and habits to disregard those demands. In the attempt to free ourselves from these temptations and habits, we become aware of what they hinder us from achieving. Thus, the "true self in us emerges," since our true self consists in commitment to those moral principles.

The prophet Ezekiel introduced an additional seminal concept: Redemption.

He defined redemption, not as the social prophets had done, merely as a collective experience actualized in the social righteousness of Israel, or of mankind. To him, redemption was an individual process.

The concepts of "Redeemer" and "redemption" among their many biblical connotations, retain the original connotation of the term "redeemer" as a person whose duty it was to assure the continuity of his family.[8]

Ezekiel's main concern is that the individual become a responsible person.

It is here that the idea of "atonement" [9] comes into its own.

The idea of atonement had its origin in mythology. The envy of the angry gods had to be appeased. That was the purpose of the offerings to them. The Only God of Holiness, however, demands men's ethical betterment, not their ritual expiation. This accounts for the opposition of the social prophets to sacrifices. Ezekiel, on the other hand, who saw in the sin against God a means of emancipation from sin, advocated their retention.[10]

---

8. Cohen presumably ascribes to Ezekiel the realization that in the idea of God is implied the function to enable the individual human being to continue as an ethical and responsible person, despite his tendency to lapse into sin.

9. The divine redemption of the individual is experienced by him as the atonement for his sins.

10. In Cohen's view, Ezekiel saw in the sacrificial cult a means of having the individual not only retain a sense of need for calling his rational self to account. The sacrificial cult was also a means of having the individual realize that such need is the result not merely of social expectation, but of the very nature of the

The reconciliation of man with God is not the ultimate goal of redemption. The final goal is the reconciliation of man with himself—the resolution of the contradictions within himself.[11]

According to the Bible, the children do not inherit the guilt of the fathers; they merely suffer because of their father's guilt. That in itself was an advance over paganism.

Jeremiah (31.29 ff.) negated the notion that children were punished for sins of their fathers. He repudiated the idea of collective sin. He did not, however, advance to the point of assigning personal responsibility for personal sin.

Ezekiel was the first to do this by addressing himself to "the soul that sins." [12]

---

cosmos, or of God. To achieve this awareness of God, the individual had to perform a symbolic act such as bringing an offering to God.

11. Cohen, however, doesn't let us forget that, to him, the main function of religion is to render the human being ethical.

12. Cohen's exposition of Ezekiel's contribution to the development, in Jewish religion, of the role of the individual brings into sharp relief an important fact about the Jewish religion as a whole. That fact is that the *Jewish religion has come nearest to the realization that to assure a future to mankind, and to render that future an improvement on the present, it is necessary to operate with both the social and the individual aspects of human life simultaneously.*

Since moral responsibility, as the extension of the law of polarity into the human situation, is the synthesis of individuality and the interactivity with the environment, to neglect one or the other pole is like trying to fly with one wing. Social reform through legislation has to be accompanied by the training of individual character through education. Social revolutions, both bloody and bloodless, operating on a collective scale only, and

Ezekiel's elaboration of the idea of personal sin proves that he knew that he was expressing a new truth.

The statement, "All souls are Mine" (Ezek. 18.4) implies that the son receives his soul not from his father but from God.

Note that Ezekiel describes "the righteous one" as engaging in good deeds, and makes no mention of any cultic or ritual duties.

Ezekiel's idea of God is different from that of his predecessors. He does not regard punishment as evidence of God's sovereignty, but as evidence of God's wish to have the wicked repent and live.

Thus Ezekiel arrived also at a new idea of man. Man can transform himself. The individual can emerge as a person who is self-aware and responsible.

Ezekiel, Chapter 18, the most profound of all prophetic writings, concludes with the proclamation that the wrong conception of sin must not be permitted to be an obstacle to repentance.

Man becomes an individual by recognizing his responsibility for his own sin. He becomes a self-conscious person, when he has the ability to change himself. Then he is the captain of his own soul. He is no longer influenced by the social behavior of his group.

The concept *teshuvah* ("repentance") implies punishment. The sinner must confess his sins to be forgiven by God.

---

religious revivals both reactionary and progressive, seeking to transform the nature of the human individual, have not forestalled in the least the world cataclysm which at present threatens mankind.

The danger that repentance might remain merely verbal is averted through its association with institutional religion.[13]

Unlike group repentance, demanded by the social prophets, Ezekiel urges personal repentance.

This is not a single or final act,[14] but a continual self-renewal, with the aid of some permanent religious forms.

Ezekiel might have done better than to attach penitential significance to the sacrificial cult. However, in his day, prayer had not yet achieved religious status.

Moreover, the political exigencies then required certain publicly recognized means for maintaining community consciousness.

Those means could not then be an *ecclesia*, since an *ecclesia* has to be attached to a state.

It therefore had to be a community, the *kahal*, which is based on inner unity and not, as is the state, on power and domination.

---

13. Institutional religion is social religion. Its cult serves as a symbolic system that helps society to articulate its collective consciousness. By being organically combined with individual repentance, social religion is likely, according to Cohen, to activate that repentance; otherwise it might remain mere wishful thinking. For institutional religion to activate the repentance of the individual, it has to be ethical. We have here a vicious circle which no philosopher or theologian has so far found a way of breaking through. The same applies to public education, from the educator's point of view.

14. That repentance is not intended to be confined to a single act, but is to constitute "a continual self-renewal," was also taught by the ancient rabbis as may be inferred from their dictum that a person should *always* engage in repentance (Shabbat 153a).

However, there was no way for the community to be then re-established, without arousing the suspicion of the non-Jewish government in power, except as a religious group, with Temple and sacrificial cult.

The situation then was in many respects analogous to that which had existed during the Deuteronomic period, when the sacrificial cult, monopolized by the Temple in Jerusalem, was necessary for combating idolatry.[15]

It may be argued that, in the sacrificial rite, the priest occupies the center of the stage, and that both the individual sinner and God recede into the background. However, there is also the great advantage that it permits the correlation between God and the individual to fulfill itself without the aid of an intermediary. The correlation is achieved through the confession of the individual sinner. The confession leads to self-purification and atonement, and not the priestly rite which has only a symbolic meaning. God "purifies" while the priest only "expiates."

But why are the sin-offerings to be brought only for unwitting sins?

Here is a point of contact with Socrates' notion that all wrong-doing is due to ignorance.[16] The community, therefore, is obliged to assist the individual to become aware of his sin.

---

15. Likewise, Ezekiel foresaw the need of reestablishing the sacrificial cult as a means of keeping alive the spirit of the Jewish nation.

16. That happens to be in accord only with ideationist rationalism. Its basic assumption is that reason dictates only what is true and right. It also assumes that the normal human being is ruled by reason. Hence, if he acts contrary to reason, it can only

Sin which can be atoned for, insofar as it is not so heinous as to cause a person to forfeit his humanity, is to be regarded as unwitting sin.

That all sin is due to error must be the affirmation of a public institution, and not be merely assumed. Hence, the institution of the sacrificial cult.[17] The awareness of our moral weakness draws us nearer to God.[18]

The sacrifice is offered "before the Lord." None but God can forgive. Neither man nor God should be a sacrifice, but only an animal. No God can bring the sacrifice, or sacrifice Himself.[19] The full significance of God's uniqueness is more evident in His attribute of Redeemer[20] than it is in His attribute of Creator.[21]

---

be because he lacks the knowledge of what is right. It is therefore the function of the community to correct the individual's mistaken notion of what is right. Theoretically, that should be the case; but practically, it works only in the case of overt crime. Ethics which is not formulated into public law is the last item on the agenda of the public.

17. That it should be possible nowadays to find a rationale for the sacrificial system only proves what one can do with ideationist rationalism. From the standpoint of functional rationalism, we prefer to depend upon Isaiah, Jeremiah and Amos, who stressed the abuses of the sacrificial system.

18. Not necessarily, as is evident from the tendency of people to excuse their moral weakness on the ground that they are "only human."

19. This is a polemic against Christianity.

20. From sin.

21. In ideationist rationalism, the attribute of Creator has only a metaphysical significance, with little or no particular relevance to ethics. On the other hand, God as Redeemer from sin helps to establish the correlation between God and man. In functional rationalism, however, the attribute of Creator lends itself, as will

The act of repentance must be "before God." It is not to be an act of God nor shared by any other being. It must be a free act of man's rational or ethical will. The sacrifice is only a symbol.

What are the specific steps called for by repentance? Self-examination, remorse, recognition, confession and action. Action consists in the repudiation of the old way of life and the adoption of a new way. A mere change of *action* is not enough; it must lead to a change in one's general behavior.[22]

Is the individual as a person a real entity or merely an

---

be seen in the next note, far more as a rationale for repentance than the attribute of Redeemer.

22. The attribute of Creator, in ideationist rationalism, implies that God is entirely apart from nature and in no way to be identified with it. In functional rationalism, however, that attribute, like all others ascribed to God, is the hypostatization of the process of creativity which goes on continually in nature, as a result of the fact that nothing in nature is static. Everything is in motion, and motion means change. Change in nature makes for entropy as well as growth. Insofar as the universe exists, it indicates that growth, or creativity, has the upper hand. That fact is the creative aspect of nature, which is hypostatized as the divine attribute of Creator.

That, it seems, is the attribute which functions in man's repentance. Being the product of self-examination, remorse, recognition, confession and action, it necessarily calls for the exercise of the highest powers of self-consciousness, and of the freedom to choose among alternatives, which is a distinctively human trait. Hence when a man engages in repentance he is really *re-creating* himself, so that his general behavior thereafter is transformed. Whence does man derive that capacity, if not from the process of creativity in the cosmos, whereby chaos is transformed into order and nature is being continually renewed? Insofar as this process of creativity enables man to improve himself as a human being,

illusion? Actually, the self is only a step, or a stage in man's reaching out toward a flying goal.[23]

Far from being an abstraction, however, the self, achieved in moments of illumination through repentance, is man's authentic being. The self owes its existence and vigor to its frequent experiencing of such moments.[24]

Likewise, the command to be holy does not refer to a static fact to be achieved once and for all, but to the process of progressively becoming holy.[25]

The aim of repentance is to become holy, and the means to it is the striving to be holy. Man himself must engage in this striving; God cannot do it for him. That is what makes man's self-sanctification an endless task.

The fact that sin is described as a "way" ("Let us examine our ways" Lam. 3.40) implies that it is not a one-time incident but an integral part of the general pattern of a person's life. Each sinful act reflects a person's character.

Since God does not share in man's repentance or effort to become holy, in what sense can He be said to help man? [26]

---

it is a manifestation of Divinity or God. The scripture: "Create in me a pure heart" (Ps. 51.12) is an expression of authentic repentance.

23. The individual, or the self, is one pole of moral responsibility, the other pole being his interaction with his social and physical environment.

24. Makes good sense in rationalism as such, whether ideationist or functional.

25. Through the divine process of creativity we can engage in self-creativity.

26. Such a question could not arise in functional rationalism. See preceding note.

The answer is that, without God, man would never achieve self-improvement, despite his endless striving for it. The possibility of achievement is implied in the reason given for man's striving, namely, "for I (God) am holy." That means that it is of the very nature of Divinity to respond with forgiveness to every act of repentance.

What does forgiveness add to repentance? Does not making for oneself a new heart [27] constitute forgiveness, thus dispensing with the need of being forgiven by God, or being redeemed by Him?

The answer is that it is important to stress that God forgives, in order to render the idea of God tenable. Otherwise, the existence of sin would contradict the idea of God.[28]

To emphasize that man, as an individual, benefits from God's forgiveness, Ezekiel metaphorically describes God in the parable of the sheep and shepherd (Ezek. 34.12,17).

This divine goodness is the basic theme also of the Psalms.

Ezekiel is aware of the paradox of possessing individuality while belonging to a people. He denotes this dual nature of man by the term "son of man." Man transcends his being "a son," by "becoming" a mature individual integrated with his people. God's forgiveness helps him to attain this maturity.[29]

---

27. A person cannot make a new heart for himself without divine help. That divine help is experienced as forgiveness of one's sins.

28. In functional rationalism, it is just as absurd to think of sin as contradicting the idea of God, as to think of man's freedom of will as contradicting the idea of God. The fact is that the idea of God, as Cohen reiterates again and again, is a correlate of the idea of man who is free to choose among alternatives, and therefore free to sin.

29. The term "son of man" in Ezekiel has no such meaning as

Unfortunately, the problem of forgiveness and the concept of "the son of man" have done much harm to the purity of monotheism.[30]

Man's awareness of his own frailty leads him to realize that without God's forgiveness and help he cannot achieve self-sanctification and regeneration. This gives rise to his trust in God.

The soul attains its individuality and maturity not by reflecting on the problem of God's existence, but by yearning for God's forgiveness.[31]

The term *emunah* in relation to God (generally as the Hebrew technical term for "religion") does not mean belief, but confidence born of a sense of security. *Emunah* implies overcoming anxiety or the sense of insecurity.

The yearning for God does not lead to mystic union with Him. Man is human and therefore sins and is in need of God's forgiveness, which is described as nearness to God, but not as a union with Him (Ps. 73.28). Sin alienates God from man; God's forgiveness restores His nearness to man.

Ezekiel's idea of individual sin and divine forgiveness is the

---

Cohen ascribes to it. In the context of the book of Ezekiel, it corresponds to the term "human being." The frequent use of that term by Ezekiel is due to the visions he beheld in his trances, during which he imagined himself beholding God and His angels. He was the only human being on the scene. When, therefore, he hears a voice calling to him while he was in a lying posture, "Son of man, stand up on your feet," he knew that he was being addressed, because he was the only "son of man," or human being, among the "sons of God" or angels.

30. This is what comes from misinterpreting ancient texts.
31. Which proves the inadequacy of ideationist rationalism.

basis of the Psalmist's portrayal of man's yearning and love for God.[32]

The lyrical spirit of the Psalmist was more potent than the polemic of the prophets to displace the sacrificial cult.[33] He exalts the humble spirit and the broken heart as the sacrifices God desires (Ps. 51.19). Humility is the proper expression of the love for God.

God's forgiveness is the logical consequence of God's goodness (Ps. 86.5).

God's goodness seeks to prevent man from relapsing into sin.

The Torah makes a clear distinction between ritual expiation (*kaparah*), which is the priest's function, and forgiveness (*selihah*) which is God's.

The concept of forgiveness is an essential element of the correlation between God and man, insofar as the ideal man must strive to attain those attributes which we ascribe to God.[34]

This concept of forgiveness does not impugn God's divinity, since the essence of Godhood is God's correlation with man. This is what the ancients meant when they said that God's attributes are manifest in His deeds.[35]

---

32. The Psalmist describes his own experience; he does not generalize.

33. In Jewish tradition, the sacrificial cult has never been displaced; it has only been suspended. Jews have prayed for its restoration several times daily during the last two thousand years.

34. In other words, what we ascribe to God should be functionally interpreted as what the ideal man should strive for.

35. Even the ancients could not help thinking along functionally rational lines, because when a person thinks not for the sake

The mutual correlation between God and man is the foundation of the moral kingdom, the Kingdom of God on earth.

God's goodness is the basis of the moral kingdom, insofar as it consists of individuals in full possession of their humanity, and not merely of social integers.[36]

Forgiveness, a cardinal principle in monotheism, is therefore an appropriate motif for the most sacred day of the year, important to the individual as well as to the community in their relation to each other.

Chapter 12
THE DAY OF ATONEMENT

All festivals, including Passover, were originally occasions of purification. Thus Sukkot was originally the main festival of purification, while Rosh Ha-Shanah and Yom Kippur were preparatory days. Later, Yom Kippur was established as the principal day of purification.

Originally Yom Kippur was not only a day of sacrificial rites, but also a popular festival in which the youth participated. It concluded with a great feast provided by the High Priest.

---

of thinking, but for the sake of knowing what to do when he is confronted with a problem of action, he cannot help thinking in functionally rational terms.

36. As a social unit only, a human being is only half-human, because at best he merely interacts with his environment in a spirit of social convention, without relating himself to the divine aspect of the cosmos. He is other-directed and not inner-directed.

The meaning of the Day of Atonement is indicated in the text: "All the assembly of Israel and the resident aliens who sojourn among them shall be forgiven, for it happened to the entire people through error" (Num. 15.26).

In the liturgy of the day, the most important section is the confession of sin. The Sages in the Talmud debated whether it should be recited publicly or privately. They eventually decided in favor of public confession, since this precludes the mystical and secretive operation of the priestly cult.

The inwardness fostered by the liturgy of the day derives from the purely ethical character of the confession. This is especially noteworthy in view of the tendency of the Sages to place ritual transgression on a par with moral transgression.

The emphasis upon the ethical is a logical consequence of the assumption that all sin is "unwitting," [1] and that God, in His goodness, forgives sin.

Of specially striking significance is the concluding prayer in the *Ne'ilah Amidah*. The concluding paragraph of the prayer, "Thou hast set man apart to stand before Thee," points to the independence and dignity of man in his correlation with God. Prostration is out of place in the confession. Man should be humble, and yet stand upright before God, as Israel stood upright at Sinai.[2]

The Sages emphasized the ethical aspect of Yom Kippur as primary, by making it a prerequisite for everyone to concili-

---

1. See ch. 11, note 16, p. 156.
2. Why then did the Jews prostrate themselves, when, on the Day of Atonement, they heard the High Priest pronounce the name YHWH?

ate his neighbor.[3] Ritual cannot substitute for ethical effort.

The Day of Atonement is thus a unique example of the development of a primitive popular festival into the highest expression [4] of ethical monotheism. On this day the Jew gives thought to the meaning and destiny of his life from the standpoint of God's goodness.

As on Rosh Ha-Shanah, so also on Yom Kippur, we are reminded of the divine judgment and redemption, in contrast to the polytheistic ideas of "doom" and "fate."

Divine judgment and redemption represent the unity of justice and love in God. That unity is celebrated on those days.

In the liturgical version of "The Thirteen Attributes" of God, the final attribute, that of exacting punishment, is omitted, in order to stress the principle of divine love. The liturgical text reads instead: *venake*—God purifies.[5]

Only monotheism is compatible with the concept of man's repeated self-renewal in achieving the spirit of holiness. This is not possible in pantheism, with its insistence on the inexorable character of natural law.[6]

---

3. How incomparably superior in ethical approach is Isaiah, chapter 58!

4. It is to be regretted that Cohen did not make more of the fact that Judaism has been evolving.

5. This is one of two instances in which the traditional liturgy deviates from the biblical doctrine concerning God. The other instance is a benediction in the daily morning prayer, where the verse in Isaiah which reads: "He maketh peace and createth evil" (Isa. 45.7) is changed to read: "He maketh peace and createth everything."

6. Strict pantheism does not recognize creativity, the function-

God, however, can declare man guiltless—*venake,* by treating man's sin as unwitting (Men. 48b).

Rabbi Akiba's statement (Mishnah, Yoma, VIII.9) expresses monotheism's essential principle. It declares that man must first purify himself, before God can purify him. There is no intermediary between God and man.

Trust in God, which derives from the experience of repentance, is Yom Kippur's teaching for the entire year.

Repentance is a life-long duty (Shab. 123a).

Judaism strongly deprecates the self-righteousness which the observance of the Law is said to foster. The Law is an instrument that deepens man's correlation with God.

It is mistakenly assumed that atonement evokes pride; actually it evokes gratitude to God and trust in Him.

As man sees it, repentance cannot be consummated unless the sinner suffer punishment.

God may declare a sinner innocent, but man cannot declare himself innocent. He must pay the penalty for his wrongdoing.

No special punishment, however, is necessary; the suffering of which man himself is the cause is the penalty. The severest punishment is to experience, as a result of our own unreliability, the frustration of our higher aspirations.[7]

---

ing of purpose, or the freedom of the human will. Its basic assumption is that there is nothing in any effect that cannot be accounted for in terms of its *efficient cause* or *vis a tergo* (see ch. 11, note 22, p. 158).

7. The terms in which Cohen spells out the punishment of the sinner verify the nature of the moral laws as conceived in

Monotheism interprets suffering as punishment for sin. That is how a person should view his own suffering. Others' sufferings, however, should be viewed with compassion.

In accepting suffering as punishment,[8] a person becomes worthy of God's goodness.

Pantheism regards the law of self-preservation as self-evident and as the basic right of man. That law is regarded as validating the identity of might and right. But the self which is thus to be preserved is merely the natural self—the biological self.

For religion, however, the self is the product of our correlation with our fellow-man and with God. Acceptance of suffering as punishment for one's own sins is necessary to complete the experience of forgiveness.

According to Maimonides, Job may be considered a prophet, by virtue of his sufferings. What he protested against was his friends' interpretation of his sufferings as a punishment for sin. As prophet, he found fault with the moral economy of human life which had to depend upon prophets.

Suffering can yield a higher good than either wealth, wisdom or piety. This is why the prophet had to suffer. Being human, even the prophet needs the maturing experience of suffering.

---

functional rationalism. They are moral responsibility, integrity, loyalty or love, and creativity. It is understandable, therefore, that the failure to live up to those laws should bring with it what Cohen designates as the severest punishment: "to suffer from our own unreliability and from the frustration of our higher aspirations."

8. Moral suffering accepted as punishment belongs to the category of *y'surin shel ahayah,* which figures in rabbinic theodicy (Ber. 5a).

Yom Kippur does not suggest the type of poetic theodicy of the Book of Job. The ritual of fasting is intended to remind us of the good that suffering may yield.[9] Suffering rather than the pleasure principle is the key to life's meaning.

In rabbinic ethics uncaused hatred is regarded as a cardinal sin. Actually, there is no justification for hatred. Causeless hatred (*sin'at hinam*) is the primary cause of human suffering.

The theory that Israel suffers for the sake of the nations which do not accept the only true God may be questioned. But there can be no doubt that it is Israel's duty to endure suffering. The individual should learn from Israel to accept suffering as a concomitant of responsibility.

Whenever the rest of the world interprets Israel's sufferings as a punishment for Israel's sin, it is in danger of losing its own soul.

In some religions, suffering is considered a sign of perfection. Hence, God is represented as suffering.

Suffering is only a means to redemption.

Redemption from sin, as well as from the suffering caused by sin, is a transitory experience in moments of ecstasy, according to the Jewish conception of redemption. Other religions strive for redemption as a permanent state of existence.

In monotheism, suffering is only one link in the chain of redemption. It is only a step toward the fulfillment of the purpose of humanity, which corresponds to the fulfillment of the idea of God as the only true Being.

---

9. What Cohen says about suffering cannot be taken seriously, much less the fact that the practice of fasting on Yom Kippur is intended to remind us of the good that suffering may yield.

Suffering should never be raised to the level of the divine.

We are gradually approaching the fulfillment of monotheism.

The historical writings of the Jews are epics placing their heroes on a pedestal. They, nevertheless, apply the same ethical standard to their heroes as to the common man.

The main point in the prophecy ascribed to Balaam, which is really Israel's conception of itself as a monotheistic people, is contained in the verse: "Lo, there is no augury in Jacob, no divination in Israel" (Num. 23.23).

The laws which command the killing of witches, and the destruction of the idolatrous nations of Canaan, must be judged in the light of the vital importance assigned to monotheism.

Tolerance is incompatible with the establishment and maintenance of monotheism.

Witchcraft and idolatry, the aberrations resulting from false conceptions of God, are the source of moral sin and of the greatest suffering.

Israel is the symbol of the redemption of the individual. And thus Israel is not merely a human aggregate, with needs and obligations, but the ideal human person incarnate.

If not for the concept of the Suffering Messiah, we would have to identify Israel as the suffering people, suffering for its sin. But Israel really suffers for the sake of God. Its suffering has given it its great vitality. In comparison with that vitality, what do power and glory amount to?

All nations suffer, and their suffering ends in political disintegration and death.

When Israel lost its state, it entered upon a higher level of existence. It took up the martyrdom to which its world-mission exposed it.

Israel's sufferings should not be viewed from the standpoint of national particularism; neither should it be treated as subject matter for the esthetic arts.

If monotheists are to be true to their mission, they must regard their suffering as a stimulus to self-sanctification and to the education and maturation for their correlation with God.

The suffering of Israel symbolizes what it means to be at one with God.

Israel's suffering leads to its at-onement with God.

The redemption of Israel depends upon the salvation of mankind.

Redemption is not a final moment in history, but realizable at every stage of the historical process.

Chapter 13
THE MESSIANIC IDEA AND MANKIND

The concept of man as a *rational* being follows from the concept of God as Creator and Lawgiver.[1] Through the corre-

---

1. This statement supplements the one at the beginning of chapter 8. There we are told that we discover the human, or the fellow-man in our neighbor, through the ethical consciousness in ourselves. Here the point is that, after discovering the human in our neighbor, we arrive at the conclusion that he, too,

lation with God, man becomes aware of his neighbor and of himself as persons. Being aware of oneself as a person is to be aware of God as the God of forgiveness. Being aware of one's neighbor as a person is to be aware of God as the God of love.

The scope of ethics is limited to the social relations regulated by the community with its laws. In dealing, however, with man in the generic sense, ethics must resort to religion,[2] with its concepts of sin and forgiveness.

---

is *rational* or *ethical*. When we analyze our own ethical consciousness, we arrive at the conception of God as Creator and Lawgiver. God as "Creator" means to Cohen that He endows man with reason (see ch. 5). God as "Lawgiver" means that God communicates to man the *laws* of reason, or ethics. By that time we become aware that our neighbor is "a rational being" or a person. At the same time we experience the fact that learning to recognize our neighbor in that way is a manifestation of God's love.

The foregoing is a roundabout way of arriving at the idea that other human beings are just as rational and ethical as we are, and that they are such is a manifestation of the love of God, who is both Creator and Lawgiver. This roundabout way of reasoning is part of ideationist rationalism. In functional rationalism, however, we make short shrift of all that, and simply proceed on the assumption that our fellow-men are just as rational and ethical as we are. Otherwise we could not *communicate* with them. The next step takes place when we try to interact with them. We then have to reckon with the laws of moral responsibility, integrity, loyalty or love, and creativity. These laws are a manifestation of God as the Power that makes for salvation. In functioning that way, they elicit the best in us, which is what love always does. They thus reveal God as the God of love.

2. Cohen maintains that, if the problem of having the ethical values function in human life were limited to organized social bodies, that problem might be solved by public opinion, plus government law. If, however, we want the ethical values to function as a means of fostering a sense of universal human brother-

From the standpoint of pure ethics, when only the individual is under consideration, it is not necessary to introduce the idea of God. That idea, however, is indispensable when mankind, as a whole, is being considered.

Religion [3] must not interfere with the autonomy of ethics.[4] Ethics is based on its own assumptions. Nevertheless, for its problems it must necessarily resort to experience.[5] Ethics does, indeed, make use of law and history; why not also of religion?

Religion [6] has evolved the idea of mankind; this is its great achievement.

In classic philosophy man is regarded as the subject of ethics. The Greek thinkers were the first to recognize in the state a prefiguration of the human microcosm, the human soul.[7]

---

hood, then we come up against the fact that no social arrangements or institutions can prevent a person from "commiting acts for which he must call his rational self into account." That makes it necessary for him "to resort to institutional or social religion, with its concepts of sin and forgiveness." A person no sooner does that than he is rationally impelled to assume the existence of God as the correlate of mankind as a whole. That, of course, is true only of a social religion which, like the Jewish religion, is monotheistic.

3. Here, too, religion is *not* synonymous, as in most instances in this book, with the idea of God. Here "religion" refers to cult and institutions.

4. Ethics "as such," based on reason, however reason be conceived.

5. This is where Cohen breaks with ideationist, particularly Platonic, dialectic. "Even pure mathematics," he states, "has to draw its problems from experience."

6. Monotheist institutional religion.

7. As in Plato's *Republic.*

Man, as such, however, remained an abstraction, an idea, and the concept of mankind did not even occur to them. Thus the barbarians were never included in the mental horizon of the Hellenes.[8]

Only after barbarians and Hellenes intermingled did the idea of the individual emerge.

Philo was the first to stress the idea of man as such. His concept of man was based on the prophetic concept of mankind.

Christianity and Islam, in postulating monotheism as the universal religion, necessarily reckoned with the idea of mankind upon whose redemption they were intent.

The conflict between the State and the Church, which raged during the Middle Ages and which still continues, did not altogether obliterate the vision of the idea of mankind.

The sciences, the arts, the Renaissance, national and international law, and the cosmopolitan philosophy of the Enlightenment further contributed to strengthening the idea of mankind.

The Reformation, the Pietist movement and the influence of Rousseau contributed to the autonomy of ethics. Kant finally succeeded in placing ethics on an autonomous basis, as part of systematic philosophy. The spirit of mankind breathes in Kant's ethics.

For Kant, mankind is an idea, not merely an empirical fact, grounded in psychology or history.

In Kant's system the idea of mankind gives rise to the concept of world citizenship. "Respect mankind in your own per-

---

8. All non-Hellenes were barbarians, in the sense of aliens, or foreigners who, according to Aristotle, were only fit to be slaves.

son as well as in the person of everyone else," is his categorical imperative.

Herder, the author of *Ideas toward a Philosophy of Humanity* and of *The Spirit of Hebrew Poetry,* recognized Messianism as integral to monotheism.

He considered the Torah as the synthesis of the concept of God as a spiritual Being and of the concept of God as author of the moral "statutes and judgments," reflecting the national spirit of Israel, manifest especially in the rise of prophecy which transcended the national boundaries.

The rise of monotheism in Israel is an inexplicable mystery.[9]

Equally so is Messianism. It is possible, however, to understand one in the light of the other.[10]

To conceive of God as the Lord of all the earth, who is acknowledged by all mankind, is to profess a cosmopolitanism which clashes with modern nationalism.[11]

How could the Messianic idea arise amidst the political disorganization which obtained in ancient Israel?

All problems of man and his fate, of his own worth and the

---

9. But a most important fact, nevertheless.

10. The essential idea in monotheism is the functioning of unifying tendencies throughout the cosmos. That fact is registered in human consciousness as unifying purpose, such as the Good, or God. Messianism likewise, represents the functioning of tendencies in mankind that lead to its ultimate unification. Thus monotheism and Messianism illumine each other.

11. But not with nationalism as such. The trouble with *modern* nationalism is that it is chauvinistic and resentful of the least interference from without, however justified.

worth of life as a whole, are bound up with the idea of Messianism.

Questioning life's worth represents the first critical stage, which leads to the notion of the destruction of the world as the penalty the world must pay for its sin.

But this raises the problem of the future, which, in turn, leads to the belief in the rise of a better state of being.

The prophets adopted the popular myth about the end of the world, as expressed in "the Day of the Lord." [12]

The assumption of a cycle of destruction and renewal belongs to the thought-world of Fate.

In monotheism world destruction was reinterpreted as World Judgment.

Zephaniah includes Israel in the World Judgment together with the other nations.

The idea of God's Judgment gave rise to the belief in God's guidance and education of mankind, leading to repentance and thus to regeneration.

Such is the progress of the idea of the "Day of the Lord" from its mythological origin as the great sacrificial feast in which the gods and men commune with one another.

By means of this reinterpretation the prophet became the

---

12. Originally it represented the belief in the ultimate victory of YHWH over the other gods, a victory that would take the form of the overthrow of Israel's enemies and the imposition of His dominion over them. With the prophet Amos, it came to be reinterpreted as the Day of Universal Judgment, when all the nations, including Israel, would be visited by all manner of calamities for their idolatries and their violation of the moral law.

social and political interpreter of history. The mythological concept of the "Day" for celebrating the triumph of force is transformed into an ethical concept based on social justice.

The biblical concept of *Sheol* foreshadows the idea of survival after death.

The myth of the Isle of the Blessed led to the belief in the immortality of the soul.

Monotheism transformed the mythological concept of survival after death by means of its idea of the infinite, which applies to time and not to space.

THE GOLDEN AGE

The mythological concept of Paradise is an answer to the question: [13] Why did God give man commandments which created in him an uneasy conscience? St. Paul also asked that question.[14]

The mythological concept of a perfect world was a preparation for Messianism which shifted that concept to the future by stressing perfectibility.

Messianism does not aim at reproducing Paradise. It assumes that man is in possession of the knowledge of good and evil. It does not regard the prehistoric era as the ideal state of existence, but as the dawn of civilization.

The conceptual aspect of the Messianic idea is so predomi-

---

13. The answer is, apparently, that man should attain that self-knowledge which, while creating in him an uneasy conscience, impels him to strive to improve himself. Man's improvement must, at least in part, be the result of his own effort.

14. His answer was: Such is the mystery of redemption from original sin.

nant that the personality of the Messiah is transcended,[15] and emphasis is placed on the Messianic Era, that is, on the future as such.

Thus arose the concept of history, with the implication that ideal humanity belongs to the future.[16]

Even the concept of God changed under the impact of Messianism. He came to be known as the creator of a new heaven and a new earth. Thus the "Day of the Lord" became "The End of Days," and the idea of man, the idea of mankind.

In mythology, the Aeon represents the destruction and regeneration of this world, without any ethical motif.[17]

In the Zagreus myth of a god who strives for the reunion of his divided parts, we have the first and last hint in mythology of any ethical connotation of the God idea.

THE DELUGE LEGEND

The influence of monotheism is evident in the story of the covenant with Noah. Noah, as the symbol of mankind, is assured of the future of the human race and of its endless development.

The promise that the earth is to exist forever implies that perfection is attainable in this world and that we need not look to a transcendent world for giving meaning to life.[18]

---

15. According to modern reinterpretation, but not according to tradition.

16. A significant comment on the significance of history.

17. Only in Jewish religion does the expectation of a better future make for moral and spiritual improvement.

18. Hence the far more important function of Messianism than of faith in the hereafter, in the roster of moral and religious values.

THE JEWISH STATE

The Jewish People, unlike the Greek People, retained its unity even after the fall of its state and was able to restore its statehood.

The division of ancient Israel was a rehearsal of Judaism's future role in the history of the world. It meant that the Kingdom of David was not to be the basis of world monotheism.[19]

Why, however, did the Jewish spirit require the Jewish People to survive, while the Greek spirit could dispense with the Greek People? [20]

---

19. That is his own idea. Jewish tradition thinks otherwise.

20. This is a most pertinent question, because the answer to it should lead us to an understanding of the Jewish religion. There can be no doubt as to the fact that the Jewish People owes its survival, its continuity, and its revival most of all to its religion. For lack of such religion, the Greeks did not survive the destruction of their city-state type of government, though their spirit, with its poetry, art and philosophy, has taken possession of Western mankind.

Just what in the content of Jewish religion has saved the Jewish People? Cohen answers that question, from the standpoint of his ideationist rationalism. The Jewish religion, according to him, revolves around two foci: monotheism and Messianism. Those two principles, unlike the poetry, art and philosophy of the Greeks, have so far not proved transferable. So long as that is the case the Jewish People has to continue in its struggle for survival. Without it, monotheism and Messianism would disappear from the human consciousness. Since those two principles are an integral element of human reason, their disappearance would constitute a deterioration of human reason. On the other hand, according to Cohen, "when monotheism becomes universal, there will be no need for Israel."

That conclusion plays marvelously into the hands of our ene-

The Greek spirit lives on in the world of poetry and art and philosophy.

Its influence continues to be felt in the life of all the nations. Likewise, when monotheism becomes universal, there will be no need for Israel.

---

mies, even the friendly ones, who contend that they have taken over the monotheism of Jewish religion as well as its Messianism. So why a Jewish People, and why a State of Israel?

There seems to be a much simpler way of accounting for the survival of the Jewish People and for the part played by Jewish religion in that survival. From the standpoint of functional rationalism, the question reads: What in the actual functioning of the Jewish religion in the life and consciousness of the Jewish People gave the Jewish People its exceptional vitality? The answer to that question is the following: The Jewish religion intensified the collective self-consciousness of the Jewish People, by fostering in every Jew an awareness of a past to be proud of and a future to look forward to, an awareness of belonging to a people whose history concerned itself mainly with the question why the Jewish People happened to be the object of God's special providence, and with a Messianism which portrayed a future in which its fondest hopes would be realized.

Is it any wonder, then, that an ancient poet, in an ecstatic moment cried out: "Who is like Thy people, like Israel, a nation one on earth?" (II Sam. 7.23). When did the Greeks ever possess national memories or national hopes comparable to those of the Jewish People? The nearest they came to anything comparable in the way of an ideal future was when Plato envisaged his *Republic*. The *Republic* contains great poetry and philosophy, but its people-making power was nil. That was demonstrated by the experiment with it, during Plato's lifetime, in the ancient city of Syracuse. Later, it was used by the Church as a vindication of its totalitarian policies.

A national self-consciousness like that of the Jewish People is not transferable as were the poetry, art and philosophy of the

But monotheism was not yet developed when the Bible was completed, and could not be entrusted at that stage to peoples that had not produced the Bible. It still needed the spiritual force of the people of the Bible. That spiritual force,

---

Greeks. The people that possesses such a national self-consciousness is intent upon living as long as the heavens and the earth exist (Jer. 33.25-26). Nothing is further from its mind than that it might disappear from the stage of history.

That implies a different conception of nationhood from Cohen's. To him, nationhood is, at best, a necessary evil at the present time, which, with the advent of better times, mankind will dispense with. In functional rationalism, however, nationhood, like family life and other types of natural groupings, is indispensable to the normal development of human nature, provided, of course, it is freed from the spirit of exclusivism, totalitarianism and absolute sovereignty.

The case of the survival of the Jewish People, not as a mere fossil, as Arnold Toynbee maintains, but with sufficient vitality to experience revival more than once through the centuries, throws light on one of the most debated problems of human concern: Is purpose, or final cause, authentic, or is it only illusory and merely a disguise for material or for efficient cause, as many scientists, especially those of positivist bent of mind, claim?

Karl Marx declared that ethical values—which supposedly belong to the category of purpose—are really nothing more than reflections of the mode of economic production, and are determined by the class in control of the instruments of production. He thus reduced the category of purpose to an illusion. If purpose is an illusion, so must all moral values like justice, freedom, equality and peace be illusions. Likewise, Freud demonstrated that we all do things in the belief that they fulfill some purpose which we have in mind, when actually we are impelled by unconscious or repressed wishes. Thus, he, too, cast doubt on the authenticity of purposeful action.

If, however, it is an indisputable fact that the Jewish People

however, could dispense with the state, since the Jewish people predated the Jewish state.[21]

This accounts for the ambiguous nature of Israel's destiny. The State was destroyed, but the People was preserved. The symbolic significance of Messianism is to remind the nations that their main striving should be the unity of mankind. Only the concept of One God could give rise to a People fit to serve as the symbol of One World.

The prophets who hoped for the revival of the Jewish state, as part of the Messianic future, had to conclude that also the enemy states, which were destined for destruction, would arise again.

Jeremiah, the tragic prophet, ruthlessly challenged the national consciousness of his people, by questioning some of its most sacred traditions.[22] Ezekiel, on the other hand, was very nation-minded.

Deutero-Isaiah was the first prophet who gave expression to the twofold aspect of the antinomy: Jewish People and Messianic mankind.

---

survived as a result of a purposeful will to live and to transmit its heritage from generation to generation, and if it tried to validate that purpose by a conception, however mythical, of its past and by a formulation, however idealistic, of its expectation—do not these facts demonstrate the intrinsic potency of purpose, or final cause? What more than that should we want to prove the functioning of other factors in human life besides matter and energy—whether we term those factors manifestations of the Good, of God, or of Divinity?

21. An argument also used by Samson Raphael Hirsch against Zionism, but not true to fact.

22. Cf. Jer. 3.16; 7.22; 31.32. He challenged certain traditions, but not the national consciousness.

The products of the human spirit necessarily reflect the life of the particular nation from which they arise. The knowledge of God, however, must have as its basis the community of mankind.

THE HOLINESS OF GOD

Holiness is morality and is therefore to be distinguished from nature [23] and its phenomena.

The uniqueness of God denotes the underlying unity of the moral principles. The God of justice is also the God of life; the God who punishes is also the God who forgives.[24]

The concept of God as creator implies that the creation and maintenance of the world are a continuous process and that the human race is imperishable.

The unity of God is a reminder to the nations to strive for the unity of mankind. Messianism is the logical consequence of monotheism.[25]

Unless monotheism is retained in its strict purity, Messianism is bound to become adulterated, as when the Messiah is identified with God.[26]

When the Messiah is regarded as capable of forgiving sin,

---

23. Only from the standpoint of *ideationist* rationalism.

24. Only from the standpoint of *functional* rationalism, for only life, or human experience, and not pure reason can teach that.

25. Cohen viewed monotheism as the analogue of Plato's conception of the Good as the Supreme Idea or Supreme Reality. That is why he saw in Messianism the logical consequence of monotheism, since Messianism meant that mankind was destined to achieve its ultimate Good.

26. The reference is to Christianity.

he usurps a function which is God's exclusively.

The function of the Messiah is to achieve the ideal mankind by uniting all men. The idea of the Messiah is not immanent in the concept of God, but in the concept of man.

THE CULTURAL UNIQUENESS OF ANCIENT ISRAEL

The absence of both science and philosophy in the culture of ancient Israel has led to a misapprehension of its creativity. Insofar as monotheism is the product of reason,[27] it compensates for this lack.

Ancient Israel had to concentrate on the idea of monotheism, even at the risk of one-sidedness, for only thus could this idea be securely established. Later, the Jewish people gave evidence also of its gifts for science and philosophy.

With respect to poetry, too, ancient Israel's culture was one-sided. At first, it produced only poetry concerning man's correlation with God and the establishment of His sovereignty over mankind.

Plato's failure to concentrate on the problem of the knowledge of God vitiated his idealism by restricting it to a class ideal.

Concentration on the knowledge of God led ancient Israel to the idea of Messianism.

The rise of prophecy, with its emphasis on the eligibility of all human beings for the attainment of the holy spirit, is

---

27. He regarded Platonism as potential monotheism, except that it failed "to concentrate on the problem of the knowledge of God."

further evidence of ancient Israel's one-sided concentration. This made possible a theocracy without clericalism or the hegemony of the priesthood. The prophets and judges were the spiritual leaders of religion and society. Moses, who was a prophet, ranked higher than Aaron the priest.

The rise of the Scribes in the Second Commonwealth was the logical outcome of prophecy. Ezra, who was a Scribe, became the founder of the religious structure of the Jewish People.

The next step was to apply the concept of revelation to the biblical canon, and then to the oral tradition, thus giving revelation a symbolic character,[28] as a special form of cognition.

The isolation of ancient Israel's culture was not an end in itself, but a means of guarding monotheism from the impact of counter-influences.

The religious one-sidedness of the ritual observance ordained by Rabbinism should be interpreted as a preparation for Messianism.[29]

Unlike the Church with the priest as mediator, Rabbinism made the laity responsible for the maintenance of the ritual system,[30] which took the place of the sacrificial cult.

---

28. Since the term "revelation," as a historical event, could not be applied to the oral tradition. It is a symbolic or metaphorical term for intuition.

29. He interpreted the rabbinic behest: "Make a fence around the Law," which led to the multiplication of ritual prohibitions, as intended to prevent alien influences from diluting the spirit of monotheism and weakening the Messianic expectations of the Jewish People.

30. Rabbinism represented the survival of Pharisaism after the

Israel's cultural self-limitation resulted in ethical rigorism.

Since God is the creator, His work must be so perfect that even evil, or whatever seems contrary to His purpose, must serve His purpose.

We have seen that social insight, which identifies suffering specifically with poverty, leads to regarding suffering not as punishment for sin.

Thus "poverty" and "piety" came to be almost synonymous. This achievement of ethical monotheism was not attained by Plato. Biblical Judaism is almost identical with ethical socialism.[31] It culminated in the prophetic struggle against kings, princes and the privileged classes.

In the Book of Psalms, the identification of the poor with the pious points to Messianism as the spiritual harmony leading to the acknowledgment of God by all men (cf. Ps. 150.6).

Ethical monotheism accounts for the fact that only that part of the people of Israel which has remained loyal to God has survived.

The concept of "the remnant of Israel" is part of the belief in the Messianic future. It also establishes the norm for the present.

The doctrine of Israel's election has similar significance. It is intended to stress the people of Israel's Messianic destiny

---

destruction of the Temple put an end to the sacrificial cult, and rendered defunct the priesthood which was the backbone of Saduceeism.

31. As contrasted with so-called scientific, or Marxist, socialism which is based on historical materialism. Cohen regarded the advent of the Messianic Kingdom or the Kingdom of God, as the culmination of the struggle for social justice in the world.

to become coextensive with mankind.[32]

The Prophets would not have dared foretell the fall of the people of Israel had they not entertained an ideal concept of that people as "the faithful remnant" which would survive.[33]

The idealization of the Messiah reflects the idealization of the People of Israel as "the faithful remnant."

When only the poor were declared fit for saintliness, David and his throne could no longer be symbolic of the Messiah. Thus the Messiah became "the servant of the Lord" (Isa. 52.13).

All Israel—indeed all mankind—must become "the servant of the Lord." Thus the Messiah ceased to be regarded as an individual. This accords with Rashi's and Kimhi's interpretations of "the servant of the Lord" as referring to Israel.

The emancipation from nationalism and opportunism derived from prophetic ethical rigorism, which, in turn, derived from ancient Israel's religious one-sidedness.

---

32. If the doctrine of election were generally understood in that sense, even though there are numerous passages in the Written and the Oral Tradition which contradict that version of the doctrine, there would be no objection against voicing it. Ethically, however, it is important not only to *be* right, but also to *appear* right. An idea is what it is taken to mean. The sense in which the doctrine of election is taken to mean by all and sundry disqualifies it from being voiced as a functioning principle in Jewish religion.

33. They could not have been prophets, or spokesmen, for and to the people of Israel, if they had not assumed that it was destined to usher in the Messianic era. In that assumption was implied its survival. Since the people as a whole did not deserve to survive, a remnant at least was bound to survive. To deserve

The prophets were the originators of the concept of world history. To them history was not merely a record of the past, but a religious vision for the future of mankind.

The fact that the prophets held on to their national consciousness in envisaging the future lends to that future a concreteness which differentiates it from the anemic myths of the "Golden Era."

National history cannot orient us to world history in the true sense of the word.[34] To comprehend the direction of world history, we have to reckon with all of mankind and cherish it in our hearts.

The Book of Deuteronomy proves clearly that, while the history of Israel is national in character, it is also an idealization based upon the historical task which Israel is called upon to achieve in the future. Such an idealization, based upon a great idea, though only a subjective one, is the most reliable guide to what is authentic.[35]

Isaiah presents the Messiah as a child, as a father,[36] and as

---

to survive, the remnant would have to consist of those who remained faithful to God.

34. Why not? On the contrary, why may not the history of a nation be an incentive to other nations to raise their collective life, with its politics, economics, culture and religion, to an ethical level? It is doubtful that mankind will ever dispense with national divisions. So far, nations have been regarded as either exempt from, or incapable of, moral responsibility. Henceforth, however, if they will not submit to the moral law, there will be no mankind.

35. See what is said above in note 20 about the role of purpose as an authentic cause of conduct in human life.

36. As child, by reason of his freedom from sin, and as father of all men.

a counsellor (Isa. 9.5). These are fitting similes for the Messiah in the role of guide for future generations.

We have seen that creation implies divine providence.[37] Likewise, Messianism implies that it is providential that men should derive their human worth from the suffering incurred in their social struggle, and not from material achievement.

The Messiah takes upon himself only men's suffering, not their guilt. As symbol of the ideal future of mankind, he is the moral Atlas of the world, not the incarnation of worldly power.

In Christianity, the Messiah takes men's guilt on himself. This only God can do. Hence, the Christian Messiah becomes God.

The poor, that is to say, the pious, are the forerunners of the Messiah, who symbolizes the moral significance of the history of mankind. According to this interpretation, life derives its true worth not from the pursuit of pleasure, but from the endurance of suffering. Though this fact may not seem to be in accord with our sense of justice, it is in accord with historical reality. However, this wrong will ultimately be righted.

The moral interpretation of history leads not only to the ascetic disdain of worldliness; it also negates the worth of power, glory, success and dominion. It exalts the spirit of humility. That enables us to note the difference between piety and humility. He who is pious represents only himself; he who is humble represents all mankind. He is aware of man's shortcomings, for he suffers from an unjust social

---

37. That refers to what Cohen has said above about God's being twice Creator, in that He also created the sense of the brotherhood of mankind (cf. above, p. 137).

order. In suffering *because* of mankind, the humble-poor suffer *for* mankind.[38]

The ideal man suffers; this truth is implied in the concept of the Messiah. Insofar as the ideal man achieves humility, he possesses the Messianic attribute described in Isaiah 11.

In Jewish ethics, humility is considered the highest virtue. It is ascribed to God Himself.[39] This explains why God is described in the Bible as particularly concerned for those who are poor, and why humility is regarded as the outstanding trait of the Messiah, who is the symbol of ideal mankind.

Prophetism did not function in a vacuum, but as part of the life of ancient Israel. Therefore, when the prophetic interpretation of the Messiah could no longer be associated with the Davidic dynasty, it had to be applied to the People of Israel as the suffering servant vis-à-vis the other nations. That the People of Israel is destined to fulfill its Messianic role, without enjoying the advantages of a state,[40] is the tragedy of Jewish peoplehood.

The history of the Jewish People verifies its Messianic destiny. In Isaiah, Chapter 53, the Messiah is represented as pleading for the sinful nations. This function enables the Jewish People to transcend tragedy and death.

---

38. This is tantamount to advising the exploited and the suppressed classes to accept their lot resignedly, as a way of bringing about the establishment of a just social order in the end. That is grist for the Marxist mill.

39. The humility symbolized by the Messiah, according to Cohen, is passive submission to exploitation and oppression. That kind of humility is hardly fit to be ascribed to God. He later corrects that inference (cf. below, p. 240).

40. Add: "And with the kind of passive resignation recommended by some of its spiritual leaders."

Injustice is an indictment against the nations. The sufferings of Israel stem from the shortcomings of the nations which have prevented the establishment of monotheism. The injustice of which Jews have been victims is an indictment against the nations.

These sufferings are also shared by the "righteous Gentiles."

The worth of the non-Jewish religions is lessened by the sufferings which their adherents inflict on Israel. This also causes pain to the "righteous Gentiles."

Humanitarian ethics finds its fulfillment in the Messianic idea, which is a protest against the "pleasure principle." This protest is shared by all religious and national groups, as long as there is among them a "faithful remnant," which tries to live up to the ideal implied in the idea of "the servant of God." [41]

The knowledge of God will ultimately be the possession of all.

Chapter 14
MESSIANISM IN THE PROPHETIC WRITINGS

Hosea was dominated by the idea of the symbolic union of God and Israel. He also foretold the reunification of Judah and Israel and the universal reign of peace (2.21; 14.6; 3.5).

---

41. Cohen exaggerates beyond all bounds the significance of the few verses in Isaiah 53, which are atypical when compared with the entire body of prophetic teachings.

Amos gave a moral interpretation of the popular belief in the advent of the Day of YHWH (8.9 ff.). The seeking after the word of YHWH marked for Amos the advent of a New Day for Israel and of the Messianic era described in the concluding verses 9.8-16.

Micah denounced idolatry and demanded "a house of God for all nations." He prophesied that a scion of the House of David would teach the nations universal peace, as pictured in Chapter 4.1-4. In the meantime, the nations would seek to destroy Zion, but they would be unaware of God's purpose, which was to bring them together, so that Zion might wreak her will against them (5.1-4, 12-14). He combined national memories with visions of the future, in which God would rule over the entire world.

In Chapter 5, Micah foresees a new David. Then will the remnant of Jacob be among the nations as the dew . . . and as a lion among the beasts of the field. Israel will assume the ambivalent role of the Messiah by bringing salvation, which has to be preceded by suffering to be shared by Israel with the other nations.

Isaiah's vision of the mountain of the Lord and the abolition of war is the same as Micah's, but it has to be read in the context of his bitter denunciation of his contemporaries (2.1-5, 10, 19, 21). In Chapter 11, the role of the Messiah is pictured as that of securing justice for the poor and ushering in the universal reign of peace and good will (cf. Hosea 2.20). He foretells the disappearance of the wicked and the spread of the knowledge of God.

After a series of chapters which prophesy the downfall of Babylon, Assyria, Philistia, Moab, Damascus, Israel and Egypt, the prophet describes the messianic era in which Egypt, Assyria and Israel will form the triad of God's chosen peoples (ch. 19).

An outstanding message of Messianic import is the vision in Chapter 25.6-8.

Compare Chapters 29.18-21; 30.26; 32.15-17. The Messiah is described as "a spirit from on high." Here too, where the main interest is in Israel, nonetheless, universal justice and peace are stressed.

Zephaniah's angry denunciation of the nations and of Judea is interrupted by Messianic prophecy (Ch. 3.9 ff.). He foretells the "pure life" and "shoulder to shoulder" unity in the worship of God. He defines the remnant of Israel as the humble and poor folk who have nothing to do with injustice and falsehood. The Messianic idea of the conversion of the nations is combined with the most sensitive description of the reinstatement of Israel. The nations will themselves bring the captive Israelites as a gift to God.

Jeremiah wrestled with the problem of reconciling the actual condition of ancient Israel with the Messianic destiny awaiting her (cf. 3.16-17; 23.1-8). That condition stood out in strong contrast to its Messianic destiny. He pictured the fulfillment of that destiny as more glorious than the redemption from Egypt, in that God would then manifest Himself as the God of righteousness (cf. 23.6; 33.16).

Of special significance is 31.30-36. The knowledge of God as the common possession of mankind is to be the practical norm for religion and ethics. As part of this knowledge will be the recognition of God as the true Redeemer of man from the power of sin.

As with Isaiah, so too Jeremiah foresees the reinstatement of Egypt, Ammon, Moab and Edom and all the other evil neighbors whose exile he had foretold (46.26; 48.47; 49.6,

39; 12.15-16) on condition that they acknowledge the God of Israel.[1]

Jeremiah foresees the conversion of the nations as a result of their own recognition of the vanity of idolatry (16.19, 20).

Ezekiel came on the scene before the Captivity, but his main role as prophet was enacted during the Captivity. He differed from his predecessors in not confining himself to the struggle against the world in behalf of monotheism. He was concerned with the practical problem of reinstating the sacrificial system. While his predecessors denounced the abuses of sacrificial worship, they did not propose its abolition.

Ezekiel did not always follow the ritual practices prescribed in the Torah.

His Messianic prophecies were not limited to the rebuilding of the state. He also expected an inner transformation.

He contrasted arrogant nationalism with Messianism. His forebodings of doom, however, are followed by tidings of salvation for the nations.

Ezekiel presented his vision of Israel's repentance as Messianism. He adapted the myth of resurrection to the fate of his people.

In Deutero-Isaiah the concept of Messianism was further spiritualized and de-nationalized, when King David's place was taken by Cyrus.

Here the difference between the national and the universal function of the Messiah becomes manifest.[2]

---

1. There is good reason to doubt Jeremiah's authorship of those chapters.
2. By the same token that Sennacherib or Nebuchadnezzar

With all this as a premise, the Messianic concept could achieve its highest idealization.

Contrary to the assumption that suffering is penalty for sin, the prophet proclaims suffering as vicarious atonement of the righteous for the sinner.

The problem of evil which agitates the Bible as a whole is transferred from the individual to the history of the nations. The paradox of Israel's suffering too is thus explained. In suffering vicariously for the nations, the People of Israel acquires the right to convert them.

To suffer for the sake of monotheism is not tragic. Jewish suffering is part of their vocation. It is needed to prove their sincerity in their mission of converting the nations to the truth. Neither love of power nor historical momentum [3] impels the Jewish People to follow this course.

The suffering of the Jews constitutes the strongest argument against the pleasure principle.[4] It is also proof of the autonomy of the ethical, for it implies indifference even to

---

could be the instrument of God's purpose to punish Israel for its sins, there is no reason why Cyrus might not be an instrument to redeem Israel from captivity and thus redeem God's name from being profaned. The difference between the national and the universal function of the Messiah is imaginary on Cohen's part.

3. Not historical momentum, but the sense of historical continuity, figures in the survival of the Jewish People. The will-to-live as a People functions as the will to keep alive the heritage of the past, and to look to the fulfillment of the promises for the future embodied in that heritage.

4. More importantly, against the negation of purpose or final cause as an authentically existential factor in the lives of people who are dedicated to a purpose. Such negation is a basic principle

the question of God's justice. God's justice will triumph only after all nations have recognized the One God.

Both Prophet and Psalmist warn [5] that the suffering of the poor should not be misinterpreted as proof of divine punishment.

The fact that those who suffer fulfill a divine mission is not regarded as a paradox. It is treated as an integral part of the history of Israel. The formula of Israel's theodicy is: "Chastisement for the sake of our peace" (Isa. 53.5).

Though Israel fails to be vindicated in the course of history—and though the nations regard the people of Israel as dead and buried—it continues to live and to perform its task for God.

The prophet emphasizes the aspects of awareness and free-will with which God's servant takes upon himself the yoke of suffering for the divine education of mankind and their atonement with God.[6]

When God's servant takes upon himself the responsibility for humanity's sin, he acts like the character in a Greek tragedy who suffers as the result of "fate." But the Bible makes it clear that the nations themselves must pay the penalty for their sins.

The history of mankind, leading to the Messianic good, will bring about the reconciliation of God with the nations, after the people of Israel will have offered itself as a victim, willing to bear suffering for the salvation of mankind.

---

in scientific positivism and in Marxism.

5. Only Cohen does the warning. The prophet and the Psalmist probably assume it.

6. The reference is to the People of Israel.

Though the story of the passion of Christ is evidently based on this poetic vision, modern Bible exegetes fail to note this connection. And yet, they claim to be literary historians rather than theologians. Would that they learned to understand that theology and religion cannot be derived from history but from reason!

The Prophet Joel (3.1-2) draws a parallel between the servant of God and the prophet. He regards the vocation of the prophet as not limited to the People of Israel. He envisages it as destined to be bestowed on all and sundry, including slaves.

The Prophet Zechariah (9.9-10) presents the same concept of the servant of God as he who gives utterance to the great slogan of Messianic religion: one world, one God. Even the name for God will be the same everywhere (14.9).

He transcends the nationhood of "the Chosen People" idea, and predicts that many nations will join Israel to become God's nation (8.22-23; 2.15).

The Prophet Malachi strikes a new note in foretelling that Elijah will bring peace to each family, before the nations are to be united.

All the pious will then constitute the Chosen People.

The most noteworthy change in the Messianic idea took place when the fate of mankind came to be considered in the light of the fate of the individual.

None of the biblical references to Messianism implies an end to human history. The concept "the end of days" does not refer to any supermundane existence. It refers to the time when the human race as a whole will put an end to its evil ways.[7]

---

7. The "end of days" is to be interpreted in terms of the

The question, why the Jews lacked belief in the resurrection of the individual, cannot be answered on the basis of their ethnic character. To ascribe that to their inherent sense of reality is only to state the question in another form.

The Messianic idea is incompatible with the so-called sense of reality. It represents a new type of super-sensate, though not supermundane, thinking.[8]

All idealism is based on that kind of super-sensate thinking. Why may it not also be achieved in rational religion as well as in scientific philosophy?

Messianism is an idealism which is unrelated to the belief in personal immortality.

Why was Plato, who laid the foundation of ethical idealism, so vacillating in his political ideas? It cannot be because of his utopianism which, like Messianism, diverts attention from the present.

Plato's utopianism, however, cannot be compared with Messianism. His blueprint for the state lacks the fundamental idea of the development of his own nation, or of other nations.[9] This proves that Messianism, with its this-worldly

---

mundane history of mankind which will end up in a World Union of the States (cf. above, p. 73).

8. The Messianic idea is based on the assumption that purpose, or final cause, is an authentically existential factor in conditioning, even if not always in determining, a result. That assumption itself is incompatible with what scientific positivists and philosophic materialists consider Reality. That assumption itself, according to ideationist rationalism, as expounded by Plato and accepted by Cohen, belongs to "supersensate, but not supermundane, thinking."

9. See above, p. 178, note 20.

idealism, as distinct from an otherworldly one, could not have evolved in scientific philosophy, but only in rational religion.

Rational religion has been able to achieve what historical politics, with its sense of reality, was unable to accomplish.[10] Messianism is the noblest fruit of monotheism. It is therefore a mistake to associate Messianism with some inherent social trait, instead of with self-conscious monotheism.[11]

Messianism is not merely a transference of the "Golden Age" from the past to the future. The concept of "Golden Age" implies innocence as a lost status, not as a goal for civilization. Since mankind is not regarded as being incorrigibly sinful, monotheism has had to project a future in which war, the great political evil, and poverty, the great economic evil, would be abolished, so that God could manifest His love and His goodness.

In the Psalms, Messianism is implied in every passage in which the Psalmist calls upon the nations to acknowledge God as the source of goodness to all mankind.[12]

When man seeks out God by loving Him, God seeks out man by bestowing His goodness upon him.[13]

---

10. Not ideationist, but functional rationalism accounts for the survival of the Jewish People.

11. From the standpoint of functional rationalism, it is a mistake to ignore the fact that monotheism, without the will-to-live of a people to live by it and for it, is empty of meaning. To be sure, an inherent social trait like the will-to-live of the Jewish People would be blind and directionless, and could not endure, if it did not have the Messianic ideal to keep it alive.

12. Particularly Psalms 96-99.

13. The rationalist approach, whether ideationist or functional, leads to a belief in God only by way of the assumption

The goodness of God, as the foundation of God's universal Kingdom, is the theme of the "new song" (Ps. 96.1).[14] It proves again that monotheism is the only true source of Messianism.

Chapter 15
IMMORTALITY AND RESURRECTION

The concept of the immortality of the soul originated in the myths associated with primitive ideas of man's relation to his family and tribe. In Greece, the concept ot immortality was not part of popular belief.

Immortality presupposes a soul. The idea of the soul has undergone many changes. At first the soul was thought of as a kind of smoke or breath. Then it denoted merely the vital function of the body. It had originally no connection with man's spiritual functions. Homer identified the soul with the diaphragm.

In Plato, by way of further development, the soul came to be synonymous with reason dealing with theoretic and practical problems. Immortality became a necessary attribute of it.

The fact, however, is that the concept of immortality does not follow from the ethical concept of the soul. Even in philosophic speculation, the concept "soul" is not a corollary of the idea of man, but of the idea of the cosmos.

---

that life can be rendered worthwhile through a sense of purpose, which, in the language of religion, is equated with loving God, or Goodness. That approach reacts on him who takes it; it makes of him a better human being.

14. Ps. 96.1; 98.1.

In the cosmos, where soul means world-soul, it denotes self-originating motion. From there it is transferred to the microcosm, where it also means self-originating motion. All souls, says Plato, are deathless.

There was a time when the soul meant a ghost that interfered with the ordinary course of events. That makes us aware of the fact that the idea of soul has been spiritualized progressively from the time when the mythical concept of the soul held sway.

Plato was as much an artist as he was a philosopher. As an artist, he was attracted by the picturesque myths of Hades. In the Middle Ages, too, the artists depicted Judgment scenes more frequently than scenes of Paradise. Plato's reference to Hades are, therefore, not to be taken literally.

Plato's poetical representation of resurrection contradicts his own assumption that the body is the prison of the soul, which he sometimes conceives as the principle of life as such, and at other times as the principle only of *ethical* life.[1]

Is the idea of resurrection inherently related to that of immortality or is it extraneous to it?

It is the function of rational religion to do with the concept of immortality what it does with other concepts of mythological religion.[2]

Both the idea of Judgment in Hades and that of resurrection imply that there is no limit to the soul's capacity for repentance and God's power of forgiveness.

---

1. That is, as synonymous with reason.
2. Here Cohen makes a bow to *functional* rationalism, in that he reinterprets the idea of immorality. Reinterpretation is possible only when the meaning of an idea is the way it functions.

Primitive burial customs derive from ignorance of the nature of the soul. The dead, provided with food and weapons, were assumed to continue living a bodily life.

The biblical narratives of the Patriarchs contain no reference to resurrection.

The concept of *Sheol* plays a negative [3] part in the Bible. With the belief in the unity of God, *Sheol* could only denote a place of punishment.

A key expression for dying is, "being gathered to his people." The term "gathered" implies the ending of one career and the beginning of another, and the term "people" implies one's clan.

A more definite suggestion is contained in the expression "Thou wilt come to thy fathers" (Gen. 15.15).

"Fathers" is the equivalent of "people." The soul, or that which gives the individual his individuality, derives from the people and its continuing history.[4]

Immortality thus comes to mean identification with the historical continuity of one's people.

This interpretation of immortality differentiates religion from mythology.

In Messianism, the differentia of religion comes to the fore, because immortality and resurrection are associated with Messianism.

---

3. Where those who die continue to exist unchanged in the same state as in the moment of death (cf. Gen. 37.35; Isa. 38.18). A conception of *Sheol* is given in Job 10.21-22.

4. Functionally, the soul of a person is the product of his individuality, plus what he derives from his interaction with "the people and its continuing history."

In Ezekiel's vision of the resurrection of the dry bones, the concept of resurrection leads to the idea of immortality as synonymous with sharing the continuity of one's people.

In addition to the principle of development implied in Messianism, there also is to be considered the idea of holiness.

The idea of holiness negates the idea of the profane, which treats as real only that which is this-worldly.[5] Holiness [6] is extended to include one's people, and is identified as the basic element in the God concept. It thus necessarily extends [7] the concept of life itself beyond the limits of this-worldly existence.

The sense of holiness gives rise to the idea of man as an individual.[8] As such, he possesses the ability, and experiences the duty, to repent. This implies the existence of a God who redeems and forgives. These ideas transcend the limits of this-worldly life.

---

5. Or only the material and the efficient causes, but not the final cause or purpose.

6. In functional rationalism, "holiness" is synonymous with Divinity. One's people becomes holy when its existence is related to a transcendent purpose, like the unity of mankind, which, in turn, is conceived as a correlate of Divinity.

7. For the individual.

8. In functional rationalism, the reverse is the case; the sense of individuality leads to a sense of holiness by the following steps: Awareness of one's individuality is normally accompanied by a sense of responsibility. Awareness of responsibility is recognized as implying relationship to one's fellow-men. The sense of responsibility is therefore the psychological polarity of selfhood and otherhood. The psychological polarity is itself a manifestation of the cosmic, or the universal, polarity of nature, whereby everything that exists simultaneously initiates action and is acted upon. That is why every time we act with a sense of responsibility, we experience life as holy or divine.

But the transcendent life, which is thus implied, is not the continuation of this-worldly life, as in the mythological cults. The very concept of holiness is intended to point to another *form* of mundane life, to the dedicated life, to living for an idea.[9]

To be holy, one must be an individual, not merely a link in any chain, even if it be a holy people.

The spiritualization of the individual is necessary to deepen the meaning of life and death.

Holiness requires that man possess the spirit of holiness.

The soul becomes spirit, because holiness requires a soul which does more than merely live.

Thus the "soul of all living" comes to mean the spirit of holiness—the spirit of man. This spirit is an idea. It designates man's task, and strengthens his will to attain holiness. This is how it determines the character of his living, his dying and his hereafter.

The Psalmist (16.10) can not reconcile the belief in a God of holiness with the thought that the pious who strive for holiness should lose at death that which has made them human and individual. He must postulate a hereafter.

Only mythology asks what happens to the soul when the body dies. Monotheism is satisfied with the affirmation that the soul does not die.

Mythology, on the other hand, does not ask what is the origin of the soul. It assumes that, like the world and the gods, the soul arises out of primeval chaos.

---

9. For a purpose that transcends one's individual interests.

Monotheism ascribes man's origin to God. God created man, so that he may achieve not only a soul, but the spirit of holiness. When man dies, his soul—become spirit—returns to God.

The spirit of man, having been formed by the spirit of holiness, continues to strive for the infinite goal of holiness.

Self-purification is an infinite task for man. He can trust in God's forgiving love. Returning to God means elevating oneself to the infinite task of holiness. What survives death is not the empirical self, but the ethical striving toward holiness.

The return to God, however, does not mean union with God. It means giving back to God what came from Him.

Monotheism guards the concept of immortality from being interpreted in terms either of pantheism or of panpsychism. It deprecates the notion of the soul's unification with God, because this would deprive man of his human differentia, of the endless task of achieving holiness.

What does the concept of immortality add to the soul's actual experience of exaltation in the fulfillment of its endless task?

The answer is: it infuses the soul with awareness of its growth. Such growth renders the soul independent of the body. And the body need not go on growing for the soul to continue its own development.

This enables us to see that it is a mistake to reinterpret Messianism in terms of immortality. It is not possible to build a bridge between the other-worldly existence of the soul and the concrete bodily substance in which the soul has to continue its existence on earth. To Messianism which is to be realized in the sphere of this-worldly existence, eternity means merely the endless history of the human race.

The concept of Messianism, which gives meaning to history as more than a record of past events,[10] was anticipated by the idea implied in the phrase "he was gathered to his Fathers." [11] The "Fathers" are the ancestors of one's national history.

The Messiah becomes in this sense the father of all men.[12] By the same token, the human soul, through its dedication to the task of holiness, becomes part of the Messianic soul.

Man as an individual is an ethical concept. He is most an individual when he embraces all of humanity in himself.

Man, as immortal, experiences in himself the sum of all ethical development, and thus has a share in the infinitely ramified transmission of mankind's spiritual life.

The foregoing considerations help us to understand more fully how the Jewish concept of immortality (*olam ha-ba*) came to be associated with the Messianic era (*atid labo*).

This association, the result of Persian influence, is responsible for the error of identifying Messianism with immortality.

This error has led to the misinterpretation of the Kingdom of God as an other-worldly domain.

The other-worldly "Kingdom of Heaven" is an eschatological idea of Christian Messianism.

The "Kingdom of God," on the other hand, rests on in-

---

10. History as progress toward an ideal goal.
11. Rather far-fetched.
12. See above, p. 187.

dividual ethical responsibility to bring this Kingdom into existence.

The prayer "Thy Kingdom come" is ambiguous. It may refer to the hereafter, or to the attainment of the moral order in this world. In the *Kaddish,* it unquestionably refers to the moral order of this world.

The concept of "Kingdom of God," [13] unlike that of "Kingdom of Heaven," implies the ever-present duty to further its establishment. It must not remain merely an object of hope and trust.[14]

Maimonides makes the proper distinction between *olam ha-ba* (the world to come) and *atid labo* (the future of this world). Neither is associated with merely physical well-being, although he does say that in *atid labo* men will be provided with all their bodily necessities, so that they will be unhampered in their spiritual quest.

Maimonides eliminated from the concept of immortality all hedonistic notions, by dissociating it from the belief in reward and punishment.[15]

Aristotle set the example of dissociating everything physical from the concept of spiritual reward. He emphasized, however, the importance of the intellect by stating that only the

---

13. The Kingdom of God is the first of the three great themes in the Additional Amidah prayer of Rosh Ha-Shanah. That validates functional, rather than ideationist, rationalism. What counts is thought-directed *action*.

14. A true and important distinction.

15. He does, however, interpret immortality as the lot only of those who, during their lifetime, engage in intellectual pursuits, and thereby cultivate their intellect. When they die their intellects are merged with the Active Intellect of the World, or God. That is their reward.

intellectual part of the soul, which only those who led a high intellectual life could possess, was immortal.[16]

Many rabbinic sayings speak of other-worldly reward in spiritual terms. Resh Lakish's view that there will be no Gehenna in the Messianic age implies that there are no eternal hell tortures.

The rabbinic phrase, "to enjoy the lustre of the Skekinah," may be interpreted as referring to moral growth or perfection.

The talmudic statement that the prophets foresaw only the Messianic future, but could not picture *olam ha-ba,* is significant; it treats *olam ha-ba* as outside the scope of the prophet's vision. The Messianic belief, however, is an indispensable part of the belief in God.

The term "nearness of God" forestalls the mystic conception of identity with God. This nearness is not an end in itself, but a means to the self-development implied in Messianism.

The concept of retribution as reward sets a task for moral civilization.

Retribution as punishment, however, is a divine mystery. It cannot be set up as a pattern for human relations. Immortality is not concerned with punishment, but with self-perfection.[17]

Immortality may, therefore, be reinterpreted as referring to the Messianic era. This era signifies the ultimate establishment of the love which, as implied in God's justice,[18] is the norm of human conduct.

---

16. Which is exactly what Maimonides believed.
17. See note 15 above.
18. This is not revaluation but transvaluation of a traditional

Thus the concept of immortality inspires reverence and love for our ancestors, as the protagonists of the Messianic orientation of history.[19]

The statement that "Messiah will not come before all the souls are rendered incarnate" means that the advent of the Messiah is not a fixed event in time. Human growth, of which the Messiah is the symbol, is endless.

The world to come and the hereafter, differentiated in mythology, are identical in monotheism. Both express man's unlimited yearning for growth.

Jewish religious philosophy tries to steer clear of all mystical concepts of immortality. It interprets reward and punishment in spiritual terms.[20]

What is the meaning of "merit of the Fathers?" To regard the individual as benefiting from the "merit of the Fathers" is to conceive the whole of mankind as balancing its account with God. This negates the concept of merit as based merely on one's own deeds.[21]

By ascribing immortality to a people and its founders, we imply that the life of the individual forms an integral part of his people's history. The individual as such cannot be said to earn merit. The merit ascribed to an individual is really the continuing merit of the Fathers of his people.

---

concept or idea, thereby assigning a function to that idea *radically* different from its original one.

19. He seems to imply that we, the descendants, confer immortality on our ancestors by cherishing reverence and love for them. They earned that reverence and love, because they give a meaning to history as more than a series of past events.

20. In vague terms, but hardly in "spiritual terms."

21. Thus removing the ethical objections to the doctrine of

In attributing merit to the Fathers, we do not imply that merit is inherited. The "Fathers" symbolize the beginning of our people's history. It is as such, and not as having been extraordinary persons, that they are credited with the merit which we enjoy.

The "merit of the Fathers" does not lessen our own responsibility or our own need for repentance and self-sanctification. It is intended merely to counteract the danger of self-righteousness.[22]

There is nothing in the concept of the "merit of the Fathers" to imply that the Fathers achieved super-erogatory merit. No matter what a man achieves, it always falls short of what he might achieve. This applies also to the Fathers.

It is absurd to interpret "the merit of the Fathers" as compensating for the sins of their descendants.[23] The entire idea is unrelated to sin. It deals only with the question whether merit can be achieved by the individual as such.

The analogy of "merit of the Fathers" to *thesaurus meritorum* of Christian theology is without foundation. The source of this erroneous analogy is the expression "the bond of life," [24] which merely denotes survival.

"The bond of life" does not presuppose any super-erogatory works which serve as amends for the sins of others.

---

reward and punishment (See below, p. 212).

22. Cf. Deut. 9.4-6; 10.15.

23. He is polemicizing the Christain conception of *thesaurus meritorum.*

24. An expression used in the prayers for the dead. It seems to imply that those for whom the prayer is recited are to be entered into a common account with those who have a surplus of good deeds which they can afford to contribute to the account of those who are spiritually bankrupt.

Moreover, the notion of super-erogatory works is inherently untenable. Even martyrdom is only a matter of performing one's duty. Many people perform their duty at the risk of life.

The Church assumes the concept of *opera super-erogatoria.* This is a denial of the infinite nature of ethical conduct.[25] Treating an ethical deed as distinct from its author, the Church objectifies the deed and makes of it, as it were, a separate entity.

This concept of the deed leads to the conclusion that it is possible to have some one else assume our responsibilities, such as taking upon himself the punishment due us.

All this stems from the assumption that it is possible to do more than one's duty. The meaning of the phrase, "He remembers the loving-kindness of the Fathers," is not that God remembers the love which the ancestors showed Him, but that He remembers the love which He showed them. The Fathers play no part in God's dispensation of reward and forgiveness.[26]

The mistake concerning "the treasure of merit" reveals the danger inherent in the problem of reward. Only the penalty which the sinner takes upon himself has ethical significance.

---

25. The idea of the infinite nature of ethical conduct means that the only limit to the good, which a person is in duty bound to do, is his actual capacity. The very concept of super-erogation is therefore untenable, since the fact that a person can do more good than the law prescribes means that his capacity is more than average, and that he has to live up to his capacity. That is as much good as he ought to do, no less.

26. Why should the merit of the Patriarchs be an exception to the statement in the Ten Commandments where we read: "And he bestows mercy. . . ." (Exod. 20.6)?

Likewise, the only kind of reward compatible with ethics is the added opportunity to do good.

Wherever the Torah promises reward, the reference is to the welfare of the nation as a whole. Even in the precept to send away the mother bird, the reward pertains to the nation, for the reward refers to the maintenance of the family unit [27] which is essential to the state. Respect for parents and the integrity of the family make for a strong and enduring state.[28]

This interpretation of reward is in keeping with the biblical spirit conveyed in the phrase "the nearness to God." Albo interprets it as signifying immortality. Insofar as immortality means sharing in the infinite development of mankind,[29] it is, indeed, a legitimate reward.

All these thoughts derive from monotheism and Messianism. We recognize in them the antithesis to the pantheistic concepts of God and of the soul. The concept of the soul, as unlimited growth of the human being, negates the idea of the universe having a soul. The universe is not ethical; it is physical and mathematical.[30]

---

27. A questionable rationalization of the law which commands that one who finds a nest has to send away the mother bird before taking the nest with the young for himself (cf. Deut. 22. 6-7).

28. The only instances in the Torah of the promise of reward to the individual for meritorious conduct are the command to honor father and mother and to send away the mother-bird before taking the young in the nest one happens to find.

29. Quite a far-fetched reinterpretation of immortality. That is a case not of revalution, but of transvaluation.

30. The universe as such is not ethical. That is why Cohen condemns Spinoza's pantheism. However the universe harbors forces which, when they operate in human life, take on ethical significance.

As all human deeds are imperfect, the very idea of abiding, constant merit is untenable. Man is always in need of being reconciled with God and dependent upon His mercy. But the concept of "merit of the Fathers" resolves the problem of individual merit,[31] while removing the ethical objections to the doctrine of reward and punishment.

"Be not like servants who serve their master for the sake of receiving a reward." "Do good for its own sake"—this is Jewish ethics.

"He who is commanded and acts, stands higher than he who is not commanded and acts." This dictum assumes the autonomous character of duty.[32]

The expression "the divine command" signifies the same as the term "moral autonomy."

The foregoing ideas are incompatible with the theological concept of "treasure of merit."

Even a martyr, then, has no special merit; he merely performs his duty.

The three laws in Judaism for which one must be ready to suffer martyrdom have no relation to other-worldly privileges.

The strict sense of duty dispenses with all notions of reward and punishment in the hereafter, and with the conception of the soul as a kind of ghost. The reference in our

31. See note 21, p. 208.
32. That is in keeping with the teaching of Kant that religion is ethics as the will of God. Since, for an act to be ethical, it has to be autonomous (i.e., inner-directed). To be truly autonomous, an act has to be done in a spirit of obedience to God who is the source of what is ethical.

prayers to "the merit of the Fathers" means that we thank God for what He did to our people in former times.

*   *   *

The problem to be considered now is that of the moral evaluation of our personal actions.

The teaching that "All who are of Israel are eligible for the life of the world to come" means that insofar as man is capable of repentance, he is eligible for immortality. No one who is righteous is damned. The absolute loss of moral worth is unthinkable.

This teaching applies not only to Jews, but to all descendants of Noah. This is the meaning of Messianism.[33]

The concept of "pious Gentiles" accords to Gentiles the right to attain the status of the pious who strive for "the spirit of holiness."

In being promised immortality and eligibility for the world to come, Gentiles are placed on an equal footing with Jews, ethically and religiously.

This teaching contrasts with the Christian dogma which, in all its forms, demands faith in Christ as a prerequisite to salvation.

According to Judaism,[34] it is enough [35] to live up to the basic ethical principles of human life.

---

33. The rabbinic teaching referred to (Mishnah, Sanhed., X, 1) refers definitely to the world to come and not to the Messianic era. It limits eligibility to a share in the world-to-come mainly to "those who are of Israel," though elsewhere the pious Gentiles are also said to be eligible.
34. Jewish religion.
35. For a non-Jew.

Maimonides' qualification that the non-Jews must recognize in Israel the true people of revelation, a fact to which Spinoza calls attention in derogation of Maimonides, refers only to those non-Jews who wish to participate in the civic life of the Jews. It does not refer to their eligibility for salvation.[36]

An examination of all the ideas and concepts related to the idea of immortality in Jewish and Platonic philosophy shows that their main purpose is to validate the concept of soul.[37]

Plato derives his idea of immortality logically and ethically from the idea of soul, viewed as the bodiless and passionless substance in man.

Jewish teaching, concerned with ethics, and not with metaphysics, does not elaborate this concept of immortality. For Judaism the soul is the spirit of holiness which, being capable of infinite development, necessarily implies immortality.

Immortality is unconditionally vouchsafed. Not even redemption from sin is a prerequisite. Immortality, however, presupposes the possibility of being redeemed from sin. The statement "that all who are of the People of Israel," that is, who belong to the Messianic order of mankind, "are eligible for the world to come," is intended to negate the notion that sin is ineradicable.

The soul is pure and, therefore, immortal. Its immortality is independent of any creedal profession, even that of monotheism.

---

36. Spinoza's understanding of Maimonides' statement is the correct one.

37. This is one of a number of instances in the book, which indicate Cohen's interest in proving that Jewish religion has much in common with the philosophy of Plato.

Immortality means that the correlation between God and man is endless.

Chapter 16
THE LAW

Polytheism satisfies man's desire to become God. Christianity retains repercussions of this striving. Jewish religion, however, keeps man strictly apart from Divinity.

This is achieved by the Law, the basis of the moral order.[1]

The Law is designated "teaching." It is not arbitrary command, but rational instruction, which sets forth the duty of man.

The Law does not concern itself with the nature of God, nor is it intended to serve as a symbol either for God or for the deification of nature. Only man is the subject of the Law.

Even in the earliest form of the Law [2]—the sacrificial system—we can already discern the monotheistic character of Judaism.

---

1. What Cohen says here about the function of the Law is implied in the text of the Torah itself. The story of the Garden of Eden is intended to present in mythical form the source of man's corruption—his desire to play the God. In the chapters that follow the Eden story, the consequences of that desire are represented as leading to the spread of violence. The rest of the Torah is an account of what God did to counteract those consequences. He created the People of Israel and gave them laws, whereby not only they might achieve abundant life, but mankind as a whole (Lev. 18.5).

2. Cohen's entire approach to the Pentateuchal Torah is from

It should be noted that sacrifices were regarded by both the prophets and the Jewish philosophers as a concession to prevailing practice.

On adopting the sacrificial system, the Torah took care to eliminate from it all pagan practices, like initiation, self-mortification and sacred prostitution, which were intended to unite man with the deity.

By deprecating this purpose of sacrifices, the Jews were able to do away with human sacrifice.

The sacrificial laws belong to the category of "statutes," in contrast with the moral laws which are designated "judgments." The purpose of these "statutes" was probably to counteract heathen practice though, in part, they were a concession to it.

Another principle basic to the Law is the lack of any distinction between what is usually termed "religion" and the other aspects of civilization.

Religion is the basis of the laws of the state. This fact had advantages, because it brought these laws within the scope of ethics. But it also had dangers, because it enabled political interests to assume the guise of ethical ideals.

The same is true of the laws of health, which, being administered by priests, might well be exploited by them for their own interest.

Likewise, the sacrificial laws, in benefiting the priests, were subject to abuse.

---

the modern documentary and evolutionary point of view. The rest, however, of his discussion of the "Law" is limited in scope, because he deals mainly with ritual practices, or ceremonial law. The civil law receives scant attention in the rest of the chapter.

Laws pertaining to the observance of the Sabbath, the festivals, the Sabbatical year, the prohibition of eating the first fruits, form a connecting link between the religious and the ethical values of the Law.

The dietary regulations are motivated by cultic reforms and by anti-mythological and hygienic [3] considerations.

How far should the Law go in keeping the Jewish people and its religion free from the danger of losing their distinctive character? The answer must be left to the evolutionary process which generally strikes a balance between inflexibility and adaptability.

The contrast between idea and practice has far-reaching implications.

The very fact that even the ritual *mitzvot,* which have not a hygienic but an educative purpose, require outward performance indicates that it is difficult to draw the line between idea and practice. This is illustrated by the ritual practices of *Tzitzit* and *Tefillin.*

In our prayers we petition that God sanctify us through His *mitzvot* and purify our hearts. This shows that the mere performance of the symbolic precept does not by itself sanctify.

The Apostle Paul sought to disparage the worth of the *mitzvot.* In doing so he misinterpreted their function. To him they were a means to immortality. For this he regarded faith in Christ more important than the Law, both ethical and ritual.

In Judaism, the Law has either an ethical or a pedagogic purpose.

---

3. Questionable.

In Christianity, all ritual practices retain that which was the original purpose of the sacrificial system, namely, to unite man with God.

Even if the Mass is interpreted symbolically, the symbolism merely dramatizes the nature of God and has no ethical purpose.

Kant was troubled by the issue which Paul had raised. Though he was inclined to side with Paul, he objected to making faith obligatory.

The issue of faith versus law is not a question of dogma but of pedagogy.

The Law cannot be compared with the "works" of the Church. The latter function as *opus operatum.* Only the Church can consecrate "works," according to Catholicism. Protestantism differs in that respect. Jewish religion teaches that whatever holiness a religious act possesses derives from the one who performs it; it is not in the category of "works."

Implied in the term *mitzvot* are the concepts of both law and duty. The former refers to God as the author; the latter to man as the one who is bound to obey.

The Law is a yoke—the yoke of God's Kingdom. His Kingdom is the Kingdom of Law—moral law. There is, however, a distinction recognized also by the Talmud between ethical laws and pedagogic *mitzvot.*

The objection to letting the Law monopolize the whole of life is valid. There are other claims which possess a sovereignty of their own.

But apart from this, there is great value in the Law's consecration of every moment of a person's life. It means the elimination of the distinction between the holy and the profane; every moment of life is rendered holy. This applies to persons as well as to actions.

The objection that the Law may monopolize all human interests does not minimize the worth of the Law. Such monopoly means that no other interests may override or set it aside. On the other hand, measures may be taken to prevent the Law from excluding important cultural interests.

Duties toward our fellow-men are stressed in the opening *mishnah* of Peah. Every one of the duties mentioned there is a social obligation. The "bestowal of loving-kindness" is of greater value than alms-giving, because it does not depend on poverty; it corresponds to the kindness God bestows upon man.

The study of Torah as the highest duty, for which no limit is set, forms a sound foundation for Jewish religion. The worship of God should be based on the knowledge of God.

In that same *mishnah,* the study of Torah is recognized as the foundation of social ethics. It is not limited to any group or class.

The duty of studying Torah accounts for the wide gap between monotheism and philosophy. In contrast with monotheism, philosophy treats the masses of men as incapable of high intellectual and spiritual attainment.

"The principal which remains for the world to come," mentioned in the same *mishnah* is to be distinguished from reward. It represents the endless growth of the human soul.[4]

In order that the study of Torah shall not lead to barren intellectualism, it must be translated into deeds which are duties.[5]

---

4. That is Cohen's reinterpretation of the idea of immortality.
5. That follows from rationalism as functional, instead of ideationist.

Although the ethical *mitzvot* are clearly differentiated from the ritual *mitzvot,* the two are treated by the Sages as being interdependent.

The distinction between the two kinds of *mitzvot,* which was also recognized by Maimonides, had already been made by his predecessor Ibn Daud, in whose footsteps he followed.

Ibn Daud in turn followed Saadia, who had drawn a distinction between *mitzvot* whose reason was comprehensible, and those which required implicit obedience regardless of any reason. Ibn Daud stated frankly that not all the parts of the Torah were of equal significance.

Maimonides, as a rationalist, tried to find reasons [6] for the various *mitzvot.* This approach is more valid than that of Ibn Daud who sought the causes or historical factors of the ritual *mitzvot.*

In the discussion of the *mitzvot,* the term "reason" cannot have the same meaning as in the discussion of God's existence, where reason means logical proof. It must mean something else in the case of *mitzvot.*

Any explanation of the *mitzvot* must start with the assumption of faith in God. It must not deal, as in the natural sciences, with cause, but with purpose, from the standpoint of the ethical nature of God and man.

This implies that the reason for the *mitzvot* consists in their being means to man's entering into relationship with God. This is no disparagement of the authoritative character of the *mitzvot* as commanded by God.

Maimonides showed himself a true follower of rationalist idealism when he demonstrated the purpose of the *mitzvot*

---

6. Rational purposes or meanings.

by postulating them to be means of knowing and, therefore, of worshipping God.

Maimonides (*Moreh* III, 31) begins with the proposition that, in the spiritual education of man, God adapts His instruction to man's unfolding nature. This is the reason for the sacrificial laws.

He distinguishes between primary and secondary purposes. Prayer has a primary purpose; sacrifice, a secondary purpose.

In Chapter 35 of the *Guide,* he classifies the *mitzvot* into fourteen categories and then divides these into two principal categories: those pertaining to interpersonal relations and those pertaining to man's relations to God. In both, the purpose is to know and honor God, for the God concept can be recognized only in the concept of the moral law.[7]

In the same spirit, he wrote the *Sefer ha-Mitzvot.*

The expression "ritual laws" was first used by Duran (1423) and Albo (*Ikkarim* 3, 25).

The most recent development of Judaism began with the German Enlightenment, and finds its principal expression in the attitude toward the ceremonial law.

Mendelssohn taught that religion was universal and that the distinctive element of Jewish religion consisted in the Law.

This is contrary to the view expounded throughout this book.

Mendelssohn tried to present the spirit of Judaism as universal. What, then, could have prompted him to reduce Jew-

---

7. This is a bold and understandable formulation of the idea of God. It is, however, Cohen's and not Maimonides' idea.

ish religion to Jewish Law? Certainly not his indifference to Jewish religion.

How is it that Mendelssohn, on the one hand, opened up to Jews and Judaism the culture and religion of reason, and on the other hand, tied them to the biblical-rabbinic yoke?

As a consequence of Mendelssohn's cultural reform, Jews have attempted to bring their religious cult into conformity with the prevailing national spirit of the peoples of which they have come to be a part.

Although the traditional forms are disintegrating, our religious cult has retained its intrinsic character.

Yielding to the national spirit of the modern nations, Reform has tried to denationalize Jewish Law.

In the past, the Law, in fostering national isolation, enabled monotheism to survive.

We must face the question: Do we still need to carry the burden of isolation for the sake of Jewish monotheism?

If the answer is in the affirmative, then the Law should remain in force. This does not mean that we should abolish the changes which have already taken place.

Is the self-segregation of the Jews compatible with Messianism?

We must realize that the need for religious separateness is distinct from the need for national isolationism.

The concept of nationhood has undergone a change in recent years.

It has become an instrument of the state.

Zionism is the product of this concept of nationalism.

Is nationhood limited to political purpose? May it not also be justified on the ground that self-segregation is necessary for the preservation of religion, which can be conserved best through the observance of the Law?

World War I demonstrated that the states must become part of a union.

By the same token, the state must adapt itself to comprise different national groups.

For this reason, we must distinguish between nation and nationality.

Zionism is a mistake, because a Jewish nation or state contravenes the concept of Messianism.[8]

It is possible for the Jews to retain enough of the separateness they need for the Messianic ideal by retaining nationality[9] within the political states where they live.

Nationality is not an end in itself, but in our case, a means of preserving our religion.

Jewish nationality should be permitted to exist as a means of maintaining its own form of monotheism.

If Jewish monotheism could be replaced by any other religion, its preservation would be unjustifiable.[10]

---

8. Events have proved Cohen's conception of Messianism to be most unrealistic and incompatible with functional rationalism.

9. The concept of nationality according to Cohen, in contrast to nationalism which is intent upon sovereign statehood, need not aim at statehood at all. Jews, for example, according to him, retain their nationality for the sake of their religion. Functionally, of course, that is absurd. A religion exists for the sake of group solidarity and not the reverse.

10. What he means is that, if Christianity could replace Jew-

But as long as, on the basis of its sources, Judaism can be shown to be a rational religion, the need for preserving it is self-evident.[11]

This does not mean that it must necessarily be the only rational religion.

Even if it were possible to experiment with the idea of replacing one religion with another, such an experiment should not be permitted. The very notion of such experimentation is absurd. It contradicts the lesson taught by the history of philosophy, that every culture or religion is an attempt to discover the truth.

When religious prejudice is given scientific form,[12] and only Christian monotheism is recognized as valid, then it is time to solve the problem rationally.

The distinctive character of Jewish monotheism is incontestable. It may reach out to all of human culture, but it will never permit itself to be replaced by any of them. The centrality of the concept of one spiritual God makes Jewish monotheism a stronghold against dogmatism, pantheism and scepticism.

---

ish monotheism, the preservation of the latter would be unjustifiable.

11. In terms of functional rationalism, the argument for the preservation of Judaism would read thus: If Judaism as a civilization can be shown, on the basis of its sources, to have been animated by the will-to-live of the Jewish People and by its purpose to make the most of its life spiritually and ethically, the need for preserving Judaism is self-evident.

12. Cohen probably refers to the Higher Criticism of the Bible, which was used by some of the leading German scholars as a justification for what has been termed "Higher anti-Semitism."

The question, however, remains: How essential is the Law?

The problem of the continuity of the Law was raised long ago.

We stand, therefore, on historical ground when we put the question: What is the relation of the Law to religion?

The answer is that, irrespective of what we may think of any of its specific laws, our religion is bound up with the Law as such.[13]

Self-segregation is the only logical and tenable policy for Jewish religion. The same is true of Jewish nationality [14] as a means of preserving, in the complexity of modern cultural life, the truth concerning God as the only God.

The Law, even if all that remains of it be the observance of Yom Kippur and the Saturday-Sabbath,[15] is necessary as a means of preventing the disappearance of pure monotheism.

The significance of the Law is not limited to its being a means to Jewish self-segregation.

The non-Jew can scarcely grasp its inherently exhilarating and fortifying influence.

The specific forms of the Law elicit some of the deepest religious emotions.

---

13. In terms of functional rationalism, this statement would read thus: Irrespective of what we may think of any of its specific laws, Judaism as a civilization requires that its religion be concerned with law as such. The Torah is not a religion only; it is a religious civilization.

14. Jewish Peoplehood.

15. If that were all that remained of the Law, it would not be Judaism, because it would not be a civilization, and it would not be Jewish religion, because for a religion to function, it has to be an every day affair.

Reforms in the Law are entirely in order, insofar as they seek to bring observance in harmony with its inner meaning.

In considering any specific law, it is important to focus on the general principle of the Law as such.

The Law applies not only to worship, but also to many domestic and civic duties.

To appreciate its significance, it has to be lived and experienced. Only then can one realize that what is designated a "yoke" is really a ladder to heaven.

The question, therefore, is not whether the Law should be retained but how it may best serve the purpose for which it is intended.

The Law itself does not lack esthetic possibilities. Witness the poetry that inheres in the observance of Yom Kippur and the erection of the *Sukkah*. The entire life of the Jew is rendered esthetically as well as religiously significant through the Law.

Far from self-segregation being its only aim, the Law seeks to imbue all of life with a sense of the divine. Far from alienating us from culture, the purpose of the Law is to give to all of culture that stability which comes from accepting the autonomy and sovereignty of ethics.

The restrictions of the Law have produced Jews who have contributed considerably to general culture in all its forms.

It is a mistake to ascribe the inner connection between the Law and public morals to personal piety. It is the impact of the Law itself.

It is, therefore, the duty of all who belong to the Jewish community to assume the responsibility for maintaining the Law as a means of assuring the future of the Jewish religion, as an act of piety toward our Fathers. Thus the principle of "the merit of the Fathers" is validated in life.[16]

The symbolical significance of the Law is bound up with its historical aspect. The Law has no intrinsic value, but the symbol calls attention to that which is of intrinsic value.

Equally as great as are the dangers inherent in the symbol is its worth.

The Law should be regarded not only as "fence to the Torah" but as an instrument for raising the level of its teachings.

If we want to get a correct idea of the Law, it is not enough merely to study the Law in the formulation of Maimonides.[17] We must ascertain the connection between religious knowledge and ethical practice, i.e., between the theory and practice of religion and pure autonomous ethics.

Chapter 17
PRAYER

The Law establishes a connection between religion and ethics and finds its chief expression in prayer.[1]

---

16. See the discussion of the "merit of the Fathers" above. Ch. 15, pp. 208, 209.

17. The study of Maimonides' formulation, however, would prove that the Law, or the Torah, is co-extensive with Judaism as a multi-dimensional civilization and not as a cult which might be reduced to the observance of the Sabbath and the Day of Atonement.

1. Far from true. The Law, or the Torah, even in the narrow sense in which it is discussed by Cohen, finds its chief expression

Without prayer, the religious cult would have continued as a ritual of sacrifices.

Prayer is typical of monotheism, which gave it its essential form. The uniqueness of monotheism found expression in prayer, since prayer is the expression of religion, as language is the expression of reason. This truly applies to Jewish prayer.

If repentance is to lead to atonement, there has to be some ethical act for purifying the self.

Repentance, as an expression of religion, implies turning to God and seeking His forgiveness. But such feelings have to be expressed; this is the purpose of prayer.

The extent to which prayer depends on thought is evident from the term *kavvanah* (devotion).[2]

Kavvanah is an ethical experience. It involves withdrawal from the turmoil of one's surroundings and concentration on one's inner life.

---

not in prayer, but in the study of Torah (cf. Mishnah, Peah, I, 1). That is a point that hardly needs laboring in view of the repeated emphasis throughout the Jewish tradition of the incomparably superior value of Torah study to that of prayer or worship. At the present time, the survival and revival of the Jewish People depend on the reinstatement of Torah study and on rendering it relevant to the contemporary moral and spiritual problems of Jewish and general life.

2. True enough. A familiar saying about *kavvanah* is that prayer without *kavvanah* is like body without a soul. But why not face the fact that, with prayers that are formalized and repeated three times a day year in and year out, as is the case with the *Amidah,* it is impossible to expect the average person to exercise *kavvanah.*

The Psalms differ from the religious poetry of the classical religions in being based on introspection; the self is the object and not the subject. The purpose is to achieve inner freedom and purity. For this, the Psalmist had to commune with God.

The nearest analogue to a psalm is a love lyric. A psalm expresses man's love for God.

Experience of love for God is no less of a miracle than monotheism.

Prayer is the only legitimate form of repentance in mature religion.[3]

Rationally, religion stands for the relation between man and God. Psychologically, religion is man's love for God expressed in prayer.

The love lyric reflects a phase of experience which signifies the epitome of life. In it that which seemed transient is invested with eternal significance.

The love lyric is addressed to the beloved who is out of reach. Hence, the idealization of the beloved and the sense of yearning.

Analogically, prayer, too, is yearning for God, who can never be seen. The seeking of God is an end in itself.

There is more to the yearning for God than the longing of human love. It includes the yearning for redemption and for emancipation from the burden of sin. It springs from the kind of anxiety which impels a person to run away from

---

3. That is intended to rule out flagellation or other forms of torment, but surely not some kind of ethical action which is necessary to prove to the penitent and to others that his penitence is sincere.

himself, to want to lose himself. It reflects man's fear of fall-
ing into despair.[4]

Man's love for God leads to his constant self-renewal.

Prayer thus confirms the reciprocal relationship between
God and man. This is where religion and ethics meet.

The individual whose worth is enhanced by repentance
and prayer is morally vindicated. This is the contribution of
religion.

Religion comes to the aid of the individual in his personal
quest for health, sustenance, or freedom from fear. It reveals
to him God's readiness to help him satisfy these needs. Awareness of all the needs for which man looks to divine assistance
constitutes the reflective element of prayer.

Once the self is brought under the aegis of religion, concern for the well-being of the self is transformed from selfishness into duty.

The self is part of the family. In being concerned about the
welfare of the family one cannot be accused of selfishness.

Here is the difference between religion and ethics. Ethically, according to Plato,[5] we dare not be more partial to our

---

4. All these psychological manifestations of the yearning for
God mean much more than the rational experience of the correlation between God and man. They are irrefutable evidence of
how much more meaningful religion becomes when we try to
understand it in terms of functional, rather than of ideationist,
rationalism.

5. Plato need not have the last word on ethics. According to
Josiah Royce loyalty is itself not only an ethical principle, but a
basic principle of all ethics. Actually loyalty is the main content
of authentic love. Loyalty is the ethical manifestation of the

kindred than to strangers. Religion, however, recognizes the special relationship between parents and children. The commandment to honor parents could have arisen only in a culture which attaches importance to the line of descent from the Fathers of the nation.

Anyone who regards prayer for one's kindred as superstitious does not know the human heart. Anxiety is a heavier burden than sin. It is, therefore, our duty to resort to prayer as a means of casting off the burden of anxiety.

Prayer presupposes faith in God who is ready to help and can do so. Whether He actually does or not is immaterial. My prayer expresses my faith in the goodness of God, and thus establishes an intimate relationship between God and me.

Prayer influences our personality. It helps us to achieve unity of personality and to overcome inner conflicts, which, in religious terminology, are designated sin. This is the psychological significance of the redemption God effects in us. Prayer is the hymn with which we celebrate this unification of personality.

Apart from the motivation of being relieved from sin, prayer has a mental hygienic value for helping the individual attain inner unity and integrity.

---

principle of organicity which operates in all animate beings. Organicity is the tendency of a *part* of a living being to interact in a direct and intensive fashion with the *whole* of the living being to which it belongs. That principle operates also in all kinds of groups, the members of which interact more intensively than with members of other groups. Hence Plato's idea that we dare not be more partial to our kindred than to strangers is unnatural and unethical. The fact, that loyalty demands that we differentiate among those toward whom we display it, is in keeping with natural, ethical and religious law.

When man prays for the highest good, he must pray, above all, for truth and honesty; for our minds and our hearts are always subject to illusion and deceit. Since man is not perfect, he must pray to grow in truthfulness.[6]

The purity of soul for which we pray in the morning prayers is the prerequisite of truthfulness. We appeal to the God of truth to help us to be truthful.

In contrast with the "Lord's Prayer," Jewish prayer includes no petition for sustenance, because those who formulated Jewish prayers sought to divert men's minds from material needs.[7]

From the connection of the *Bet ha-Kenesset* with the *Bet ha-Midrash* we infer that prayer presupposes reflection and study.

From King Solomon's dedicatory prayer it is evident that the main purpose of the Temple was to serve as a place of prayer.

It is often said that public prayer defeats the purposes which only individual prayer can accomplish. The truth, however, is that the individual has to enter into relationship with God. For this he needs his fellow-men, who will collectively constitute the Kingdom of God.

The *Alenu* prayer implies that the community is the foun-

---

6. If our spiritual leaders would formulate realistic and heartfelt prayers for the acquisition of ethical traits and habits, there would be no need of writing treatises on the need for prayer.

7. If Cohen had consulted a traditional prayer book, he would have come across, in the week-day *Amidah*, the prayer for a blessed crop and the following in the prayers after meals: ". . . O our God, our Father, feed us, nourish us, sustain, support and relieve us."

dation of the Messianic Kingdom. Though that Kingdom belongs to the future, we must strive for it in the present. This idea is also conveyed in the *Kaddish*.

The community is required to set the stage for the Messianic era. The prayer of the individual must, therefore, be part of the prayer of the community.

The existence and maintenance of the community should be the main theme of prayer.[8]

Through prayer, the community attains religious worth. This has enabled the Jews to survive as a stateless people.

The benediction, "Thou crownest Israel with glory" indicates that the glorification of Israel is a means to the glorification of God.

The "I" of the Psalms refers to the People of Israel. It is the people of Israel who in the Psalms express their love for God. Love for God is thus blended with love for the People of Israel.

The community represents Jewish religion as well as Jewish peoplehood.

This is not parochialism, for there are many references to mankind in Jewish liturgy, as in the benediction "Thou graciously bestowest knowledge upon man." The emphasis is on "man."

The prayers serve as a socializing influence which comes to fruition in the synagogue. Synagogal prayer unites and equalizes all who share in it. It does not replace individual prayer, but provides the individual with an immediate purpose, in addition to the divine purpose on which he should set his

---

8. Of public prayer.

heart. The problem of the language of Jewish prayer, like the problem of Jewish law, should be viewed from the vantage point of the function of prayer as a means of preserving Jewish identity.

We should reckon equally with the following two principles: a) As part of the non-Jewish civilization, we must learn to pray in the language of that civilization, and b) As a means of conserving Jewish identity, we should retain the original Hebrew.

There is an abundance of spiritual treasure in the traditional prayers in which biblical and rabbinic phrases are interwoven. Through those prayers, the Jewish spirit has continued to give expression not necessarily to new ideas, but certainly to new emotional values.

The objection that emphasis on Hebrew in the prayers contradicts the principle that we must reckon with the civilization of our environment is untenable. A knowledge of the religious values in their original language deepens the understanding of our cultural heritage.

The principal contents of our prayer book are expressive of the basic Jewish beliefs. A remarkable source of the statement of these beliefs is the Rosh Hashanah *Mussaf*.

Prayer is the principal religious instrument for attaining the ideal of the human spirit.

Prayer, the language of the correlation between man and God, is also the language of Messianism and, therefore, universal. It is also the means of articulating the ideals of the individual.

He who cannot pray cannot divest himself of his finitude with its pettiness and its anxieties. Prayer is religion in action.[9]

---

9. It would be truer to say that ethical conduct is religion in

Chapter 18
THE VIRTUES

There is only one moral goodness, but there are many virtues. Moral goodness, as a divine attribute, is holiness. Virtues are those divine attributes which apply to man. Jewish teaching emphasizes that there is a definite distinction between holiness and the virtues.

In the ethics of pure will, virtue is defined as the path to goodness.

From the ethical standpoint, it is also necessary to differentiate between the attitude of the reflective will and that of the affective will. The former gives rise to an awareness of dignity; the latter, to an awareness of love.

Dignity is a term that may be used to denote the essence of God. In the Trisagion, *kavod* is wrongly translated "glory." It should be rendered "dignity," and be understood as God's goodness which "fills all the earth."

By the same token, dignity is a synonym for man's essence, i.e., his personality. Messianic humanity implies the universal recognition of the dignity of every human individual.

---

action and that prayer is religion as inner experience.

This chapter is on the whole an illuminating exposition of the function of prayer. That is largely due to the fact that Cohen treats prayer from the standpoint of psychology and not of philosophy. This leads him to note carefully the role of formal worship and public prayer. In the last analysis, he has to resort to functional rationalism to get at the basic significance of "religion in action."

Love is a manifestation of the affective will. It represents the correlation between God and man.

There are four types of love: God's love for man, man's love for God, man's love for fellow-man, and man's love for himself.

The Mishnah enumerates ten virtues (Ab. Zarah 20b), assigning a special position to humility, which applies not so much to the correlation between man and God as to the correlation between man and his fellow-man and between man and himself.

The interpretation of the virtues as paths to goodness harmonizes with the implications of the Hebrew terms for virtue: *middah* (measure) and *ma'alah* (step).

Freedom of the will makes of the virtues *ma'alot,* i.e., "steps" in the process of approaching God through self-perfection. The highest step is religious martyrdom. Maintenance of life is not the highest "step" in Judaism.

In attempting to find a basis in Judaism for the classification of the virtues, in keeping with the principles of the ethics of pure will, we find that "truth" is a term for God.

Theoretical and ethical truth are mutually dependent; this is the law of truth. That is also the basic meaning of the God idea. Hence, the identity of religion with reason.

The main significance of the idea of God's uniqueness is that the concept of God is the only one with which all ethical concepts must reckon.

In addition to theoretical and ethical truth there is also esthetic truth.

Since religion cannot be based on either scientific truth alone or ethical truth alone, it must be predicated on the harmonization of both.

Scriptures identify truth with God. The term "truth" there does not have any philosophical connotations, but simply denotes soundness and firmness.[1]

The rabbis speak of truth as the seal of God (Shab. 55a). In Scriptures, truth is one of the thirteen attributes of God. Also, the wisdom of Israel's laws implies the recognition of their truth [2] (Mal. 2.6-7).

Truth is the only absolute value which is not relative to any other.[3] Maimonides, therefore, does not hesitate to ascribe it to God.

The virtues of sincerity [4] and truthfulness in man correspond to the divine attribute of truth.

---

1. That should have suggested to Cohen the functional conception of truth as authenticity. It was the fact that things appeared differently from what they were actually or authentically that started the first Greek thinkers on their search for what was authentic beneath appearance. Functionally, appearance which is not authentic is the source of maladjustment and harm. There cannot be proper, healthful or creative adjustment to one's human or physical environment, except on the basis of what that environment is authentically. To depend merely on appearance is all too often to fall into a trap. Hence the significance of truth as authenticity. Because adjustment to what is authentic enables man to fulfill himself, authenticity is an aspect or attribute of divinity, godhood, goodness, or God. In Jeremiah 10.10 we read: "YHWH is an authentic God."

2. The truth of Israel's laws is in their being a guide to what should be man's adjustment to his authentically human and physical environment. That constitutes the wisdom as well as the divinity of those laws.

3. That is because truth is synonymous with authenticity.

4. If sincerity is synonymous with authenticity, it is certainly

The prophets opposed sacrifices for the same reason that they opposed idolatry: the insincerity frequently associated with them.

In polytheism, prayer is more in the nature of a hymn than of prayer. In polytheism, the object one prays for belongs to a particular deity. In Judaism, the object of prayer is the self. There is no need for any intervention between the self and God. Symbolism endangers sincerity in prayer.

Truth is the foundation of sincerity, and sincerity is the essence of ethical man.

Those who ask, "How could the Jewish people survive?" overlook the vital power that inheres in religious sincerity.

The sincerity of the Jews' God-consciousness is the true reason of their resistance to the plastic arts. It also accounts for the great power of the lyric poetry of the Psalms.

If it seems strange that God should have revealed Himself to only one people, let us remember that ancient Israel's monotheism evolved into Messianism which is intended for the entire world, and that "Chosen People," "Zion," and "Messiah" are symbolic of the future of mankind.

Sincerity in religion is also assured by the regard for reason in Jewish tradition.

The unity of religion with rational knowledge is a guarantee of sincerity in all human affairs, especially in scientific

---

a virtue. But it is, more often than not, uncritical and lacking in discrimination between the authentic and inauthentic. In that case it is liable to do more harm than good, and is therefore anything but a virtue.

research. God is the principle of truth that undergirds the interconnection among all branches of knowledge.

The duty of truthfulness is stressed repeatedly: Ex. 23.7; Lev. 19.11,12; Hos. 4.1; Zech. 7.9; Ps. 31.19; 85.12; 101.7; 119.163; 120.2; Prov. 12.19, 22; 23.23. And the following in the Talmud: Hul. 94a; Sanh. 92a; B.M. 48a.

While the sense of human dignity motivates the pure will on the human scene as a whole, love [5] motivates virtue within the more limited circles of the family, the clan, the people and various purposive associations. However, when love alone is the motive, it is apt to mislead.

Truthfulness [6] is an absolute virtue. It sets for man a task greater than he is able to cope with, as no one can ascertain the nature of truth.

Our limited knowledge of truth should lead us to be humble and diffident. Humility in no way impugns one's dignity, but it makes for love [7] and forbearance in human relations.

In the Psalmist's conception of God, truth and love are united (Ps. 85.11).

Humility, which must go with truthfulness, cannot appropriately be ascribed to God. It is ascribed, however, to Moses. Indeed, it is the only specific virtue ascribed to Moses. From this we may infer its importance.

Humility is ascribed to God in order to set a pattern for man. Unlike love and justice, which can logically be ascribed

---

5. That is why authentic love is essentially loyalty, and loyalty is love.

6. Truthfulness is synonymous with authenticity.

7. Humility does not make for love, but it removes the obstacles in its way.

to God, humility can be ascribed to Him only in the sense that He loves the humble.[8]

In emphasizing humility, Jewish ethics differs from both classical and post-classical Greek ethics (cf. Zeph. 2.3; Prov. 15.33; 18.12).

Humility is regarded as the outstanding trait of the Messiah, and thus of the Messianic consciousness and of Messianic humanity. No matter how much civilization may advance, it can never dispense with this virtue.

Judaism teaches that one who is humble before God is also humble toward his fellow-men.

Chapter 19
RIGHTEOUSNESS

Righteousness is equated with holiness. It is the attribute of the Messiah.

Like humility, righteousness is a way to piety.

Whether righteousness can be fully achieved is doubtful; nevertheless it is a primary ideal.

Only through righteousness can the state fulfill the purpose of religion [1] and become a theocracy.[2]

---

8. Isaiah 57.15.

1. A religion without a civilization is empty; a civilization without religion is blind and directionless. Hence Jewish religion can function normally only as an integral part of Judaism as a civilization.

2. Theocracy is generally associated with an organized church

The principle of righteousness led to the limitation of those property rights which are the bulwark of egoism and opportunism. This is the significance of the laws concerning the Sabbath, the Sabbatical year and the prescribed gifts to the poor.

The extremes to which the principle of justice are carried is evident from the fact that the Sabbath has been established for the sake of the slave and the laborer. Moreover, the Torah revolves entirely about Israel's emancipation from slavery.

From the applications of the principle of righteousness in the Bible, we infer that righteousness can be stimulated best by love. This is evident also in those cases where righteousness is subordinated to the interests of peace.[3]

Paradoxically, the principle of love as applied to righteousness throws light on the meaning of vicarious suffering. Though proscribed, on principle, by Moses and Ezekiel, vicarious suffering is a matter of experience. In early Mosaism (Ex. 20.5), vicarious suffering is interpreted as vicarious punishment. The only way to eradicate this notion was to do what Judaism did later, when it interpreted vicarious suffering as endured in a spirit of love by the victims of poverty, suffering for the sins of their exploiters.[4]

Deutero-Isaiah makes this interpretation the basis of his Messianic version of the history of the People of Israel, which envisages the entire nation as chosen for suffering, because

---

based on clericalism. That is furthest from Cohen's mind. To him a theocracy is a civilization permeated by the spirit of rational religion.

3. Mishnah, Gittin V, 8.
4. All this is pure imagination.

of the mistakes or sins of its fellow-nations.[5] This is the true meaning of the doctrine of Divine election.

Vicarious suffering does not contradict the idea of righteousness. It is not a punishment, but an inevitable consequence of God's justice which culminates in love—the love which shines brightest in the human soul when it suffers martyrdom.

Chapter 20
HEROISM

Since all virtues are derived from the attributes of God,[1]

---

5. Cohen's interpretation of the sufferings of the Jewish People for the sins of the nations and cruelties they inflict on the Jews is neither ideationist nor functional rationalism. It is rationalization at its worst. It is not even making a virtue out of necessity. Passive submission to man's inhumanity is a questionable virtue. This rationalization of the passive attitude toward the abnormal kind of existence in exile has obstructed any effort of the Jewish People to put an end to its homelessness. It is in keeping with Cohen's opposition to Zionism.

What is particularly objectionable in Cohen's rationalization of passive submission to exploitation and oppression is that it is based on fifteen obscure verses in Deutero-Isaiah which, even if Cohen's interpretation of them be the correct one, are entirely atypical in relation to the rest of Jewish Scriptures.

1. To understand why, according to Cohen, all virtues are derived from God, we have to remember the following: first, that God is synonymous with the rational order of the world; secondly, that insofar as man acts ethically he acts in keeping with the rational order, and thus, in the language of religion, in con-

the question arises: Where does heroism belong? Heroism, taken literally, is implied in the attribute of God as "man of war"

Heroism is also implied in the human attribute of "long-suffering" (Prov. 16.32).

---

formity with one or another attribute of God. Since, then, heroism is ethical, it ought to correspond to some trait, or attribute, of God. That God is described as "a man of war," or as being long-suffering, according to Cohen, proves that heroism is conceived as a divine trait. This shows to what lengths ideationist rationalism has to go to prove its case.

In functional rationalism, it is essential to determine first the rationality of the virtue itself. That involves making sure of the way it functions, of the conditions and the consequences of its functioning. Only then may it be projected onto Divinity, or the idea of a rational world order, and thus related to some attribute of God.

The reverse procedure, however, of immediately relating what is regarded as a virtue to an attribute of God, is a dangerous one, because it fails to establish the authenticity or genuineness of the virtue in question. This is the mistake Cohen commits in the case of heroism. Is the conduct of the Japanese suicide squads, which carried out the brutal commands of their superiors, heroism? Had he analyzed the virtue of genuine heroism, he would have discovered that it is such only when displayed in behalf of responsibility, integrity, loyalty or love and creativity. As a matter of fact, if any of these traits is missing, the heroism is not genuine, but either sheer recklessness or extreme self-assertiveness. On the other hand, when heroism is genuine it is the result of the concurrent interaction of all those cosmic forces which enable man to achieve his salvation.

It is surprising that Cohen has nothing to say about the courage with which it should be the function of religion to imbue a person when disaster befalls him, when he is the victim of a pain-

The Jewish interpretation of heroism is expressed in the rabbinic saying that he "who conquers his evil inclination is a hero" (Ab. IV.1). Here is a point of contact with Greek ethics, which likewise extols the control of sensuality. In the war of reason against licentiousness, there is little difference between monotheism and polytheism.

Nevertheless, monotheism has made its special contribution also. Because of its religious teaching, Judaism may well boast of being superior in its ethics to Platonism. This superiority emerges not only in all important questions pertaining

---

ful and fatal disease, or suffers the loss of those dear and near to him as a result of some tragic accident. What else is such courage, if not true heroism? What is there in rational religion, or in a rational conception of God, to help a person endure the worst that may befall him?

There is, it seems, an answer to this question from the standpoint of functional rationalism. As pointed out frequently in this book, one of the aspects of the cosmos, or rational order of the universe, is creativity. It is that aspect which is not deterred by the process of entropy, disintegration or death. The world not only goes on, but seems to be spurred on by these destructive forces to greater activity. Thereby not only are losses caused by the destruction and death made good, but an even higher and more complex level of existence is achieved.

The heroism of a Franz Rosenzweig, who for years was confined to bed with creeping paralysis which robbed him of control over his limbs and of the power of speech, or of the thousands in the concentration camps who underwent the most cruel torments conceivable and still managed to remain unbroken in spirit, is a manifestation of the creativity which is one of the attributes of God as the rational order of the universe.

Hence the basis in the Bible for the idea of heroism or courage is not "God is a man of war," but the affirmation of God as Creator.

to the individual and the state, but also in those pertaining to metaphysics.[2]

According to Plato heroism consists in flight from this world. He regards the body as the prison of the soul. Such heroism, however, comes to a tragic end. On the other hand, in Judaism, the hero is he who stands the test in that which makes him human, as the result of his correlation with God. Insofar as man is faithful to that correlation, he cannot be frustrated, since "the word of our Lord endures forever" (Isa. 40.8).

In martyrdom, justice and heroism are combined. Heroism marks the triumph of that which is distinctively human; justice combined with love signalizes the triumph of the divine.

Jewish martyrdom is unique. Socrates was a martyr for his own theories.[3] But the Jew is a martyr for the God of mankind, for the religious ideal of the unity of mankind, as expressed in Messianism.

All Jewish religious duties are summed up in the *mitzvah* of "the sanctification of God's name."[4] Self-sanctification is the epitome of religious ethics, for when I sanctify myself, I sanctify God, that is, achieve full awareness of God's holiness.

Kiddush ha-shem is martyrdom not for the salvation of

---

2. The reference is to Plato's conception of the human soul as distinct from, and as surviving the disintegration of, the body.

3. That is entirely unfair to Socrates. He was a martyr for the truth. As such he reflected a trait of Divinity, namely, truth or authenticity.

4. To sanctify God's name, in terms of religious rationalism, means to act out in one's own life whatever attributes we ascribe to God.

one's soul, but in the service of history.[5]

"Christ crucified" is symbolical [6] of the People of Israel as poetically pictured in Deutero-Isaiah. Why this is so is a riddle which future historians and philosophers will have to probe. In the meantime, the Jew must be prepared to suffer martyrdom for the unity of mankind, as taught by pure monotheism.

Chapter 21
LOYALTY [1]

Emunah, loyalty, is derived from a root which denotes firmness. The covenant is an instrument of loyalty. Remembrance is the psychological aspect of loyalty, and may serve as a means to active virtue. The Torah, therefore, motivates love for the stranger [2] by the remembrance of what the Israelites had experienced in Egypt.

Remembrance leads to gratitude,[3] which is a specific form of loyalty. Gratitude may not be demanded by him to whom

---

5. That is in keeping with his reinterpretation of the belief in the immortality of the soul (see ch. 15, p. 199).

6. *Should* be symbolical to the Christian world.

1. Loyalty is a manifestation of *cosmic* organicity in collective organisms like families and nations.

2. Functionally, love is synonymous with loyalty, and is displayed under the identical circumstances.

3. Gratitude is the awareness and recognition of dependence, which are essential to the awareness and recognition of interdependence, a trait of the rational order of the world, or of God.

it is owed, but it is the duty of him who is indebted for some favor. Moreover, a person owes it to himself to be grateful for the sake of his own inner harmony.

The importance of loyalty in marriage may be inferred from the liberal Jewish divorce laws, which presuppose that only mutual loyalty of husband and wife adds meaning and purpose to their marriage bond.

The family is rooted in loyalty. The duty of the father to teach his son Torah is the basis of the community's and the state's duty to educate the child.

Thus the Torah, in its widely ramified aspects, becomes a life-long manifestation of loyalty to one's people. The Jews had their poor, but they had no illiterate proletariat.

Justice leads to social service. The limitations of institutional charity are well known. Justice, therefore, has to be supplemented by the virtue of personal almsgiving, a form of loyalty to oneself and to one's fellow-men.

Another aspect of loyalty is the soul's expression of gratitude. As such it motivates the benedictions with which prayers of petition conclude.

What psychological unity is to consciousness in general, loyalty is to ethical consciousness.[4] The purpose of all benedictions of gratitude is to stimulate our loyalty.

Both justice and heroism have to be supplemented by the auxiliary virtue of loyalty. Humility, too, is a form of loyalty.

---

4. That is consistent with the conception of loyalty as a manifestation of the cosmic principle of organicity.

Chapter 22
PEACE

Peace implies equity, and is therefore a qualification of absolute justice. Like loyalty, it is an auxiliary virtue.

The Greeks referred to the harmonious synthesis of the virtues as *sophrosynē,* which corresponds to the concept of "humanity" as interpreted in *The Ethics of Pure Will,* as well as to the biblical concept of "peace."

God's attribute of peace implies "long-suffering" and "forgiving sin."

The sum of all the virtues and the unity of human nature are contained in the attribute of peace. The Messiah is called "the Prince of Peace."

The priestly benediction reads: "The Lord lift up his countenance to thee and give thee peace." When read in the light of God's response to the prayer of Moses that God show His Glory to him, we gather that "peace" is the "countenance" of God, and the consequences of peace are "the other side" of God, as it were.

Peace is the divine attribute of perfection, and the loftiest ideal of human ethics.

That God "makes peace" implies that peace combined with truth is the highest purpose of human life.

Contrary to Heraclitus' teaching that war is the begetter of all things, Jewish religion posits peace as their source and purpose.

God represents the harmonization of ethics and nature.

Through peace, love is freed and directed to man's noblest task of self-perfection, which is inner peace.

Inner peace is the contentment flowing from the awareness of divine providence.

Many of our Sages, who were poor artisans and day laborers, and our people, as a whole, during the darkest periods of their history, found contentment and peace in the study of Torah. Their inner peace did not depend upon material security, but upon the contentment of reason. It was rooted in awareness of the historical significance of Judaism for humanity. Neither piety nor the observance of the laws could have kept alive the devotion which gave rise to this inner peace.

Messianism is the bond which unites present mankind with mankind of the ideal future.

Inner peace, said Bahya, makes for that inner unity which enables us to experience the unity of God.

Inner peace tames our wild passions, but does not impede our noble feelings. In order to attain such peace, we must learn to distinguish between emotions which have an integrating effect and those which lead to disintegration.

Psychology and ethics have not solved the problem of whether hatred is an original disposition, or the abnormal transformation of some other impulse.

However, the religious teachings pertaining to the virtues aim at combatting hatred. The pursuit of peace leads to the elimination of hatred.

Many precepts forbid hatred. This, however, is not sufficient. We must know how to overcome hatred. The answer is given in the talmudic term "groundless hatred," which should be interpreted to mean that hatred as such is without foundation, that the very fact that one human being hates another is irrational. Hatred is illusion based on ignorance and misunderstanding.

No individual and no nation can have inner peace as long as there is no freedom from war. Messianism unites the individual with mankind. For our own inner peace, we need assurance that national hatreds will be eliminated from the civilized consciousness.

Peoples do not hate each other. Greed and envy are real, but hatred is illusion. We should set no stock by the "historical wisdom" which claims that hatred is an inborn human impulse and part of the cosmic order. Bacteria are engaged in a struggle for existence, but they do not hate one another, as men do.

It is important not only to stress the need for peace, but also to unmask the raving image of hatred.

Pessimism is a mystical doctrine opposed to reason and faith in God. Monotheism and its Messianic goal make for optimism. Faith in the striving for peace as the meaning of history is a religious duty.

The two signs of inner peace are sympathy and joy.

Though sympathy is merely a form of sensitiveness, religion utilizes it as an instrument for peace and for love of fellow-man. That love, at its purest, is reflected in the human face and brings forth tears, as does sorrow.

Sympathy acts as a corrective of strict justice. This is implied in the saying: "Judge everyone in the scale of merit." The pursuit of peace evokes compassion which is higher than justice.

In personal relations, the pursuit of peace is the basis for mutual reconciliation among people and reconciliation with oneself.

A second sign of peace is joy. According to Kant, to share joy is harder than to share sorrow. This statement overlooks the part of joy in sympathy. Joy can be experienced, even if the occasion does not affect us personally, provided it enhances our realization of life's worth.

If there were any truth to the pessimistic view that man is evil at heart, and that sharing joy is not as natural as sharing sorrow, there could be no peace in the world and no path that leads to virtue. Fellow-feeling in the experience of a noble deed proves the power and genuineness of peace. Man's yearning for the good makes for peace.

The Jewish festivals have joy as their purpose. The poor must be given a share in the common rejoicing. Thus the way to achieve peace is made clear, for the meaning of the festival is to reconcile the poor to their fate.[1] Thus the Sabbath inaugurated the abolition of slavery. It brings joy by holding out the hope for the time when all men will be free and will share their knowledge and their toil.

Of all the virtues, the pursuit of peace has the greatest magical influence.

Peace is the aim of human life to which all other aims are secondary.

It is the spirit of holiness. It is the Messiah.

The spirit of peace in the rejoicing of the festivals is a distinctive trait of the Jewish temperament. On Sabbath and festivals the Jew indulged in frolic and pleasantry, combined with joy in intellectual and spiritual contemplation, no matter how sad his weekdays were. The persecuted Jew would

---

1. The one fly in the ointment of inspiring ideas in which this chapter abounds.

then forget his enemies. What made that miracle possible, if not the so-called "yoke of the Torah?"

The Jewish religious spirit precludes hatred and revenge. The Jew's unshakable faith in the better future of mankind gave him inner peace. Messianism is and ever will remain the foundation of Jewish consciousness.

Death is not the end of life, but merely a conclusion of a chapter. It marks a new beginning which Judaism interprets as the realization of peace.

Death is the kingdom of peace. He who is at peace with himself and with his fellow-men cannot fear death.

Judaism does not think of God as a judge who condemns souls to hell. He is a judge who forgives. The worthy life our Fathers led should fill us with peace and hope.

In the solidarity of the generations the Jew achieves his immortality.

In Hebrew, *olam* means both "eternity" and "world," thus identifying the immortality of man with the eternity of the world. It denies the myth which pictures the world as ending in a cataclysm to be followed by renewal.

PART THREE

Modern Rationales
of Judaism

CHAPTER I

A MODERN ESOTERIC RATIONALE *

A modern esoteric rationale for Judaism is not an attempt to interpret Judaism in terms of some dominant philosophy of our day. It is rather an attempt to formulate a life pattern on the basis of the Jewish tradition for those of the intellectual élite who wish to experience Divinity as a felt presence. They are not satisfied with mere conformity to the religious practices of their community, nor with the mere acceptance of its religious beliefs. They wish to experience in direct and immediate fashion the actual presence of God and His response to their yearnings and prayers. They are content with nothing less than perceptible evidence of such response in some effect on their environment, their physical condition or their mental state.

Every religious civilization generally produces a group of spiritually sensitive people who are dissatisfied with the mechanical fashion in which their contemporaries live their religion. When some individual in that group happens to possess what is generally described as personal magnetism, or what is technically termed "charisma," the other members of that group defer to him and accept him as their spiritual leader. They come to depend upon him for stimulation and guidance in practical matters, but mainly for transmitting to them something of his own experience of the Divine Presence. In biblical times nazirites and prophets formed themselves into charismatic guilds for that purpose. During the

---

* Based on a chapter in a forthcoming volume in the series *The Library of Living Philosophers: The Philosophy of Martin Buber,* ed. by Paul Arthur Schilpp and Maurice Friedman, The Open Court Publishing Co.

latter part of the Second Commonwealth era the Essenes
constituted such a guild. On the European continent, during
the feudal period, there seemed to have developed an ascetic
movement known as German Ḥasidism, which is reflected in
the *Sefer Ḥasidim* by R. Judah ben Samuel he-Ḥasid (d.
1217). During the latter part of the eighteenth and the first
part of the nineteenth century there flourished in East European countries the Ḥasidic movement. At its height, Ḥasidism was directed as much, if not more, against the Haskalah,
or Jewish enlightenment movement, as against the dry
legalistic spirit of Talmudism.

Toward the end of the nineteenth century, however, Ḥasidism became a mere backwater alongside the mainstream of
Jewish life. By mere chance, a highly gifted youth was
introduced at that very time into the world of Ḥasidism.
That youth was Martin Buber. He was fascinated by its way
of life. Its effect on his personality, however, remained dormant until it was suffused with western culture. The opportunity to promulgate a westernized form of Ḥasidism
presented itself to Buber when the Zionist movement came
upon the scene and he learned of Ahad Ha-Am's spiritual
version of its aims. Buber thenceforth made it his life mission to provide Zionism with a rationale for Judaism. That
rationale was not to be based on classical philosophy. It was
to be an original kind of spiritual or religious humanism that
was based on Ḥasidism minus its theurgic or magical excres-
cences. Accordingly, what follows is not a summary of the
content of Buber's esoteric rationale, but rather a description of the method he employed in formulating it. Some of
the important insights, however, of Buber's thinking necessarily come into view.

Hermann Cohen assumed that his *Religion der Vernunft*
would provide modern Judaism with a rationale for its existence as Maimonides' *Guide for the Perplexed* had provided
medieval Judaism. By the same token might Martin Buber's

writings be regarded as providing modern Judaism with the type of rationale which is analogous to that of Judah Hallevi's *Al Khazari* for medieval Judaism. The fact that Judah Hallevi preceded Maimonides, whereas Martin Buber follows Hermann Cohen does not affect the parallelism. Of main interest is the fact that *non-Jewish* influence had determined the *pro-philosophic* attitude of Maimonides who was an avowed disciple of Aristotle and the *anti-philosophic* attitude of Judah Hallevi whose *Al Khazari* is modeled both in form and content on Al Ghazali's *Destruction of Philosophers.* Likewise it was the non-Jewish influence of Kant's thinking that is recognizable in Hermann Cohen's *Religion der Vernunft,* and Kierkegaard's anti-philosophic attitude that is chacterististic of Martin Buber's writings on Judaism. Again like Maimonides, who asserted the Jewish differentia of his own thinking by contesting Aristotle's conception of eternal matter, Buber asserts his Jewish differentia by contesting Kierkegaard's absolutization of the individual.

MARTIN BUBER'S ANTI-PHILOSOPHIC RATIONALE

Buber does not profess to be the creator of a philosophic system. He, in fact, questions the very possibility of embodying living truth, or reality as it actually exists and operates, in any systematic hierarchy of ideas. His main contribution to the ordering of thought consists fundamentally in his proposal of a new method in the art of living, a method he came to designate as "the life of dialogue." The numerous essays, lectures and short works in which his thoughts find expression possess the unique quality of being designed, as he puts it, "to meet the needs of particular moments, and bear the mark of time." Whatever idea he has occasion to expound emerges from the very depth of his character and his innermost being. The wide range of his intellect and its highly integrated power are a guarantee for the viability of his pronouncements. There is such a decided consistency and coherence in the multitude of his writings that it is possible to identify the pattern of his thinking.

The pattern is not, I believe, merely the unfolding of a central insight, such as Maurice S. Friedman places at the head of his work on *Martin Buber*. He there quotes Buber as describing his own standpoint as the "narrow ridge." Friedman interprets that standpoint as "the paradoxical unity of what one usually understands only as alternatives—I and Thou, love and justice, dependence and freedom, the love of God and the fear of God, passion and direction, good and evil, unity and duality." Friedman's statement is, indeed, a comprehensive summary of virtually everything that Buber has written, but it fails to furnish the key to an understanding of "the quality and significance of Martin Buber's life and thought." In my opinion, the one piece of writing that provides the key to that understanding is the essay entitled "Plato and Isaiah" which was delivered by Buber as an inaugural lecture at the Hebrew University in 1938, when he was in his sixty-first year. It sounds a note which justifies Friedman's characterization of Buber as "spokesman for Judaism before the world" (*Martin Buber*, p. 9). But, in order to derive from that address the key-principle of Buber's interpretation of Judaism, we need to know some of the main facts and factors which form the background of that address.

A knowledge of that background is indispensable particularly to an insight into Buber's attitude toward philosophy and tradition. That attitude was not arrived at as a result merely of intellectual exploration. It was definitely a response, or, to use the formula Buber recommends as a principle of true living, "a responsible decision," in answer to the concrete situation in which he found himself. Rather than detracting, therefore, from the validity of Buber's attitude toward philosophy and tradition, it confirms its validity, at least within the framework of that concrete situation. For that reason none of the details in the following description of Buber's early background should be considered irrelevant to our main theme.

As a young lad, Buber grew up in the home of his grandfather, Solomon Buber, who, in addition to being a Hebrew scholar and a well-to-do merchant, was an adherent of Ḥasidism. He would often take his grandchild with him on periodic trips to the Ḥasidic community of Sadagora in Galicia. The profound impression which the Ḥasidic manifestation of Jewish religion then made on the lad was a determining influence of his career in later years. As a student in the University of Vienna, young Buber came under the influences of Simmel, Dilthey and Bergson, and made a special study of the mystics of the Renaissance and the Reformation.

During the last decade of the nineteenth and the first of this century, the Zionist movement gained world attention, and the Jews themselves had to take a decisive step that would insure their survival as a people. Those were the years when the Jews in Europe were confronted by a modernized Western civilization in which anti-Semitism was gaining headway. It took Theodore Herzl to foresee that this anti-Semitism would ultimately aim at nothing less than to render the entire European continent *Judenrein*. The response which he finally succeeded in eliciting from the Jews was Zionism and the rebirth of Jewish collective consciousness.

Modernized Western civilization had emancipated the Jews from their political disabilities and status as aliens, with the expectation that they would become absorbed by the general population and disappear as a distinct social entity. Most Jews in Central and Western Europe, however, met that expectation half-way. In fact, the statesmen themselves, who advocated the emancipation of the Jews, had proposed a compromise: the renunciation of their nationhood and the retention of their religious beliefs and practices. That compromise was enough to make of the Jews a conspicuous minority that could serve as a scapegoat for the many economic ills to which the newly born states were subject. Thus arose the modern form of Jew-hatred known as anti-Semitism which throve in Central Europe, and from there spread to the East and to the West. This new form of Jew-hatred was no longer motivated by the Christian myth, but by the rising cult of modern nationalism. The Dreyfus case was the most dramatic outburst of anti-Semitism which had been simmering for several decades, as Herzlian Zionism was the most dramatic outburst of Jewish consciousness which had been in the making during that same period, under the influence of the modern European national movements.

Young Buber, whom the university education had alienated from Judaism, was brought back to it by Zionism. At first it was the political Zionism of Herzl, but almost immediately he discerned its shortcomings as being mainly "anti-anti-Semitism." He yearned for some more profound rationale than that of escape from persecution. He looked to Zionism to transform both the inner and outer life of the Jewish People. "We must strive for nothing less," he wrote after his long experience with the movement, "than the concrete transformation of our life as a whole. The process of transforming our inner lives must be expressed in the transformation of our outer life, of the life of the individual as well as that of the community. And the effect must be reciprocal, the change in the external arrangements of our life must be reflected in, and renew, our inner life time and again. Up to now, Zionist theory has not adequately realized the importance of this mutual influence" (*Israel and the World*, "Hebrew Humanism," p. 245).

No wonder he soon came under the spell of Ahad Ha-Am, to whom the return to Eretz Yisrael was to be a means to the renaissance of the Jewish People. But before long that spell seemed to be broken. Ahad Ha-Am's version of Judaism reborn appeared to Buber to be a synthetic product, in which Western culture had more of a share than the Judaism of tradition. He could not reconcile himself to Ahad Ha-Am's conception of Judaism, in which the belief in God played no role. Both the ineradicable influence of Ḥasidism and his own conviction that human life could have no worth or meaning without God kept him from identifying himself with Ahad Ha-Am's "cultural Zionism." A Judaism, however ethical and idealistic, which was not based on faith in God was for Buber incapable of resuscitating the Jewish People.

Without a God-inspired zeal, Zionism was likely to be merely a quixotic attempt to imitate under next-to-impossible conditions the nationalist adventures of the awakened European peoples. The latter had, to begin with, the most important and indispensable asset, namely, lands which they could call their own. The Jews had no such asset. They first had to recover the land from which they had been exiled many centuries before, and which the Arabs regarded as their inalienable possession. To overcome that insuperable obstacle nothing less than the resumption of the covenant relationship between the Jewish People and God would have to be the avowed aim of Zionism. Zionism could not succeed, unless it were animated by a Messianic spirit.

For the Jews to evince such a spirit, Buber concluded, they had to be disillusioned concerning the true character of contemporary Western civilization which had held out to them the promise of universal reason, enlightenment and progress. They had to be made to realize to what extent this very civilization which was insidiously, even if not always violently, seeking to destroy them body and soul was intrinsically incapable of even understanding what man is, to say nothing of helping him to achieve salvation. Jews should rather look to their own spiritual heritage for the method of salvation of which mankind was desperately in need. Nothing less than an unprecedented spiritual awakening, as part of their effort to

recover their ancient homeland, was therefore needed to re-
call them to their vocation of being a holy people, and an
example of justice and peace to the rest of the world.

This was the final decision which Buber arrived at, after
he had withdrawn for a few years from public and literary
activity in order to learn at first hand, and if possible to relive, the revelational experience recorded in the Bible and
the unique mode of communal life fostered by Ḥasidism in
its prime. What he came out with from that intellectual and
spiritual hibernation is best summed up in the address on
"Plato and Isaiah."

That address was delivered in the fateful year of 1938,
when the world was in the grip of the demonic frenzy let
loose by Hitler. It was spoken at the Hebrew University, as
Buber took his place on its faculty. He then, no doubt,
wished to give expression to the idea which had obsessed him
during all the years in which he had been engaged in preparing the Jews for their proper role in Zion. From that standpoint, the very title of that address is highly significant.
Plato is the symbol of philosophic thinking, and Isaiah of
Jewish religious tradition. Accordingly, the all-embracing
principle which he tried to set forth on that occasion was
that the Jews should not look to the philosophy of the West
for inspiration or guidance in their great enterprise of rebuilding their land and their People. The only dependable
source of inspiration and guidance is their own religious tradition. The following is the substance of the argument advanced in that address:

Plato entertained a life-long ambition to found a republic
in accordance with his concept of justice, in the hope that he
would thereby influence the existing states to follow the example of that republic. Realizing how much human life
depended upon the nature of the state, and noting how poorly
governed all states were, he came to the conclusion that the
only way to remedy that evil was to have philosophers do the

governing, or to have the governors become philosophers. The problem of finding the right kind of political leaders was to be solved either by having philosophers come to power, or by educating as philosophers those who already possessed power.

The absurdity of that solution has been pointed out by Kant. Power and reason, he said in effect, do not go together. The most that can be expected is that power should at least not suppress the voice of reason. Plato, however, was convinced that his theory would work. He went so far as to train his disciple Dion to head a republic that was to be established in Sicily, and he himself journeyed thither several times to help Dion with his task, without making any headway. In the end, Dion was assassinated by a fellow-disciple of Plato and all of Plato's expectations came to naught.

"Why did Plato fail?" asks Buber. Instead of answering that question, Buber proceeds to describe another type of failure, that of the Prophet Isaiah. Isaiah is commissioned by God to bring a message of reproof to King Uzziah for his misrule. But Isaiah is warned that his message will not be heeded—except by a small "remnant." Isaiah is made aware that "failure is an integral part of the way he must take."

Isaiah has a conception both of "spirit" and of "power" different from that of Plato. According to Isaiah, neither the one nor the other is properly the possession of man. They have to be gifts from God. The prophet, as a man of spirit, must not expect to exercise power. The king, as a man of power, is answerable to God. In contrast with Plato, who regarded his own soul as perfect, Isaiah acknowledged himself as unclean. Plato had a fully worked out plan for the structure of the just state. On the other hand, all that Isaiah did was to criticize the existing state and to demand of the people and the government that they heed the will of God who was the true King. The will of God cannot be mediated by priests who possess power, but only by prophets who lack it.

Isaiah did not address his message only to King Uzziah but also to the people. He sought to impress upon them that, if they were to be worthy of having God as their King, they would have to become a genuine people, a people free from the divisive effect of injustice and inequality. Every individual among his hearers was thus made to feel responsible for the conduct of the state to which he belonged. Moreover, Isaiah warned Israel not to engage in power politics and not to become involved in international intrigues. To survive amid the great world powers, Israel had to prove by example that it could make peace a reality in its internal life.

Isaiah also failed as did Plato later on. The fact, however, that we Jews still exist as a people proves that Isaiah's failure was different from Plato's. There were some of Isaiah's contemporaries who not only took his admonition seriously, but who also transmitted it to their descendants. It has become the religious tradition of the Jewish People, whom it has kept alive by giving them a purpose to live for. Plato's philosophy, on the other hand, articulated in his *Republic,* has remained a classic for classroom study. Such is the difference between philosophy and religious tradition, a difference summed up in the following statement:

> The prophet's spirit does not, like Plato's, believe that he possesses an abstract and general, a timeless concept of truth. He receives one message for one situation. That is exactly why after thousands of years his words still address the changing situations in history.

Here, at last, we have the key idea to Martin Buber's writings. It is the idea that the Jews have what to live for as a People. Western civilization has produced philosophers, but the Jews have had their prophets. Western civilization excels in the discoveries of science and the inventions of technology, but it has little to offer in the way of helping man achieve his human destiny. Judaism has not contributed to science or technology, but mankind cannot achieve unity and peace without the divine message which is embodied in the Jewish religious tradition.

Buber recalls the spiritual illumination which Pascal experienced when he suddenly discovered that the God he believed in and prayed to was the "God of Abraham, God of Isaac, God of Jacob—not of the philosophers and scholars. He turned, not from a state of being where there was no God to one where there was a God, but from the God of the philosophers to the God of Abraham" (*Israel and the World*, "The Love of God and the Idea of Deity," p. 53).

Thus Pascal, himself a great representative of Western thought, found philosophic thought inadequate as a means of helping man to live. That should suffice to prove that the Jews do not have to depend for their spiritual fulfillment upon the philosophic thinking of Western civilization. On the contrary, they have the opportunity and the responsibility to bring to mankind the only truth concerning God that can transform mankind. What mankind needs is the awareness that God is not a mere idea of the mind, but an infinite and absolute reality that exists independently of it; and that salvation depends upon man's self-commitment with his entire being in thought, feeling and action to faith in this living God. This truth has to be translated into life by the Jewish People in the land of its origin, amid conditions which would permit all of its political, economic, social and cultural activities to be permeated by the revelational spirit that prevailed during Bible days, and that was temporarily revived in the Ḥasidic movement.

The foregoing thesis, maintained by Buber, can be best brought into sharp relief by being contrasted with its antithesis which was promulgated by Hermann Cohen, the founder in Marburg University of Neo-Kantianism. Like Buber, Hermann Cohen too, had for a time been alienated from Judaism, but unlike Buber who came back to Judaism through Zionism, Cohen came back through Kantianism. For Cohen, too, the belief in God is the heart of Judaism. But there the resemblance ends. Whereas to Cohen the belief in God is the belief in the validity of the idea, arrived at through a process of reasoning like that pursued by Kant in his *Critique of Practical Reason,* to Buber such a God can have no practical significance for human life.

Buber regards Cohen as a great "system-creator," but considers his efforts wasted. "Cohen," he says, "has constructed the last home for the God of the philosophers" (*Eclipse of God,* "The Love of God and the Idea of Deity," p. 74). He then proceeds to disprove Cohen's argument in defense of *idea* as reality and as capable of being loved. Cohen asks: "How can one love anything, save an idea?" thereby implying that to be loved, God must be conceived as Idea. In reply, Buber rightly points out that, while an idea can be loved, it cannot be conceived as loving. The point that Buber next makes is that Cohen, in spite of himself, really conceives God existentially. Buber accepts Rosenzweig's interpretation of Cohen, that "Cohen's idea of God should not be taken to mean that God is only an idea in Cohen's eyes" (*Eclipse of God,* p. 79), and he refers to Cohen as "the philosopher who is overwhelmed by faith."

To the average person who follows that debate between Cohen and Buber, the difference may sound little more than that between tweedledum and tweedledee. As such, however, it is likely to appear only when taken out of the life context in which that debate was conducted. The life context is the situation in which the Jews found themselves in the first decade of this century vis-à-vis present-day Western civilization. Buber was convinced that the cause of authentic and vital religion demanded that the Jews become a nation once again and resume the broken continuity of its existence in Eretz Yisrael. On the other hand, Cohen as sincerely and eloquently argued that the cause of religion demanded that

Jews retain their *nationality* (as distinct from "nationhood," and as the equivalent of "community") but otherwise become integrated into the State of which they were citizens, and there demonstrate the truth of monotheism by carrying it out to its ethical conclusions.

Buber's philosophy of reality, or of religion, is as much of an apology for his "Utopian Zionism" as Cohen's is for his "Universal Judaism." Both would probably resent the notion that pragmatic considerations had anything to do with the formulation of their respective God concepts. To Buber, however, that fact should not be objectionable in the least. On the contrary, it harmonizes fully with his own principle that concreteness is the only gate to reality; and what is more concrete than the existential situation? He himself makes use of that principle in his interpretation of Kierkegaard's central category of the "Single One" (*Between Man and Man,* "The Question to the Single One," p. 40).

Apart from pragmatic consequences, however, any system of thought deserves to be weighed in terms of its inner consistency. Even when, as in the case of existentialist systems, paradox is not only not deprecated but even treated with great respect, there are limits beyond which we cannot afford to go even in paradox. Thus, although Buber himself allows considerable room for paradox in his own thinking, he refuses to go along with Kierkegaard in the latter's version of the story of Abraham's willingness to sacrifice his son Isaac at God's command, the paradox in this instance being that faith in God may on occasion demand human sacrifice. Of course, once you admit the legitimacy of paradox, there is really no point at which it can be halted. Thus even Kierkegaard's paradox is accepted as normal when we consider killing for one's country the height of ethical behavior.

Nevertheless, Buber's entire thought pattern does reveal so much coherence that its contribution to the understanding of philosophy and tradition merits examination. Certainly his strictures of classical, or speculative, philosophy should not be disregarded. They constitute serious reasons why idea-tionist philosophy as such cannot get at the heart of reality. The following five shortcomings of philosophy refer only to ideationist philosophy:

1. In the first place, philosophy has to resort to the method of generalization. In order to generalize, it has to abstract from concrete objects or situations some one aspect or quality that is common to a number of them, and study it as though it possessed independent reality. It thus comes to treat as reality that which is only an idea and to ignore the existential reality which is always an organic complex of aspects or qual-ities.

2. Secondly, philosophy seeks to discover the regularities of laws that obtain in the processes whereby things and persons interact with one another and with their environment. That leads to the conclusion that all of reality is dominated by an inherent principle of unbreakable iron necessity. Thus hu-man freedom, without which there can be no moral or spir-itual responsibility, cannot but be treated from a philosophi-cal standpoint as mere illusion.

3. Thirdly, philosophy is committed to the epistemological problem of "How do we know what we know, and that what we know is neither dream nor delusion?" Consequently the only kind of "I" or "personality" that it deals with is the subjective one, of which the entire content of knowledge is the object. That fact reduces even one's personality to a sub-jective idea, devoid of that ontological reality which is es-sential to the belief that personality itself is existentially real, existentially effective, and existentially responsible.

4. Philosophy has shown itself unable to answer satisfac-torily the question which is basic to a sense of security or at-homeness in the world. That is because it is unable to answer the question of "What is man, what unique quality in him

enables him to be self-aware, and to distinguish between what he is and does, on the one hand, and what he ought to be and do, on the other?"

5. Philosophy has reduced God to an idea which is a creation, or expression, of the human mind. In the words of Kant, which are quoted by Buber, "God is only an idea of reason, but one possessing the greatest practical internal and external reality" (*Eclipse of God,* p. 70). This kind of God is not a living God. If faith in God is to make a difference in a person's life, it has to mean standing in a relationship to God as a living entity that is independent of man.

All of the foregoing five indictments which Buber brings against the philosophers of Western civilization are implied in the one sweeping indictment which he elaborates in what is the most sustained argument in all his writings. I refer to the last chapter of his *Between Man and Man,* entitled "What Is Man?" There he states in full the case against philosophy. He gives a comprehensive and penetrating, though brief, analysis of the outstanding systems of thought from Aristotle to our own day, from the standpoint of what he regards as the most basic of all questions, namely, "What is Man?" Remarkably enough, that entire section of the book is a summary of his inaugural course of lectures at the Hebrew University as Professor of Social Philosophy, delivered in 1938, after he had delivered the inaugural address on "Plato and Isaiah." We cannot but conclude that those lectures were intended to elaborate in detail what we have found to be the main thesis of the inaugural address: We Jews have nothing to learn from Western civilization as to how to rebuild our own civilization. The following is a summary of that long chapter in *Between Man and Man:*

Buber credits Kant with having been the first to articulate the crucial question concerning the uniqueness of man, the question which was to be the subject of a new philosophical discipline, namely, philosophical anthropology. Kant himself, however, did not even undertake to answer that question. According to Buber, it is inherently impossible for philosophy to deal with that question, in the manner in which the philosophers since Kant, with the possible exception of Feuerbach, have dealt with it. They have all dealt with the question of "What is man?" as though each individual human being were an encapsulated entity. To prove his case, Buber passes in review one great philosopher after another only to find that each one makes the mistake of considering the person as self-contained, instead of in the light of "the wholeness of its essential relations to what is."

Buber introduces at this point a very significant observation with regard to the history of the human spirit. He distinguishes between "epochs of habitation" (i.e., at-homeness in the world) and "epochs of homelessness." The former are the pre-Copernican epochs, and the latter are the post-Copernican epochs. Plato, Aristotle, Augustine, Aquinas, Cusanus, Pico della Mirandola and Malebranche conceived man as housed in a self-enclosed universe. Though they all sensed something of the mystery of man as no less marvellous than the mystery of nature, the feeling of man's at-homeness in that universe neutralized any possible interest they might have had into probing more deeply into the mystery of man.

Post-Copernican cosmology, however, has made it impossible for man to form any tenable image of the universe. The resulting sense of human homelessness and solitude has given new poignancy to the problem of "What is man?" That is the problem of which Pascal became keenly aware. He discerned in man's capacity to reflect about life and the world a daring challenge to the universe, even though the universe crush him with its infinite might. The realization that man's daring to measure himself against the universe constituted man's uniqueness was the beginning of a new approach to the problem. More recently, Hegel attempted to recover for man the sense of security and at-homeness in the world by substituting the universe of infinite time for the universe of infinite space. Man's new house is to be time, in the form of history whose meaning can be learned and understood (*ibid.*, p. 139). Karl Marx's variation of the Hegelian dialectic, by substituting economic determinism for abstract reason as the substance of the dialectic in time, tried to serve the same purpose of making man feel at home in the world. Buber, however, argues that the sense of security which Hegel and Karl Marx believed they had succeeded in recovering for man was deceptive. For, neither the one nor the other could *guarantee* that salvation would ensue in the future. In fact, their respective promises of salvation, Hegel's through the German State and Marx's through the triumph of the proletariat, turned out to be a mirage.

The first thinker, according to Buber, who came to actual grips with the problem of "What is man?" was Nietzsche. Nietzsche's answer was that man is "the animal that is not yet established." Man is a creature in transition from the subhuman to the superman. But when Nietzsche tries to describe the transition and the goal, he goes off on a tangent. He misrepresents the actual history of man's sense of guilt, and is mistaken in his assumption that man's will to self-fulfillment is intrinsically the will to "increase in power." Since Nietzsche lacked a correct knowledge of the empirical facts concerning human life, no reliance can be placed upon his fantastic notions concerning man's place in the universe, however poetically and majestically he expressed them.

In the meantime, man's sense of insecurity has become more painful, due to what Buber characterizes as the nature of the modern crisis, namely, "man's lagging behind his works." That is the idea usually expressed in the concept of civilization as having grown into man's Frankenstein. The first genuinely satisfying answer, according to Buber, that dealt with that question in all its terrifying significance is one that was given a century ago, but which has begun to be appreciated only in recent years. That is Kierkegaard's answer, which is based not on philosophy but upon religious tradition. Kierkegaard maintains that the only way in which man can identify his true being and achieve his destiny is through faith. But it must be faith that is lived in the wholeness of human life and not merely verbalized into a conceptional translation.

Buber has avowed his indebtedness to Kierkegaard (cf. *The Eclipse of God,* p. 149) for what he himself has been pleading in all his works: the formulation of a *theological anthropology* based on a *religious tradition.* The existential nature of man is to be sought not in thought, or reason, nor in the will to power, but in "the stages and conditions of life itself: guilt, fear, despair, decision, the prospect of one's own death and the prospect of salvation." Buber next subjects to criticism the more recent philosophies of man, those of Heidegger, Husserl and Scheler. Each of these philosophies, being secular in character, renounces Kierkegaard's theological presuppositions, and consequently, according to Buber, was bound to fail in one respect or another to reckon with the totality of man's nature.

The inevitable conclusion which Buber would have us draw from the foregoing analysis of philosophic thought since Aristotle is that philosophy is inherently precluded from enabling man to translate "into the reality of his life the one characteristic element which cannot be found anywhere else in the universe." That is the point implied in Buber's contrasting Isaiah the prophet with Plato the first great philosopher whose thinking, however modified, has set once for all the pattern to all subsequent philosophizing. None of the philosophies has exerted a creative or permanent influence on human life. Isaiah's influence, on the other hand, has been creative and permanent. The existence of the Jewish People testifies to that. Isaiah is as typical of religious tradition as Plato is of philosophic thought. What then, are the intrinsic qualities of authentic religious tradition which, according to Buber, renders it indispensable to life?

The Jewish religious tradition, according to Buber, is the indispensable means of achieving that inner transformation of the Jewish People, both individually and communally, without which the outer transformation which Zionism has been fostering is less than half the task. He quotes what Conrad Burdach, a scholar noted for his researches into the Renaissance period, has to say in comment on Dante's statement: "The greatest desire Nature has implanted in everything from its beginning is the desire to return to its origin." To which Burdach adds that it is the goal of humanism "to return to the human origin, not by way of speculative thought, but by way of a *concrete transformation* of the whole inner life."

These quotations are introduced by Buber in his essay on "Hebrew Humanism." There he states in the most lucid terms what the Jews must do, in order to "return to their origin," since only there will they find the "factor of spiritual power" which must accompany the material factor. Every word in that long statement throws light upon the place which the Jewish religious tradition has held in Buber's thinking and career. For lack of space I shall quote only the most striking passages in that essay which throw light on what Buber understood by the Jews' "return to their origin."

"It cannot be achieved," he writes, "by any spiritual power save the primordial spirit of Israel, the spirit which has made us as we are, and to which we must continually account for the extent to which our character has remained steadfast in the face of our destiny. This spirit has not vanished. The way to it is still open; it is still possible for us to encounter it. *The Book still lies before us, and the voice speaks forth from it as on the first day. But we must not dictate what it should and what it should not tell us* (italics mine). . . . What it does have to tell us, and what no other voice in the world can teach us with such simple power, is that there is truth and that there are lies, and that human life cannot persist or have meaning save in the decision in behalf of truth and against lies; that there is right and wrong, and that the salvation of man depends on choosing what is right and rejecting what is wrong. . . . The *humanitas* which speaks from this Book today, as it has always done, is the unity of human life under one divine direction which divides right from wrong and truth from lies as unconditionally as the words of the Creator divided light from darkness. . . . What matters is that in every hour of decision we are aware of our responsibility and summon our conscience to weigh exactly how much is necessary to preserve the community, and accept just so much and no more; that we do not interpret the will-to-power as a demand made by life itself. . . . The men in the Bible are sinners like ourselves, but there is one sin they do not commit, our arch-sin: they do not dare confine God to a circumscribed space or division of life, to religion. . . . He who has been reared in our Hebrew biblical humanism resists patriotic bombast which clouds the gulf between the demand of life and the desire of the will-to-power. He resists the whispering of false popularity which is the opposite of true service to the people. . . . He knows that, in the final analysis, the only thing that can help his people is what is true and right in the light of the age-old decision . . . . That is the meaning in contemporary language of the 'return to the origins of our being' " (*Israel and the World*, "Hebrew Humanism," pp. 245-247).

In his essay on "National Education" (*Israel and the World*, pp. 160 ff.) Buber dilates on the place of tradition in all national movements and in every kind of national education. He emphasizes the need of imbuing the minds of the rising generations with "the great spiritual values whose source is the origin of their people." There are three possible attitudes to a religious tradition, of which only one is desirable. That is the positive attitude. It expresses itself in allowing "the forces inherent in the beginnings to shape present-day life in accordance with present-day needs." Undesirable, of course, is the negative attitude, which rejects all tradition as "neither credible, nor usable, nor timely." Equally undesirable, however, is what Buber terms the "ficticious" attitude. That is characteristic of people who boast of their tradition without believing in it, even teaching it to their children, but not with the purpose of having them seriously integrate it into actual life.

Buber is convinced that the Jewish Bible has the power "to guide the life of the man of today" (*Israel and the World,* "The Man of Today and the Jewish Bible," p. 92). "The Bible," says Buber, "has, in the form of a glorified remembrance, given vivid, decisive expression to an ever-recurrent happening. In the infinite language of events and situations, eternally changing but plain to the truly attentive, transcendence speaks to our hearts at the essential moments of personal life. And there is a language in which we can answer it; it is the language of our actions and attitudes, our reactions and our abstentions; the totality of these answers is what we may call our answering-for-ourselves in the most proper sense of the expression. This fundamental interpretation of our existence we owe to the Hebrew Bible; and whenever we truly read it, our self-understanding is truly deepened" (*At the Turning,* pp. 49-50).

Buber is very much concerned that the continuity of the Jewish religious tradition be not misinterpreted as resistance to spontaneity and change. He often keeps on reminding the reader: "Let me reiterate that such continuity does not imply the preservation of the old, but the ceaseless begetting and giving birth to the same single spirit, and its continuous integration into life" (*Israel and the World,* "Teaching and Deed," p. 143). "Only the teachings truly rejuvenated can

liberate us from limitations and bind us to the unconditional, so that spiritualized and spirited, united within the
circle of the eternal union, we may recognize one another and
ourselves, and, empowered by the fathomless laws of history,
hold out against the powers moving on the surface of history"
(*ibid.,* p. 144). This is what religious tradition can do, when
the adherents of a movement "absorb and transform what
they have absorbed in response to the demands of the hour."
He condemns in no uncertain terms the acceptance of tradition and law as what he calls "a once for all." Such a frozen
tradition only "prevents meeting with God in the lived concrete . . . The very symbols which man uses to address God
often stand in the way of that address" (*ibid.*).

The significance which Buber attaches to a functioning religious tradition is due to his regarding it as an indispensable
instrument of the collective memory. "We Jews," he writes,
"are a community based on memory. A common memory has
kept us together and enabled us to survive. This does not
mean that we based our life on any one particular past, even
on the loftiest of the pasts; it simply means that one generation passed on to the next a memory which gained in scope—
for new destiny and new emotional life were constantly ac-
cruing to it—and which realized itself in a way we can call
organic. The expanding memory was more than a spiritual
motif; it was a power which sustained, fed, and quickened
Jewish existence itself. I might even say that these memories
realized themselves biologically, for in their strength the
Jewish substance was renewed" (*Israel and the World,* "Why
We Should Study Jewish Sources," p. 145). No wonder Buber
regards nothing so ominous in contemporary Jewish life as
"the disappearance of the collective memory and the passion
for handing down" (*ibid.,* p. 147), in other words, the failure
to keep the Jewish religious tradition alive.

Buber recognizes clearly that the Jewish tradition owes its
ability to function as the memory of the Jewish People, and

the retention of its religious character, to the fact that *it is the product of the collective life of the Jewish People.* "In the case of some peoples," he writes, "such as the Chinese, the Jews, and the Greeks, lonely thinkers thought of the absolute as such, in its utmost metaphysical purity; but the actual life of the people was not influenced by those thoughts. Reverence for the absolute can become the life-principle of a people only when the people itself puts it into practice as a people, and not in the sphere of abstract thought, but in actual life. Reverence of the absolute does not mean metaphysical ideation, but religious event" (*Israel and the World,* "The Gods of the Nations and God," p. 198).

The one truth which the Bible, as the basic religious tradition of the Jews, proclaims as its main teaching is that their ancestors had entered Eretz Yisrael with a sense of commitment to a mission from above to set up a just way of life throughout their generations. It was to be "a way of life that cannot be realized by individuals in the sphere of their private existence, but only by a nation in the establishment of its society" (*Israel and the World,* "The Land and Its Possession," p. 229). The serious religious crisis in the throes of which the entire world finds itself has had a destructive impact on the Jews. "The true solution," Buber wrote to Gandhi, "can only issue from the life of a community which begins to carry out the will of God, often without being aware of doing so, without believing that God exists and that this is His will . . . This is the innermost truth of the Jewish life in the land; perhaps it may be of significance for the solution of this crisis of faith not only for Jewry but for all humanity. You, Mahatma Gandhi, who know of the connection between tradition and future, should not associate yourself with those who pass over our cause without understanding or sympathy" (*ibid.,* 230-231). We thus have in the appeal to Gandhi evidence of how strongly Buber is convinced that a vital and functioning religious tradition is the product of the interaction of a people with its physical environment, and cannot be the outcome of lonely thinkers engaged in metaphysical speculation, however spiritual and sublime. Elsewhere in passing, he states simply: "I hold that Jewry can gain an effective and more than merely stimulating share in the building of a steadfast world of peace only in its own community and not in scattered members" (*Between Man and Man*, "Dialogue," p. 5).

Ḥasidism had provided Buber with the main fuel, so to speak, for the flame of his Jewishness which was kindled by Zionism. Buber regarded Ḥasidism as "the one great attempt in the history of the Diaspora to make a reality of the original choice (for the true God and against Baal), and to found a true and just community based on religious principles" (*Israel and the World*, "On National Education," p. 159). Nevertheless he was not blind to its corruption and failure, which he ascribed mainly to the fact that it did not aim "for the self-determination of the people, or to state it differently, because its connections with Palestine were only sporadic and not influenced by the desire for national liberation . . . But," he adds, "finally the Jewish national movement, either consciously or unconsciously took up the age-old social message, and impelled by it, set up as the goal of national education the pattern of the new type of man, of the man who can translate ideas into life, who along with the national idea will satisfy the longing for a great communal life" (*ibid.*, "On National Education," p. 159).

In the light of what we have found in the foregoing discussion to be Buber's attitude toward philosophic thought and religious tradition, we might be inclined to say that Buber prefers to regard himself as standing on the shoulders of the Jewish religious tradition and seeing beyond it rather than as standing on the shoulders of philosophic thought and seeing beyond it. He apparently believes that philosophic thought, no matter how deeply it may try to explore the truth about reality, can never know it, because it starts out with the wrong premise, by assuming the existence of a self-enclosed mind, on the one hand, and of a world that is completely outside it and heterogeneous to it, on the other. This premise is particularly misleading when the matter of concern is the salvation of man, or the attainment of that which is uniquely and fully human in him.

An objective and fair evaluation seems to point to the fact that Buber has consistently followed his own standard of "the narrow ridge," in the new synthesis which he achieved between the two. His pattern of thought on the subject in question is far from being anything like that of the medieval theologians who sought to harmonize tradition with philosophy. It is truly a third alternative to both of them, in the sense of implying their mutual supplementation. But this conclusion seems to be contradicted by what he himself keeps on emphasizing. He gives the impression that he considers the Jewish religious tradition as self-sufficient, and capable of answering the needs of every new situation as it arises, without any recourse whatever to philosophic thinking.

Take for example, the following: after referring to the *halutz* (the Jewish pioneer in Eretz Yisrael) as motivated by the will to realize the ideal human community, which is "a union of persons living together, a union founded on the direct and just relations of all to all," Buber adds: "The *halutz* does not draw his will to realize this ideal out of himself, or out of his era, or out of the Western world; nor does he derive it from the occidental socialism of his country. Whether he knows it or not, whether or not he likes it, he is animated by the age-old Jewish longing to incorporate social truth in the life of individuals living with one another, the longing to translate the idea of a true community into reality. The new type of human being such as the *halutz* promised to become is a result of the development of very early traits.

What we call 'Israel' is not merely the result of biological and historical development; it is the product of a decision, made long ago, the decision in favor of a God of justice and against a god of instinctive egoism, etc." (*Israel and the World*, "Learning and Education," pp. 158-159).

This statement could not emphasize more strongly the adequacy of the Jewish religious tradition for enabling man to achieve spiritual security and fulfillment. In view of what we have shown to have prompted Buber to take this extreme position with regard to philosophic thought vs. the Jewish religious tradition, that emphasis is understandable. But in a thinker of the stature of Buber we do not like to see overstatement of a case. We should have preferred to have seen him keep to the "narrow ridge," despite the strong temptation to depart from it, even though by so doing he might have been able to display less fervor as a prophet and greater consistency as a thinker.

It would take us far afield to explore the problem of the extent to which Zionism and the entire modern Jewish renaissance would have been impossible without the impact of Western civilization of our day. No one can question the influence of modern secularist nationalism on contemporary Jewish life in all its positive and negative aspects. In the words of Salo Baron, "Reflecting in many ways the ideologies shaped under the peculiar conditions of their varying environments, often helping to formulate new nationalist theories, various segments of Jewry searched for a comprehensive rationale of their own to maintain their world-wide ethnic and religious unity" (*Modern Nationalism and Religion*, p. 213). Modern secularist nationalism, which has exerted a revolutionizing influence on contemporary Jewish life and thought, including that of Buber himself, is the unmistakable product of contemporary Western philosophic thought.

No less true is it that in the reinterpretation of the religious tradition, on the assumption that it must not be conceived as "a once for all," and that it has to be renewed by each generation in response to the highest needs which only a genuinely spiritual community can define—in all of these qualifications of the religious tradition, we cannot help but discern the influence of philosophic thought. Karl Mannheim, as a philosopher, has arrived at exactly the same conclusion as did Buber concerning the role of religious tradition. "The complete penetration of life by religion," he writes, "will only occur, if those who represent the religious tradition are once more able to go back to the genuine sources of religious experience and do not think that the habitual and institutional forms of religion will suffice for the reconstruction of man and society" (*Diagnosis of Our Time,* p. 27).

Moreover, from the side of philosophic thought itself, one may question whether it could not of itself evolve a pattern of human life calculated to bring about a type of human community that would be capable of enabling its members to achieve spiritual self-fulfillment, and at the same time contribute to world peace and well-being. However cynical we may be about the establishment of the United States, its Declaration of Independence and its Federal Constitution do represent the deliberate commitment of a great people to the creation of a community founded on the principles of freedom, justice and peace. Even the initial policy recommended by Washington, of avoiding entangling alliances with other powers, brings to mind the ancient prophetic warnings against entering into alliances with the world empires of those days.

Who, indeed, inspired the founders of the United States to build such a nation, if not Aristotle, Locke and Rousseau? To be sure, with the vast increase of population and the growing threat from the Old World, the United States has strayed from the dream of its founders. But it has nevertheless had a Jefferson, a Lincoln and a Wilson among its political leaders, and an Emerson, a William James and a John Dewey among its philosophers, to keep it ever mindful of its spiritual mission. What is interesting about all of them is that they managed to achieve their spiritual conception of the American People without the "benefit of clergy." One has only to glance at Dewey's *A Common Faith* to discover how much in common there is between his ideas about the normal relation of religion to community life and Buber's ideas on the same subject in his *Israel and the World,* or how the two thinkers independently arrive at the same distinction between the two possible kinds of faith that make a difference in people's lives.

The fact is that it is possible for Western thought to be inherently self-corrective and to arrive at conclusions virtually identical with those of Buber concerning the basic shortcomings it has harbored hitherto, as well as concerning the need for entering into living relation with other individuals as a means of entering into relations with Reality that is independent of us. What more striking proof of this self-corrective capacity inherent in philosophy than the phenomenon "Bergson," whose influence on Buber is no less recognizable than that of Kierkegaard. "Our thought," we read on the very first page of Bergson's *Creative Evolution,* "in its purely logical form, is incapable of presenting the true nature of life, the full meaning of the evolutionary movement. Created by life, in definite circumstances, to act on definite things, how can it embrace life, of which it is only an emanation or an aspect?" *(ibid.,* Introduction, p. ix).

Buber himself has occasion to refer frequently to the inherently self-corrective character of philosophic thinking. The sophists, according to him, played such a role. "The function of the sophists, and consequently of their like in later times," writes Buber, "has been recognized as the functions of dissolving and preparing. . . . As Protagoras leads toward his contemporary Socrates, Stirner leads toward his contemporary Kierkegaard . . . . What Stirner, with his destructive power successfully attacks is the surrogate for a reality that is no longer believed." *(Between Man and Man,*

"The Question to the Single One," pp. 44-45). As far as philosophy's ability to realize that only through the attitude of faith and the interaction of organic community life can man achieve what is essential to his becoming fully human, it is a pity that Buber should have limited his survey of philosophic thought to continental philosophers. Apparently accepting the continental estimate of American thinkers as not being philosophers but only "pragmatists," he ignores their existence entirely.

It is a fact, however, that the very conception of ideas as "instruments," which the human mind employs in its attempts to get at reality, stresses the same principle as happens to be the central truth of Buber's own philosophic thinking. "Instrumentalism" is as emphatic as Buber in deprecating the tendency of generalizations to falsify reality. American thinkers like Lewis Mumford and Baker Brownell have arrived by means of that "instrumentalism" at conclusions concerning the role and function of community that coincide entirely with those of Buber. Note, for example, the following typical statements by them:

"Men are individually nothing," writes Mumford, "except in relation to that greater reality Man. And Man himself is nought, except in relation to that greater reality which he calls divine. Thought, art, love, are all intimations of this divinity, flickerings of man-made filaments that connect in our imaginations with distant flashes in the dark impenetrable sky (*Faith for Living*, p. 210).

And Baker Brownell, on the very first page of his book entitled *The Human Community: Its Philosophy for a Time of Crisis*, has this to say: "As William James suggests, we must continue to start freshly with integral situations, not with conceptional terms. Though specialism and term-creating ways of thought have their importance, they are not in themselves sufficient unto life. The inner unity and substantiation of things, which James approaches through what he calls *con-*

junctive relations (italics mine), must be recognized in any vital procedure. These are the influences of our experiences. Central in them, a creator of confluence, as it were, is the community."

And here is another paragraph from a section of Brownell's book, entitled "Corrupted by Universals." "Through the technique of the universal, whatever that may mean, our western theory, as well as that of most of India, has withdrawn the sacred essence of things from the humid context of living . . . Thus the dualisms emerged. These, suggests Dewey—unlike Plato—answer no problems, take us nowhere, and leave us stalemated in the strategy of life" (*ibid.*, p. 223). This time it is not Plato and Isaiah, but Plato and Dewey who are set off against each other, to the disadvantage of continental philosophy.

All of which proves that the sharp distinction which Buber draws between philosophic thought and religious tradition does not hold water. The fact is that it all depends upon the philosopher's perspective, and upon how much latitude one allows oneself in reinterpreting a religious tradition. How far Buber avails himself of such latitude may be inferred from the way he equates the traditional belief in Creation with the modern belief in evolution, and the traditional belief in revelation with the modern increase of knowledge. It is only with regard to the traditional belief in *salvation* that he assumes we have nothing to learn from philosophy. Is that quite true? Why does he not subscribe to the traditional conception of bodily resurrection, or of reward and punishment in the hereafter? When he reinterprets the fear of God to mean something entirely different from what it has meant in tradition, namely, awareness of the incomprehensibility of God's being, does he not avail himself of ideas which emanate from philosophic thought?

If philosophic thought were as radically heterogeneous to the spiritual teachings of the religious tradition as Buber states, it could not possibly illuminate that tradition and give it that creatively adaptive capacity which Buber himself has demonstrated in his *The Prophetic Faith*. I am inclined to disagree with Buber's suggestion that the Jewish religious tradition is intrinsically capable of *indefinite unfolding*. Actually that tradition has, in the course of its existence, undergone the very *metamorphosis* which Buber negates, and to which he himself, as "the spokesman of Judaism before the world," has been one of the greatest contributors. The religious tradition owes that metamorphosis to philosophic thinking, and it is fortunate that Buber is highly expert in both. With a slight modification, Franz Rosenzweig's saying still holds: "Divine truth wishes to be implored with both hands," that of philosphy and that of tradition.

As stated at the beginning of this chapter, the appeal of Buber's rationale for Jewish existence is inherently esoteric and limited to those Jewish intellectuals who look to religion to open up to them areas of experience that transcend both science and philosophy. As long as there are Jews of that type, there is no reason why they should not be provided with the kind of rationale which meets their need. The dogmatism that would rule out more than one absolutely true rationale for Jewish existence ignores the intellectual freedom which has come to be a *sine qua non* of being human. Jewish existence will henceforth have to be compatible with the inevitable variety of human minds.

The purpose of this text is by no means that of formulating the one and only tenable rationale. Instead, that purpose is to reckon with the spiritual need of the overwhelming number of Jewish intellectuals for whom Jewish existence has become meaningless and purposeless, because the struggle for mere survival has diverted their minds from the meaning and purpose of Jewish existence. The need, however, for developing a rationale and ideology for a Jewish future in terms that would put a stop to the stampede of our Jewish intellectuals from Jewish life can no longer be postponed, for their number is legion and is rapidly increasing.

Chapter II

A MODERN FUNCTIONAL RATIONALE

Few Jews of our generation know Jewish life, both from within and from without, as intimately as does Dr. Nahum Goldmann. That is why we should give heed to the warning he sounded at the opening session of the World Conference on Jewish Education which convened in Jerusalem during the second week of August, 1962:

"The two decisive forces and motivations," said Dr. Goldmann, "which secured Jewish existence and identity in the past centuries, namely, the strength of the Jewish religion which dominated the totality of Jewish life on the one hand, and the persecutions of the Jewish people on the other, have lost their effectiveness today. The major part of the Jewish people is no more guided in its day-to-day life by the laws and regulations of Jewish religion, and imminent physical danger by persecution does not exist for the overwhelming majority of the Jewish people. Under such conditions the Jewish people can easily lose its Jewish identity for the lack of incentives and motivations which would impel it to remain Jewish. The danger is not one of a dramatic breakaway or even of a conscious denial of their Jewishness, but of a slow and anonymous process of erosion, of the lack of any real motive and reason for remaining Jewish; of losing all inspiring values and contents of their existence and life as Jews, which must inevitably lead to indifference, ignorance, and finally— to the definite loss of any Jewish consciousness" (*Jewish Education,* vol. 33, no. 2, p. 73).

A most ominous sign for the future of Diaspora Judaism is the stampede of Jewish intellectuals away from the Jewish

People. There is hardly any need to document that fact. Can any one think of many Nobel Prize winners of Jewish parentage who identified themselves with Jewish life, to say nothing of Jewish religion? Einstein, who was driven back to the Jewish People as much by anti-Semitism as by his ethical sense, was an exception who proved the rule. Yet even Einstein's return was counterbalanced by Bergson's, Freud's and Berenson's self-alienation. Their contribution to human culture does not have to be measured by Nobel prizes.

What is true of the Jewish intellectuals of first rank is equally true of those of second, third and fourth rank. "Why is it," asks Edwin Wolf 2nd, president of The National Foundation for Jewish Culture, "that hundreds, if not thousands of the most esteemed scientists, humanists, economists, artists, musicians, writers and intellectuals of all kinds, men and women who were born Jews, have left or are leaving Jewish life?" (*The Jewish Digest,* Feb., 1963). Twice the magazine *Commentary* took a poll of Jewish intellectuals in their prime, only to find that with few exceptions their common attitude toward Jewish life and association was one of escapism, and in some cases even self-hatred and anti-Semitism. In case some are inclined to think that such escapism is a passing phenomenon, let me remind them that a recent poll taken of students on a number of college campuses does not augur well for any subsidence of the wave of escapism on the part of Jewish intellectuals of the next generation. As one of those students put it: "I want to think as a person, not as a Jew-person. I wouldn't touch a Hillel Foundation with a ten-foot pole."

Nothing except the threat of physical extermination can be worse for the future of Judaism than the self-alienation of the Jewish intellectuals. A people that is of minority status must have great confidence in itself, great faith in its own *raison d'être,* if it is not to be intimidated by the handicaps that go with having minority status. To whom can it look for encouragement and validation in its struggle for existence, if not to its men and women of intellect, who identify themselves with it for its sake? A Jewish People, or civilization, that cannot retain its intellectuals is, indeed, a fossil. Were that condition to become permanent and inescapable for Jews outside Israel, those Zionists who write off Diaspora Jewry would be vindicated.

Before accepting that conclusion, however, it is necessary to consider the following: In the first place, it is significant that Sholom Aleichem's play, *It Is Hard to Be a Jew,* dealt with a Jewish student in a Gentile university. Evidently it is the intellectual Jew who is not only more sensitized to frustration; he all too often has his intellectual ambitions frustrated merely because he is a Jew. Secondly, if we expect the intellectual Jew to remain loyal to the Jewish People, then we ought to arm him with an indefeasible and inexpugnable rationale for standing his ground. Though many Jewish intellectuals would desert their Jewish People under any and all circumstances, many others would remain at their post.

The fact that the Jewish People has survived to our own day, and by what it has achieved through Zionism, can laugh off Toynbee's characterization of it as a fossil, is due to its having been able in the past to retain the loyal adherence of the intellectual Jew at two critical junctures: one, during the Graeco-Roman period, through Philo, and the other during the era of Arabic domination of the West, through Maimonides. The Jewish intellectual of Philo's era was a disciple of Plato. The Jewish intellectual of Maimonides' era was an Aristotelian. Both Philo and Maimonides, each in his own way, mastered the dominant philosophy of his era and utilized it to reconcile the Jewish intellectuals of his day to Jewish tradition. Both formulated the rationale for Judaism to fit the world-outlook of those who were inclined to challenge it.

The modern intellectual, whether Jew or non-Jew, does not philosophize along classical lines. Classical philosophy has for him a historical value as the product of speculative imagination, provided it does not degenerate into medieval mysticism or modern emotive vebiage. His is an altogether different realm of thought. It differs not only from that of Plato and Aristotle, but even from that of Kant and the post-Kantians. Those ideationist philosophies can no longer provide Judaism with a rationale that is likely to put a halt to the escapism of Jewish intellectuals.

None of the four movements in Judaism, the three denominational and the one secular, appeals to the spiritually-minded intellectual Jew. He would want Judaism to reckon with a conception of God that is based on experience as authentic as the sense of moral responsibility, and not merely on tradition, whether revealed or philosophic. He would want the Jewish way of life to stress the primacy of ethical values, and to have the Jewish rituals activate such consciousness of God as to evoke the conscience of man. He would like to see the Jews striving to evolve a civilization in Zion that is based on freedom, justice and good will, and endeavoring, in the Diaspora, to help the native civilizations of the countries where they live achieve those same goals. In brief, he would want the Jews to covenant themselves anew to strive to become "a People in the image of God," not the God of tradition nor of classical philosophy, but God as the Power within ourselves and within nature as a whole that impels and helps men and nations to become fully human.

From the standpoint of Jewish existence, the present predicament in Jewish life began to develop in the beginning of the nineteenth century. It differs from any past Jewish situation in the following three respects:

1) In pre-modern times, Jews throughout the world professed implicit faith in the divine authorship of the Mosaic Torah, and subscribed to the binding authority of the rabbinic interpretation of that Torah. Modern enlightenment has undermined that faith and has deprived Jewish life of

any authoritative guidance, either for belief or practice, that might act as a unifying bond among Jews.

2) Throughout the past, all Jews had implicit faith in the ultimate resumption of national life in Eretz Yisrael, their ancient homeland which figured in their consciousness, each time they engaged in their thrice daily prayers and recited the benedictions after each meal. The granting of civic rights to the Jews, which changed their status from aliens to citizens, has been an invitation to the Jews to renounce their sense of national solidarity and their expectation to return to Eretz Yisrael.

3) Throughout the past, the will of the Jews to survive as a people was reinforced by the religious climate of the non-Jewish world. The Judeo-Christian tradition then existed in fact, whereas now it exists only in name. In Jewish law, Christians and Moslems were not regarded as idolators. The reason given for that attitude toward them is that they believed in the creation of the universe by God out of nothing and in all the miracles recorded in the Bible. The concept "Judeo-Christian tradition" was thus actually given legal status (cf. Moshe Rivkes, Comment on *Shulkan Arukh, Hoshen Mishpat,* Hilkot Hovel 425.5). The Jews occupied an important place in the Christian and Moslem world-outlook. Even though that fact led to their being victims of relentless persecution, it fortified their determination to suffer martyrdom for their religion. Nowadays, however, the challenge to Judaism emanates from the intellectual climate which challenges all traditional religions as being outlived and irrelevant. Though they still seem to play a role in the life of men and nations, they are definitely in retreat.

"The two Catholic religious civilizations," writes A. N. Whitehead, "are Christianity and Buddhism, and—if we are to judge by the comparison of their position now with what it has been—both of them are in decay. They have lost their ancient hold on the world" (*Religion in the Making,* 1926,

p. 44). In Soviet Russia and its satellites the traditional religions are being systematically extirpated. The most telling symptoms of the ultimate elimination of the traditional religions from the practical affairs of human life are: first, the establishment of the United States on the principle of separation of Church and State; and, secondly, the progressive elimination of religion as personal commitment from the curricula of colleges and universities.

Each of the foregoing three factors in the present situation contributes in large measure to the disintegration of Jewish life. Each of them elicits the question: Why remain a Jew? It is the third factor, however—namely, the secularist, rationalist climate of opinion—which is the most challenging and which has to be countered with a rationale in terms of which Jews would have to engage in the following: 1) reconstitute themselves as a people, so as to recover, at least for part of their number, political autonomy in Eretz Yisrael, and for those in the Diaspora, at least spiritual autonomy, and, 2) foster *a credible psychological equivalent,* for our day, of the traditional attitude toward the Torah as divinely revealed.

The kind of rationale which might achieve the foregoing results cannot be based on any of the classical philosophies, in part or as a whole, which influenced the thinking of Hermann Cohen or of the Reform movement in Judaism. It has to be based on the same type of inductive approach to reality as that which has opened up new horizons of experience and knowledge in all other fields of human concern. If the approach of the ideationist philosophies may be said to have been dialectic and deductive, that of the functionalist philosophies may be said to be operative and inductive.

The contrast between the two types of philosophy is reflected in the contrast between the way they conceive their objective. Both types of philosophy have the same objective: to identify what is authentic behind the illusory world of evanescent phenomena. To the ideationists, authenticity is that which is static, identical, and immutable behind the ceaseless stream of changing phenomena. To the functionalists, authenticity is that which is prognostic, reliable and creative. To the classicists, the criterion of what is authentic is *semper idem;* to the moderns, it would be *semper melius.* To the classicists, the Golden Age was in the past. According to their theologians, we are all condemned to suffer the consequences of original sin; to the moderns "the best is yet to be."

It was a comparatively easy task for the traditional theologians like Philo and Maimonides among the Jews, and for Augustine and Thomas Aquinas among the Christians, to make peace between their respective religions and their respective classic philosophies, the Platonic or Aristotelian. That was the case because religion and philosophy in the past conceived as authentic that which was static or immutable. Religion for them pointed to God and His law as authentic because of those attributes. Philosophy, likewise, pointed to the ideas as that which in all things is their static, identical, or immutable element. On the other hand, things visible, audible or tangible were illusory and unreal. Hence revelation and reason could not but express the same truth, even if in different language. That was the basic assumption of all pre-modern theologians as well as of most pre-modern intellectuals.

The overwhelming majority of modern-minded intellectuals can no longer be persuaded to regard the limitless range of the data of experience as illusion, and to accept some limited series of abstract ideas as authenticity. They refuse to accept the sharp dualism between experience and idea. There can be no experience without ideas, nor ideas without experience. Since experience implies either acting or being acted upon, all thought is thought of, for, or about, action of some kind. Since all action is change from one state of being to another, the thought that is related to action is the element of continuity in change. Einstein's formula $E = mc^2$ is the formula for the element of continuity in the vast manifold of physical data. Authenticity therefore for the scientifically minded person is any process or changing situation, insofar as we can identify in it an element of continuity.

What has all this to do with a rationale for Judaism? It means that, as Jews, we cannot do without Judaism as a religious civilization; nor can we do with Judaism as it has come down to us from pre-modern times. Henceforth Jewish religion, or the religious aspect of Jewish civilization, must be *au courant* with the most advanced thought and the most progressive social aspiration, and at the same time be *inherently continuous* with the religion of the Bible and the Talmud. For such continuity to be possible, there must be a functioning and identifiable Jewish People. To become a people once more, the Jews have to build a state, and to reconstitute themselves as a People on the basis of a new type of polity. Such a deliberate and difficult task cannot be undertaken, much less be achieved, unless motivated by some high purpose. *For us Jews there can be no higher purpose than that of exemplifying the art of so living individually and collectively as to contribute to the intellectual, moral and spiritual progress of mankind.*

To achieve that goal calls, in the first place, for a conception of God that is compatible with what has come to be regarded as the most helpful and creative approach to the philosophic problem of what is authentic in human experience. That rules out the traditional conception of God as a Person, in the image of man, raised to the degree of infinite perfection. It also rules out the idea of God as formulated in the philosophic tradition, whether as first cause, as final cause, as inherently in no need of logical proof, or as guarantor for the ultimate triumph of the right. God, who in the Jewish religious tradition figures as creator, law-giver, and source of righteousness and mercy, will have to mean to the modern intellectual Jew that aspect of nature as a whole which makes for the maximum fulfillment of man's highest ethical and creative potentialities.

That is the God of whom we have immediate experience whenever we deliberately act out of a sense of responsibility, honesty, loyalty or love, and creativity. Such ethical conduct reflects cosmic traits which are manifest throughout the universe. Those traits are respectively: polarity, authenticity, organicity, and creativity. The concurrent functioning of these cosmic traits in man elicit from him the best he can be and do, and enable him to bear the worst that may befall him. Moreover, as a correlate of the ideal mankind to be, or of the Messianic future as envisaged by the prophets, that concurrent functioning of cosmic traits is Divinity. Though not spelled out in these terms, this is, in effect, how Hermann Cohen would have us conceive God. The fact that he identifies God as purely an "idea" robs the belief in God of the feeling of authenticity. Cohen's answer to the question: "How can one love an idea?" is: "How is it possible to love anything but an idea?" (*Religion der Vernunft,* p. 187). Only to a tender-minded ideationist is such an answer acceptable.

If we Jews wish to exemplify what it means to make self-and-world improvement the goal of human life, we have to continue the process inaugurated by our traditional Torah. That process consists of ordering our collective life as a spiritually autonomous people, in accord with the Covenant which Moses had our ancestors make with God, the Creator of the world, who is also the God of all mankind. That Covenant which has been renewed several times in the course of our three-thousand-year-old history is, in effect, a Constitution which confers upon us the status of an organic society entitled to exist in perpetuity. It is spelled out into a way of life which is intended to make of us "a People in the image of God."

That way of life has always differed from the way of life

promulgated by other religions and by the traditional philosophies. It has always stressed the role which the organic collective group plays in the moulding of the life of the individual. That way of life still implies the empirically tested fact that, unless the nation, the people, or any other community to which a person belongs, is more than an organization of power, that person must find it difficult, if not impossible, to act justly and to love mercy and to walk humbly with his God. Ancient Stoicism, which was a religious philosophy, or a philosophical religion, assumed the opposite. Stoicism maintained that, if every individual person would attend to his own moral development, society would take care of itself. That assumption has proved to be a mistake.

Jewish religion recognizes intuitively that the humanization of man cannot take place only through each human being, individually, aiming at his own salvation. Also the nation as a whole, to which the individual belongs, has to be animated by the divine traits of moral responsibility, authenticity, loyalty or love, and creativity, in relation to each of its members and to all other nations. Only then is the individual likely to achieve those traits in his relation to all with whom he has occasion to interact. This is what is meant by being "a People in the image of God." This is what the Mosaic Torah aimed at having the people of Israel become. Not only the people of Israel, but every people can and should become "a people in the image of God." When that comes about, the Messianic Age will have arrived.

Now that the Jews have established the State of Israel, they have the opportunity of demonstrating there what it means for a nation to become "a People in the image of God." It must be remembered that the State of Israel is a project of the entire Jewish People, and not merely of those who inhabit it. Jews throughout the Diaspora have made its establishment possible, not merely as a home for those who were homeless, but as a land where the purpose spelled out in the

Torah of having the Israelites become "a People in the image of God" might be resumed. That is the philosophy of Judaism which A. D. Gordon, the most ideologically constructive pioneer of the Zionist movement, lived and taught.

What of those Jews, however, who wish to remain in the Diaspora? For them to adopt the program which Hermann Cohen's philosophy calls for is tantamount to spiritual suicide. In Germany, where Cohen expected his program to meet with fulfillment within at most a half-century, most Jews who could not escape in time were exterminated. As long as nations either tacitly or admittedly strive to become peoples in the Nietzchean image of the "Blond Beast," there is every reason in the world why the Jews everywhere should reaffirm and reactivate their corporate status as a People. They owe it to the God of mankind to insure the security and spiritual development of the State of Israel, and to promote in each country of which they are citizens all such measures as will make also of its nation "a people in the image of God." To achieve that purpose, Jews, as a living, united, Zion-centered, trans-national people, must strive to become what Cohen himself regarded as having been the prophetic conception of Israel: "Not merely a human aggregate with needs and obligations, but the ideal human person incarnate" (*Religion der Vernunft,* p. 275).

The foregoing account of the direction which Judaism and the Jewish People must take, if they are to survive in the present-day world, is radically different from that implied in Hermann Cohen's *Religion der Vernunft.* That difference is due, not so much to the difference between the philosophies which are their respective starting points, as to the difference between a realistic and an unrealistic grasp of the *facts* of life, or the *data of experience.* Cohen was at first too steeped in Kantian ideationism, and later too absorbed in the task of revising it and evolving Neo-Kantianism, to realize that the German nation, whose world-outlook was influenced by a cruel anti-Semitic religious fanatic like Luther, was not the kind of nation to adopt the Messianic ideal of ethical socialism. He did not realize that religion was many, and that each religion was an integral and non-transferrable part of a particular civilization. In his study of the Jewish sources, *he failed to note that Judaism was an evolving religious civilization, and not merely a religion.* He failed, as it were, to see the wood for the trees in it.

Only with that as a hypothesis, are we in a position to state specifically, first, why none of the rationales which contributed to the survival of Judaism in pre-modern times is any longer relevant, and, secondly, what are the criteria of relevance in a rationale for our day.

The rationale inherent in the Torah itself proved to be inadequate, as we have seen, as soon as Jews came under the influence of Greek culture and philosophy. Both Philo and Maimonides elaborated rationales of the kind that were standard in pre-modern times also for Christianity and Islam. That standard was based on the assumption that their respective religious traditions had been supernaturally revealed by God. Their validity was beyond question. Hence they could not possibly be in conflict with reason, since both revelation and reason sought to enable man to know what was the true, or authentic, way of life by which he could achieve salvation. Accordingly, the function of reason in pre-modern times was regarded as being merely that of confirming the validity of the religious tradition, not only as a whole, but also in all its details of belief and practice.

With the advent of modernism, however, a radical change in the foregoing assumption took place. The faith in the religious tradition has been shaken by the scientific study of its origin and development. Its limitations and fallibility have been established beyond a doubt. Hence the function of a rationale for validating religious tradition has come to be that of *selecting* from it that which is compatible with reason, which is the last court of appeal. That is what Hermann Cohen has attempted in his *Religion der Vernunft*. A modern rationale for Judaism must follow, if not in substance, at least in form, his new approach to the problem of validating the Jewish religious tradition. It has to *select* and *validate* those beliefs and practices in that tradition which, either in their original meaning or in some reinterpretation of it, are compatible with the dictates of reason.

Why, then, has Cohen's rationale for Judaism proved to be inadequate? The answer is to be found in his inadequate conception of the function of reason itself. While he correctly regards reason as a means of identifying what is authentic in experience, he misconceives authenticity by identifying it with what is static and immutable. Moreover, with regard to religion, he correctly stresses its ethical function as primary, but he misconceives the scope of ethics as limited to interpersonal relations. He overlooks what he himself implies in his discussion of Messianism as the correlate of the idea of God, namely, the fact that ethics applies also to intergroup and international as well as to interpersonal relations. Consequently, the very primacy of ethics in Jewish religion calls for the permanent and creative survival of Jewish peoplehood, a survival that is inconceivable without rootedness in its original homeland.

Despite the inadequacy of Cohen's rationale for Judaism, we can learn from it what are the criteria of an objective and adequate rationale for Judaism of our day. In the first place, such a rationale has to *select* from the Judaism of the past those beliefs and practices which, either in their original or in a reinterpreted form, are compatible with what we now recognize to be authentic. To be authentic, Judaism as a civilization, or way of life, has to prescribe a world-outlook and a conception of God that can impel and direct us to live, in our intergroup and international relations, in a spirit of moral responsibility, honestly, lovingly, and creatively, and so to live in our interpersonal relations as to leave the world the better and the happier for our having lived.

In the American, or any other free political environment outside the State of Israel, one who is born a Jew, especially if he is of a reflective turn of mind, cannot automatically remain a Jew. As soon as he becomes mature enough to think on his own, he has to accept his remaining a Jew as a matter of choice and deliberate commitment. Such commitment is generally assumed as being merely a matter of accepting the traditional idea of God and observing the ritual practices associated with that idea. Actually, however, to choose to remain a Jew is a three dimensional affair. It involves choosing to belong to the Jewish People, to believe in Jewish religion, and to practice the Jewish way of life. In terms of contemporary philosophy, Judaism as an evolving religious civilization is *existentially* Jewish peoplehood, *essentially* Jewish religion, and *functionally* the Jewish way of life.

If the average intellectual Jew, therefore, is to be convinced that he ought to remain a Jew, he has to be assured, in the first place, that the Jewish People, which is at present in a state of formlessness, is on the way to being reconstituted. Secondly, he has to be made to realize that the Jewish conception of God has not been static and immutable, but on the contrary, has been evolving *pari passu* with the progress of the human mind. And, finally, he has to be made aware that the Jewish way of life is capable of giving primacy to those values which are essential to human survival and progress. Each of these three Jewish objectives will now be discussed in detail.

The reconstitution of the Jewish People is an incomparably far more difficult goal to attain than was the establishment of the State of Israel. It took fifty years of Jewish organized campaigning in behalf of Zionism before the nations of the world took cognizance of the collective voice of the Jewish

People and recognized its claim that it was entitled to a homeland in (what was then) Palestine. It took, in addition, the annihilation of more than one-third of the Jewish People and the desperate courage of a quarter of a million Jews in Palestine to compel the United Nations to sanction the existence of the State of Israel.

When we survey the present condition of world Jewry, from the standpoint of the possible emergence of a united Jewish People, we are liable to conclude that such a consummation is not merely utopian—it is quixotic. Unless we have faith in the capacity of the Jewish People to experience resurrection, there is no need to discuss the matter any further. Unless we can relive in our very bones the vision of Ezekiel in the Valley of the Dead Bones, no plea for the reconstitution of the Jewish People is of any avail. On the other hand, wishful thinking alone, however ardent, will not bring about the resurrection. Yearning has to be translated into planned effort to resuscitate whatever life still inheres in the Jewish People, and to remotivate whatever urge to go on living it still retains.

Two lines of effort to resuscitate whatever life still inheres in the Jewish People have to be initiated forthwith. Collectively, all existing institutions and organizations in Jewish life should reformulate their purposes and redirect their activities on a communal basis, as though the Jewish People were already reconstituted; individually, every Jew should habituate himself to think and act as though the Jewish People were already a reality. Judaism must henceforth be taught and preached with the aim in view of fostering the state of mind known as an affirmative Jewish consciousness. In other words, our immediate task is to provide the reconstitution of the Jewish People with a thoroughly valid *raison d'être*, so that the individual Jew, in striving for that reconstitution and in ordering his own life, as though it were already a fact, would enjoy the experience of living a more rational and more moral life than he would otherwise.

In the entire history of religion we do not find any people other than the People of Israel that set up such a goal for itself. Probably Moses in the wilderness and Samuel in Eretz Yisrael conceived that ambitious aim for the People of Israel. The Divinity, in whose name Moses gave direction to the life of the Israelites, could not be conceived as divided among a number of divine beings. The God who sent Elijah to rebuke Ahab for being a party to the crime of killing Naboth had to be known also as the God who gave rain. That is how the ancient Israelites arrived at the intuition that the Power that supplied their physical needs expected that they would use those supplies in accordance with His law of righteousness. To be authentic, Divinity had to be conceived as one and indivisible. Accordingly, the God of Israel could not brook the worship of other gods.

The Israelite tribes, who were constituted as a people by means of a covenant with this one and indivisible God, found it difficult to rise to the spiritual heights of a Moses or a Samuel and to live up to the terms of the covenant. But the influence of these men of God lived on among small groups of devotees to their teachings, and in later centuries it produced the great prophets whose words are recorded in the Bible. For the first time in the history of religion we meet what is, in effect, a people engaging in self-evaluation and self-criticism. The prophets assumed that the religion as practiced by their contemporaries was a corruption of the religion their ancestors had been taught in the wilderness. Thus Jeremiah explicitly denounces the sacrificial cult as an alien form of worship which had been adopted by the People of Israel (7.22).

The incentive to reconstitute the Jewish People cannot be the belief in the divine chosenness of the Jewish People. If we really believed that God had singled out the Jews for some high destiny, we would see no need for trying to reconstitute our People; we would leave that to God. Nor can we depend upon the sense of mission to convert the rest of the world to ethical monotheism. What we need is to believe in the inherent genius of Jewish peoplehood to elicit from the individual Jew the best of which he is capable. Where else can we expect to find evidences of that genius if not in our religious tradition?

However, that tradition, in the form in which it has come down to us, is dated. It was relevant to climes and times other than our own. If the pulse of peoplehood still throbs within us, we can get our tradition to be relevant to the unprecedented conditions of our day. It has to keep pace intellectually with the most advanced thinking and with the most advanced social action. If our religious tradition is to meet these requirements, its doctrines have to be reinterpreted and its laws have to be revised, in the light of what is most conducive to the good and fulfilled life on an individual and collective scale. Such light can be shed only by an understanding of the nature of religion itself, and of its role in the life of men and nations. All that presupposes a complete transformation of our habits of thought and action as Jews. Nothing less than such transformation will get us to believe in the great potential of the Jewish People, and to take the necessary measures to reconstitute it.

A genuine understanding of religion is precluded by the conventional notions about it. They all boil down to the assumption that, whereas politics, economics, science, technics, art and morals have their respective sources in normal and communicable experience, and tend to improve with the growth of experience, religion derives from a source of truth that transcends that kind of experience, and is not affected by it. Only those who have access to that transcendent source of truth are supposed to be able to mediate it to their fellowmen. It is generally assumed that for the mass man religion must remain an object only of vicarious and not of direct experience. It is therefore to be exempt from the kind of free inquiry to which we ordinarily subject experiences of a secular character.

As long as the experience on which religion was based in the past helped to make life more bearable than it would otherwise have been, the fact that it was of a vicarious and not of a personal character was of little consequence. When the acceptance of that vicarious experience, as though it were personal experience, contributed to one's social status, and when, in addition, it helped one maintain an even keel through life's storms, religion was no problem. That the particular group to which one belonged, as was the case with Jews throughout the centuries, possessed no military power or prestige, and that to be identified with it invited hostility and persecution, did not matter, as long as the original experience on which Jewish religion was based was firmly believed to be historical. That is no longer the case. The overwhelming majority of the Jews throughout the world no longer believe that the events which are recorded in the Mosaic Torah, and which throughout the centuries have served as the unimpeachable rationale for Jewish existence, ever took place. That is an incomparably more serious challenge to Jewish existence than that with which Maimonides had to cope in his *Guide for the Perplexed*.

At the present time many Jews manage to sidle out of Jewish life, without shocking their Jewish friends and acquaintances; at the same time they augment their chances of being accepted by Gentile society. Why should they take the trouble to transmit the Jewish religious tradition to their children, since they no longer believe in the historicity of the events on which it is based? Why, in the words of Arthur Koestler, should they place an unnecessary burden on their children's shoulders? There are those who maintain that Jews who had been alienated from Judaism have of late been returning to it. The fact is that in most instances the Jewish children are the ones who, seeing their Christian playmates or classmates identified with the religion of their parents, pressure their own parents for some kind of religious identification. This is particularly true of the suburban areas into which Jews are moving from the large cities.

Some Jewish parents, to be sure, gratify those wishes of their children. They first organize a religious school and hire teachers for the Sunday School. Those teachers, likely as not, form study groups for adults. Before long ground is bought and a costly synagogue is put up. That kind of religious activity, being "other directed" from the start, does not strike deep roots. The members of the building committee, who have never missed a fund raising meeting, seldom step into the synagogue after the dedication ceremonies are over. Jews have come to be known as "Seventh Day Absentists." The synagogue movements may somewhat retard the process of absorption of the Jews by the rest of the population, but they cannot stop it. Perhaps that process would be stopped altogether, if Jews would realize that they have the opportunity to experience through Judaism the thrill of human self-fulfillment which transcends all worldly success.

Nowadays the Damocles sword has been transformed into a super-monster of fifty megatons—the equivalent of 50 million tons of TNT, and the caves of the rocks and the holes of the ground into which Isaiah bade his contemporaries to hide in terror are taking the form of bomb shelters. All this has come about because the dominant religions of the world have condoned war, and have been more interested in advancing their own power and prestige than in improving human character and promoting international peace. If, by some miracle, mankind is spared the cataclysm which threatens it at present, *every* religion will have to be transformed into an agency for universal justice, freedom and peace. Should not the Jews take the first step in that direction, by making their religion into an instrument for the moral and spiritual humanization of man? It was for such a purpose that the Jewish religion came into being. Though diverted again and again from that purpose through their own ineptitude and through the hostility of the nations, the Jewish People is still being haunted by it. The establishment of the State of Israel, and the renascence of Jewish life there, are likely to reactivate that purpose, so that *throwing in one's lot with the Jewish People can come to mean living for that which might save mankind from impending doom, and which might render human life itself worthwhile.* In order that this become the meaning of involvement in Jewish life, our notions of religion in general, and of Jewish religion in particular, have to undergo a radical revision.

Religion can no longer operate *with* a tradition which speaks in terms that are alien to the *personal* experience of the average intellectual man or woman. On the other hand, it cannot operate *without* a tradition. An authentic religion is not the same as a personal philosophy of life. Its main function is to involve the individual in the social and spiritual heritage of a historic society and to commit him to the transmission of that heritage. A religion is even *more* than what its tradition expressly expects its adherents to believe about God, and what it expects them to do in order to earn His grace. It tacitly, though no less firmly, expects its adherents to identify themselves with all the generations of their forebears who created that tradition and lived by it. Self-involvement in the social and spiritual heritage, and commitment to transmit it, are bound to transform the vicarious experience of the reality of God into a personal experience.

A verse in the first Psalm describes the ideal human being as follows: "His desire is in the Torah of the Eternal, and in his Torah he meditates day and night." The Sages in commenting on this verse add: "Through the study of Torah, the follower of God transforms what was God's Torah into his own Torah." The Prophet Isaiah, on the other hand, gives a vivid description of a religious tradition which is not integrated into one's personal experience in the following scripture: "This people draw near me with their mouth and honor me with their lips, while their hearts are far removed; their religion is a mockery, a mere tradition learned by rote" (Isa. 29.13).

For a religious tradition to become a part of our personal experience nowadays, it has to possess the authenticity we associate with scientific fact. It has to convey the kind of literal meaning which we can integrate into our normal experience. No religious tradition can do that, unless its supernaturalism is translated into naturalistic terms. That, however, is a small price a people has to pay for the sense of historic continuity which confers meaning and zest upon its career in the world. The fact is that our own Jewish tradition can without difficulty be translated into naturalist religious experience.

The traditions of all the great religions arose during the first or archaic period of civilization, when the individual mind had not yet emerged. That may be designated as the stage of spontaneous thinking. In time, when the individual mind began to emerge, civilization attained the stage of speculative thinking. Finally, the era in which we live began to dawn with the rise of modern science in the sixteenth century. Our era may therefore be characterized as the stage of scientific thinking. It is evident, of course, that this stylized separation of the different stages of a civilization does not mean that each stage corresponds to a particular era of that civilization. Survivals of the archaic period of a people's culture exist contemporaneously with the most advanced products of the latest period. That is particularly true of religious culture which, more than any other, suffers from lag. That fact currently complicates the problem of religion in general. If, however, we are to disentangle that problem, *we have to*

limit our consideration to those Jews who nowadays are sci-
entifically oriented. We should help them find in Jewish re-
ligion their vocation as members of a reconstituted Jewish
people.

To be able to help them, however, we have to communicate
with them in terms of their universe of discourse. We must
realize that those who have become imbued with the spirit
and method of scientific thinking cannot but regard traditional religion as outdated. Its conception of God as a personal Being, its stories of miracles by which He made His
presence known, its creed concerning the reward of the righteous and the punishment of the wicked, its claim to be in
possession of the ultimate truth about man, society and the
world as a whole and of the key to salvation, are as obsolete
as is the biblical mind-picture of the earth with a windowed
heaven overarching it. There is hardly any need for recount-
ing what the scientific study of the biblical text has done to
undermine its reliability as a source of moral and religious
truth. The general public, whether Jewish or non-Jewish, by
dint of their *cultural* lag, manage to live complacently, with
their minds divided between their intelligence which they
use on week days and their will to believe which they exercise
on Sabbaths. In the daily issues of peace and war which agi-
tate mankind, the traditional religion is, by dint of its supernaturalism, condemned to sheer irrelevance and ultimately
to fossilization or disappearance.

The only reason that traditional religion is not entirely
dead, and even seems to flourish again, is that the human being actually needs and wants religion, religion that shall give
ethical purpose and meaning to his life as a human being.
Mankind is today hungering for the peace of mind which can
come only with the end of all war, both civil and international. There was a time when people believed that with the
progress of science and technology it would be possible to
abolish disease, poverty, ignorance and war. It was assumed

that man would then be able to dispense with religion, which was supposed to evoke supernatural means for the abolition of those evils. While, however, the improvement in the physical condition of human life has progressed in arithmetical proportion, the menace of conflicting interests and of global war leading to the annihilation of the human race has grown in geometric proportions. Such is the outcome of progress in science and technology, unaccompanied by equal progress in morality and religion.

How can we resolve the dilemma in which man finds himself? He has mastered tremendous powers which can both create and destroy, but he has failed to achieve the self-mastery which is needed to bring them under control. None of the sciences, not even the human sciences like psychology or sociology, can teach man self-mastery. They can only describe what man is and does. They have no authority to command what he ought to be or do, no rational influence to which man must submit, if he is to achieve self-mastery. Nor can traditional religion any longer exercise any influence, because of its dependence upon the belief in the supernatural, which lies beyond the realm of human experience.

The only way out of that dilemma is to evolve the kind of religion which can command self-mastery, without resort to the supernatural. That means, in the first place, extending scientific research in the domain of the natural, in order to find there the *sources* of those moral and spiritual tendencies in man which have elicited whatever degree of self-mastery has brought him to the present stage of his development. Secondly, it means fostering a conception of Godhood or Divinity which identifies it with those sources of the moral and spiritual tendencies in man. Those sources do exist in the domain of nature, or of the cosmos as a whole. In their concurrence and interactivity they constitute Godhood, or the Power that makes for man's self-mastery and for his salvation or fulfillment.

None of the historical religions other than that of the Jewish People is capable of undergoing the reconstruction which is essential to rendering it relevant to the urgent needs of contemporary mankind. That is the case because of the unique character of the Jewish religion. *It is the only religion of mankind, which, from its very inception, has been based on the on-going history of a people in its relation to mankind.* Most Bible scholars misunderstand the religion of the Hebrew Bible when they maintain that it belongs to the ancient class of national religions. They are misled by the fact that God in that Bible is given the name *Yahweh,* and is designated the God of Israel. They fail to realize that any possible comparison with other deities is negated by the word *ehad,* which occasionally means "The only authentic one" as well as "lone" (cf. II Sam. 7.23; Ezek. 37.22; Koh. 4.8; I Chr. 17.21). Accordingly the great rallying cry: "Hear, O Israel, Yahweh is our God, Yahweh is *ehad,*" calls upon Israel to recognize Yahweh as the only authentic God. Such an idea as that there is actually only one god who is an authentic deity was absolutely inconceivable to the other peoples of the world. It could have been entertained only by a people that conceived all mankind as intrinsically a unit, and its division into nations as only a temporary condition which will come to an end when Yahweh will be acknowledged King over all the earth. "On that day shall Yahweh be the only God and His name the lone One" (Zach. 14.9).

The truth is that the resemblance of biblical religion to the national religions of ancient times is entirely incidental. That resemblance is completely nullified by the obsessive emphases throughout Jewish tradition on the solity or onliness of the God of Israel. "He alone is God and there is none other beside him" is the keynote of the religion of Israel in *all* stages of its development. That means that our ancestors had a totally different notion of what constituted Divinity or Godhood from that which prevailed in the rest of the world. The ancient national religions regarded Godhood as residing principally in the visible objects, whether animate or inanimate, of the physical world. Those religions inherited from primitive religions that sense of kinship between human beings and the animal world which found expression in animal worship among so highly civilized a people as the ancient Egyptians. Not so in Jewish religion, which put man on a pedestal, as the purpose of creation. Man as the possessor of self-awareness and of the freedom to choose among alternative courses of action belongs to a higher order of being than the beasts. *Moreover, Jewish religion has always assumed that, for man to maintain his God-likeness, he has to be the product of a people which orders its life in accordance with the will of God, or God-given Torah. That was the kind of people ancient Israel aspired to become.* Thus, in our present way of speaking, built into the Jewish consciousness is the striving to have the Jewish People foster a type of civilization that is calculated to render man fully and divinely human.

All of this is implied in what the Bible has to say about God and His relation to ancient Israel. This fact must now be made explicit and be grasped by us Jews, if we wish to understand the miracle of Jewish history. The Jews have almost always been a people at the mercy of great world empires. Our ancestors came into being as a people during an interlude in the struggles between the East (Mesopotamia) and the West (Egypt) in ancient times. The Jewish People has managed to impress itself on the consciousness of the Western nations and of many Eastern ones. They have gone to the extent of virtually forgetting their own past and adopting the past of the Jewish People as though it were their own past.

It is true that the Western and the Near Eastern nations have used the past of the Jewish People merely as a preface to their own kind of religion, the Christian nations for theirs and the Moslem nations for theirs. *As long, however, as the*

Jewish People is alive, it has the opportunity to demonstrate the true function of religion as being to make of each people or nation a medium for the nurturing of the ideal human type that would be an embodiment of Divinity or the Divine aspect of the cosmos. To qualify for such a vocation Jews have to relearn the true meaning and function of their own historical religion, as a religion based on the ongoing history of a people. They have also to become fully aware that a people with a historical religion like the Jewish religion is blessed with an extraordinary capacity for spiritual growth and creativity.

The past of the Jewish People can be shown to have been a record of its determination to subject its life and destiny to the will of the one and only authentic Divinity. Its intuition that Divinity to be authentic had to be the Creator of the world and the Lawgiver of righteousness happens to coincide with the fact that creativity and righteousness are indispensable to the life of men and nations. That does not mean that the Jewish People as a whole was aware from the very beginning of the specific implications of its religious intuition. It has needed contact with other civilizations and cultures to outgrow the primitive and immature ideas it associated with Divinity, before it could learn to identify as the operation of cosmic processes those human traits of moral responsibility, authenticity, loyalty or love and creativity which make for the good and abundant life we term salvation.

Moreover, the criterion which the prophets stressed for the authenticity of a religion was that it must give primacy to ethical conduct in all of men's dealings with one another. This, together with peoplehood as providing the milieu for the manifestation of Divinity, gave rise to a new type of religion. Divinity came to be regarded as manifest principally in those of man's desires and needs which were the expression of his ethical and spiritual potentialities. Stated in terms of contemporary experience, this new conception of Divinity, which emerges from the prophets' criticism of the religion of their contemporaries, means that *Divinity is to be beheld in the moral and spiritual uses to which man puts the power he acquires through his manipulation of the forces of nature.*

All this must lead to but one conclusion: stated in terms of the most urgent human needs, the Jewish People is committed *to the promulgation of that belief in God which can impel man to create a social order based on freedom, justice, peace and love.* That commitment is spelled out in its Torah which is as ongoing and evolving as the Jewish People itself, and to which is applied the designation of "thy life and the length of thy days" (Deut. 30.20). Jewish religion is the only religion which has grown not merely out of the life, but out of the self-conscious history of a people. Its method of apotheosizing its own history might be adopted by all nations in search of spiritual homogeneity that is compatible with political freedom and theological diversity.

We Jews, therefore, have to transpose our traditional religion, which is set to the key of supernaturalism, into the key of naturalism, by tracing its ethical strivings to laws inherent in the cosmos. In doing so, we shall effect the same kind of spiritual and moral revolution as our ancestors did when they proclaimed that there was only one God, and that it was Him alone they and all the rest of mankind should acknowledge as God. That is henceforth to be our vocation. That is a sufficiently valid and inspiring purpose to motivate us to reconstitute ourselves as a People, to reinterpret our religious tradition in the light of that vocation, and to revise our way of life so as to render it effective as a means to our becoming a People in the image of God.

The type of religion which we Jews as a People, and which mankind as a whole, urgently need as a means to *survival* has to consist, or take the form, of *moral responsibility in action.* Moral responsibility, as said above, is the cosmic, and there-

fore the divine, law of polarity which functions in man as
conscience, the source of his rights and his duties. Rights derive from the selfhood or independence of the individual;
duties derive from his interdependence or interaction with
others. Rights without duties are brute might; duties without
rights are sheer slavery. The combination of the two which
go into the making of moral responsibility enables man to
fulfill himself as a human being, and so to live as to leave the
world the better and happier for his having lived.

The meaning of moral responsibility in action is spelled
out in what may be termed the divine rule formulated by
Hillel. That rule states: "If I am not for myself, who will be
for me? And being for my own self what am I? And if not
now, when?" Every individual life is rich, full and meaningful to the extent that it is consciously interlinked with the
lives of one's fellowmen. The isolated egoist who lives only
for himself lives an irresponsible life. The way to apply that
rule is indicated by the question: "If not now, when?" That
means that we have to utilize *immediately* every actual occasion and opportunity to translate both our independence
and interdependence into action. That is further spelled out
by an additional statement in the Talmud: "A person should
regard himself as though his deeds have been weighted in the
balance and as though half of them were in the scale of merit
and the other half in the scale of demerit. The next deed
which he is about to perform will determine his fate and that
of the rest of the world" (Kiddushin 40b). That implies that
each act we commit carries with it consequences for which
we are responsible at the very moment we act.

Religion as moral responsibility in action is needed to rid
us of three fatal illusions. First is the illusion of *collectivism*.
That illusion is due to the tendency to put the blame for the
wrong we commit upon the kind of society to which we belong. We underestimate the extent to which each of us individually initiates action. We like to imagine that we are mere

driftwood, swept along by the irresistible tide of social forces, political, economic or cultural. The Eichmann trial and execution, which took place in Israel, was needed as a demonstration of the principle that individual irresponsibility is an illusion. His plea that he was a mere helpless cog in a vast machine was shown to be a lie. As long as a person is sane enough to distinguish between right and wrong, he is responsible for what he does, no matter how great the social pressure that is exerted upon him.

The illusion of collectivism prevents us from realizing that each of us has a share in whatever preventable harm comes to others, however remote they may be from us. Recently a pugilist was killed in the boxing ring. A number of investigations were started to determine who was to blame for his death, whether it was the referee, the manager or the other pugilist. Norman Cousins pointed out that the blame ought to have been put on the prevailing *mores,* which regard prizefighting as a perfectly proper enterprise and vehicle of entertainment. Actually, everyone of the spectators whose presence made it possible for the boxing match to take place, and the millions who watched on television, had a share in the pugilist's death.

The more involved an individual is in activities of a far-reaching character the greater the field of his responsibility. That is especially true of those who exercise leadership in politics, industry and science. With regard to the last, Einstein wrote to leading scientists who held a conference in Italy, in 1950: "The unleashed power of the atom has changed everything but our way of thinking. We need essentially a new way of thinking if mankind is to survive."

The fundamental error of Communism consists in maintaining that the class to which an individual belongs determines his thinking. Hence, according to Communism, it is impossible for a person who belongs to the capitalist class to realize that he, as an individual, is responsible for depriving his employees of the "surplus value" which they create through their labor. That assumption is refuted by the fact that if not for Karl Marx, who as a banker's son belonged to the capitalist class, there would have been no Communism.

Edmond Cahn, in his book, *The Predicament of Modern Man,* tells the story of a district attorney who prosecuted an innocent young man in a case of murder and had him convicted to life imprisonment on the basis of the most circumstantial evidence, all because the district attorney had to prove the town safe for an international exposition that was held there. "Increasingly," writes Cahn, "since the beginnings of the modern period, we citizens find ourselves identified with the oppressing district attorney. Representative government has implicated us. It has made us participants—accomplices, if you will—in deeds done in our name and by our authority. The new predicament of democratic man is the moral involvement in the misdeeds of government."

A most forthright statement with regard to the far-reaching extent of the moral responsibility of each of us was President Kennedy's pronouncement on the Mississippi crisis: "Neither Mississippi nor any other state deserves to be charged with all the accumulated wrongs of the last hundred years of race relations to the extent that there has been failure. The responsibility for that failure must be shared by us all, by every state, by every citizen."

The second illusion of which moral responsibility is needed to rid us is that of "rugged individualism." That is the illusion that society is composed of individuals, each individual struggling to avoid pain and to secure as much pleasure as he can. Political and social relations are not supposed to have more than a superficial effect on the nature of the individual. The individual remains the same unchanged spiritually isolated atom. Most psychoanalytic theory and existentialist philosophy have revived that illusion of psychological atomism. That kind of individualism is like conceiving a net to be a collection of holes divided by twine.

The economic system based upon that illusion is that the competition among individuals is indispensable as a means of keeping goods and services at the lowest price. Pressure of population is regarded as necessary in order to keep wages near subsistence level. To assure an abundant labor supply, it is advisable not to disturb the improvidence of the poor. The *laissez-faire* policy (or so-called freedom), which is a corollary of this "rugged individualism," is supposed to work well not only within each state, but also among states in their relations to one another. Such is the philosophy of national isolationism.

Economically, it means making each country self-sufficient by developing its natural resources and banning foreign imports, and at the same time competing with other countries for the economic domination over foreign nations which are rendered dependent on its imports.

Politically, it means absolute sovereignty and refusal to reckon with world opinion or to submit to international law. The inevitable outcome of such international policy is a continuous state of cold war, which is liable, at the least provocation, to break out into shooting war. The illusion of individualism, whether of the person or of the state, is nothing but utter selfishness and the height of irresponsibility.

A third illusion from which the religion of moral responsibility in action should rid us is that you cannot change human nature. The argument runs: You cannot eradicate the law of self-preservation—as though the self to be preserved were encapsulated in an individual body. The fact is that the law of self-preservation operates in human society as a whole. Now that all human beings throughout the world have become inextricably bound up with one another, through the rapidity of transportation and communication and the threat of immediate world cataclysm, the survival of the human race has become impossible, unless human nature in the individual and in the collective undergoes a veritable metamorphosis.

It is true that traditional religion has always held out a distant prospect of such a metamorphosis. It has pictured the Messianic era when even the ravenous beasts would become tame. In the meantime, however, man has acquired far more power than he possesses the ability to bring under the control of moral responsibility. Never has Hillel's question, "And if not now, when?" been so pertinent and so ominous, unless forthwith answered in the spirit in which it is asked. That spirit is implied in the first two questions, the answer to which must be the combination and coalescence of what is true and good in collectivism with what is true and good in individualism, in independence and in interdependence. That combination of moral forces, which the conscience has to exert, must be the answer to that which has become the burning problem of our every-day existence: How to outlaw war and the manufacture of armaments. If not now, when?

The religion of moral responsibility in action can no longer afford to confine itself to vague abstractions about Deity and the moral law. It must be specific and concrete. It must address itself to all civilizations and peoples in terms of their respective memories, experiences, and problems and hopes. In other words, it has to be indigenous and not imported. Like the Jewish religion, the religion of active moral responsibility has to be universal in form and specific in content, speak in the name of humanity as a whole and be relevant to the particular interests of each particular nation.

The *purpose* of Jewish existence is to be a People in the image of God. The *meaning* of Jewish existence is to foster in ourselves as Jews, and to awaken in the rest of the world, a sense of moral responsibility in action.

The tendency to delight in contemplating lofty ideas like

the foregoing without translating them into action ultimately leads to despair of man's capacity to tame the beast in him.

"If not now, when?" Hillel reminded us.

The threat of global war and total annihilation of the human race is no longer a mere nightmare. It is an ominous reality at our very doorsteps, from which the most ingeniously contrived air raid shelters will not save us.

The moral responsibility of forestalling that dread possibility devolves on all of us individually and collectively. We dare not escape that responsibility by taking refuge in the claim of individual powerlessness. We act irresponsibly, in the first place, when we do not belong to some spiritual group that exists for the purpose of fostering moral and religious values. And we act irresponsibly when we do not persuade such groups to give primacy to the task of arousing the conscience of mankind to the imperative need of putting an end to all international and civil wars.

We Jews have a Day of Atonement for fasting and prayer, for the forgiveness of sins and the resolve to improve morally and spiritually. If we are to take ourselves and our religion seriously, we should observe the Day of Atonement primarily as a day of protest against the waging of war, and of appeal to all other spiritual bodies also to dedicate a day for fasting and prayer for like protest. Then will those in the seats of authority among the nations of the world be impelled to give heed, and use their power, to render the earth safe for mankind.

EPILOGUE

We Jews, as a permanent corporate entity, have in common a collective consciousness, known as Jewish consciousness. It has its roots in the Hebrew Bible. The oldest part of this Bible, known as "Torah," functioned in the lives of our ancient ancestors as a Declaration of Dependence upon the God of Mankind and as a Code of Law, governing their relations to that God and to one another.

Later there were added to Torah the other parts of the Bible, which have become part of the Jewish canon. They consist of history, prophecy, liturgy and wisdom; and together with Torah they constituted the foundation of the religio-cultural life of our forebears throughout the centuries of exile and dispersion. In the form of Written and Oral Torah, the religio-cultural heritage of the Jews helped to maintain their unity and solidarity, despite the lack of political unity since the destruction of the Second Commonwealth in the year 70 C.E.

The status of the Jews since then until the last quarter of the eighteenth century was a twofold one: that of a nation in exile, with their nationhood *in potentia,* and that of an *ecclesia (Knesset Yisrael)* based on Torah both Written and Oral. Every Jewish community throughout those centuries was governed by the rabbinate as the judicial arm and by lay leadership as the executive arm. There was no need for a legislative arm. On rare occasions, a leading rabbi issued an amendment to the Torah code, as in the case of Rabbenu Gershom, who issued a ban against polygamy that was accepted by other rabbis.

The foregoing form of religio-cultural polity, which was common to all Jews, together with their enforced segregation,

320

rendered unnecessary the issuance of any formal declaration as to their status both as a nation in exile and as an *ecclesia,* or religious community.

Both of the foregoing aspects of the status of Jews as a corporate entity became defunct as the result of the civil emancipation. Emancipation put an end to the alienage of the Jews and to their enforced segregation, and it integrated them into Western culture which, despite its retention of its Christian ecclesiastical polity, has become predominantly naturalist and secularist.

It is doubtful whether the corporate character of Jewish society would have survived, had the civic equality granted the Jews been unqualified and had it been extended to include economic, cultural and social equality. A limited and diminishing group of traditionalist Jews would probably have managed to segregate themselves from the general community and have survived as a spiritual backwater, remote from the main current of civilization. The overwhelming majority of the Jews would have been absorbed by the general population.

The lag, however, in the political and moral progress of the continental nations that granted civic rights to the Jews they harbored helped to keep alive the collective consciousness of the Jews, despite the break of most of them with their traditional religious solidarity as a result of the spread of secularism.

Thanks, on the other hand, to whatever collective consciousness most Jews still retained, they succeeded in organizing the Zionist movement, in reclaiming the greater part of their ancient homeland, and in establishing there a modern state known as the State of Israel.

Apart from its serving as a home for Jews who are homeless elsewhere, the State of Israel has rehabilitated the Jewish collective consciousness to the extent of arousing in it the desire to have all Jews throughout the world achieve, as a corporate entity, a status which would confer upon Jewish existence worthwhile purpose and directive meaning.

Such status can no longer be that of nation either *in esse* or *in potentia*. Nor can it be that of an *ecclesia,* as was the case throughout the centuries of exile. The status of a nation would require that the overwhelming majority of the Jews in the world settle in Israel. Moreover, it would, under present conditions, raise the problem of double loyalty for Jews living outside Israel. The reason the status of the Jews cannot any longer be that of an *ecclesia* is that it would require all Jews uniformly to subscribe to an authoritarian set of religious dogmas and to a regimen of religious practices. That is a condition which is entirely impracticable.

The inescapable conclusion is that the continued survival of the Jews as a corporate entity has to be compatible with a sense of historic continuity, despite the changes in the purpose and meaning of Jewish existence, and with a limited degree of diversity of religious belief and practice within functioning unity and solidarity.

To that end Jews have to evolve a third type of societal status, as an alternative to nationhood and churchhood (*ecclesia*), namely, that of peoplehood. All Jews should henceforth know themselves and be known by the rest of the world as a religio-cultural, or Torah, People.

The Jewish People shall henceforth be constituted of all Jews who are imbued with a collective Jewish consciousness, which functions in their lives as a source of inspiration and guidance in their strivings to achieve ethical and spiritual self-fulfillment.

No corporate entity can function without an agency to organize it and interpret its will in the form of laws or principles for those who constitute it. A nation has its government; a church has its hierarchy. Both exercise will that is authoritarian. A people, on the other hand, cannot exercise authoritarian will, since those who belong to it do so of their own *free* will. The only kind of agency that the Jews as a religio-cultural People can afford to submit to is one which by virtue of its intrinsic character can exercise moral and spiritual influence. It can only recommend, but not coerce.

It is a historic, though generally slighted, fact that what made it possible for the Jews as a People to outlive the mightiest nations and empires, and to endure the inhuman treatment of a world of enemies, was their implicit belief that God Himself had dictated the contents of the Pentateuchal Torah to Moses. That implicit belief provided our ancestors with sensate evidence of the existence of the God of mankind and of his special concern with them. Many Jews nowadays maintain that, since such belief has become obsolete, there can be no purpose or meaning to Jewish existence. Many more, however, like Hermann Cohen and other thinkers, despite their inability to subscribe to the traditional belief concerning the divine authorship of the Torah, somehow assume that they can continue to find purpose and meaning to Jewish existence. For that assumption to be valid it has to be related to an awareness of the reality of God that is based upon *personal and immediate experience.* Since there is no *sensate* object, whether historical or natural, that can yield personal and immediate experience of the reality of God, some *mental state* has to serve as the source of one's personal experience of the reality of God.

This book sets forth three distinct mental states, each of which has been proposed as the most likely source of personal experience of the reality of God. Hermann Cohen assumed that reason, exercised along metaphysical lines suggested by Kant, but brought into stricter lines with logic, impelled one to arrive at the certainty of God's existence. Martin Buber identifies as a personal experience of the reality of God the universalization of our emotional reaction to our fellowman as a "Thou" instead of as an "It." I, on the other hand, assume that rather than the intellect, as with Hermann Cohen, or feeling, as with Martin Buber, *the human will,* as it functions in one's conscience, is the most reliable and universal medium through which one can experience most vividly the reality of God.

The first person to have hit upon this idea and to have discovered that this idea was the distinctive contribution of Hebraism to world civilization, as distinct from that of Hellenism, was Matthew Arnold. He summarized that idea in the phrase "God as the Power that makes for righteousness— not ourselves." By "not ourselves," he meant to say that righteousness was not a human convention but a law inherent in the very nature of reality.

The reason I have found it necessary to modify Matthew Arnold's formulation of what God should mean to us is that I believe that his formulation could give a more accurate account of the *functional* approach to the meaning of God, by describing God as the Power that makes for man's salvation, or fullfillment as a human being. To be sure, righteousness is an indispensable means to salvation, but only when it achieves that result does its divine source assert itself.

Righteousness is evidently not merely a contemplative or an emotional experience, or virtue. It is definitely a form of action accompanied by a conative experience, and therefore a manifestation of the human will. The question which then suggests itself is: Why not identify righteousness with conscience? In view of the popular saying "Conscience is the voice of God," should not Matthew Arnold rather have defined God as the Power that makes for conscience?

The evident answer is that the dictates of conscience are not necessarily righteous. The conscience of a deluded fanatic may compel him to commit murder. Certainly the conscience of an ignorant person may misdirect him as to the difference between right and wrong. Conscience as such is experienced as the obligation to do what is felt to be right and to refrain from what is felt to be wrong. But there is nothing in that feeling itself to guarantee the authenticity of the rightness or wrongness. Conscience may be no more than a hunch, an intuitive guess, or the echo of public opinion. To be the voice of God, conscience has to undergo life-long training in knowledge, faith and courage. Only an educated conscience can know what righteousness is. No conscience can be regarded as properly educated unless it elicit behavior which, on a magnified scale, would lead to *universal* freedom, justice and good-will. Such behavior can arise only from an active functioning of moral responsibility. Moral responsibility is the synthesis of human independence and interdependence. It is the human manifestation of the cosmic law of polarity—the synthesis of individuation and interaction. *That is the kind of conscience which enables one to experience the reality of God as the Power that makes for salvation or human fulfillment in this world.*

Such education of the conscience will have to become the preoccupation of every Jew. Unlike, however, the education of the mind, the subject matter for which has been organized and systematized, little of anything has been done to organize and systematize either the subject matter or the method to be used for the education of the conscience. That is an enormous but indispensable task to which rabbis, educators, psychologists, sociologists and others who are expert in the human sciences and in the cultural humanities should be required to apply themselves. This new cultural content should be integrated into the Jewish religious tradition with a view to using the latter as a guide to ethical human behavior and to authentic experience of the reality of God.

The integration of contemporary knowledge concerning the improvement of human nature and human society into the cultural and spiritual heritage of the Jewish People is the process of expanding the Torah, both in concept and in content. That process was achieved twice before. The Torah was first expanded during the era of the Second Commonwealth, when the Jews came in contact with Persian civilization after it had adopted the religion of Zoroaster. The Jews then accepted from that civilization the belief in the resurrection of the dead and in salvation as attainable only in the hereafter. As a result, they had to reinterpret the Written Torah, in the light of this new outlook on man and God. That reinterpretation gave rise to the Oral Torah. About a thousand years later, the intellectual Jewish élite came under the influence of Greek philosophy, with its emphasis on the incorporeality of God and the immutability of His will. That necessitated a second reinterpretation of both the Written and the Oral Torah along lines such as Saadia Gaon and Moses Maimonides indicated in their writings. Likewise in our day, the Jewish religious tradition, or Torah, has to be reinterpreted and expanded for the third time, in order that it become a means of educating the conscience of the Jew. Thus, in addition to "Written Torah," and "Oral Torah," we have to evolve what Ahad Ha-Am suggested—*Torah sh'belev,* "Torah of the Educated Heart." Such Torah will supply purpose and meaning to Jewish existence and impel the Jewish People to make of itself a People in the image of God.